THE DEPOSITIONS

ALSO BY THOMAS LYNCH

Prose

Apparition & Late Fictions

The Good Funeral

Booking Passage

Bodies in Motion and at Rest

The Undertaking

Poetry

The Sin-Eater

Walking Papers

Still Life in Milford

Grimalkin & Other Poems

Skating with Heather Grace

THE DEPOSITIONS

NEW AND SELECTED ESSAYS ON BEING AND CEASING TO BE

THOMAS LYNCH

FOREWORD BY ALAN BALL

W. W. NORTON & COMPANY
Independent Publishers Since 1923

This book is for Gordon Lish

Printed in the United States of America
First Edition

For information about special discounts for bulk purchases, please contact W. W. Norton Special Sales at specialsales@wwnorton.com or 800-233-4830

Manufacturing by LSC Communications, Harrisonburg
Book design by JAM Design
Production manager: Lauren Abbate

Library of Congress Cataloging-in-Publication Data

Names: Lynch, Thomas, 1948– author. | Ball, Alan, 1957– writer of foreword.
Title: The depositions : new and selected essays on being and ceasing to be / Thomas Lynch ; foreword by Alan Ball.
Other titles: Essays on being and ceasing to be
Description: First edition. | New York : W. W. Norton & Company, 2019.
Identifiers: LCCN 2019032130 | ISBN 9781324003977 (hardcover) | ISBN 9781324003984 (epub)
Subjects: LCSH: Life. | Death. | Identity (Psychology) | Loss (Psychology) | Meaning (Philosophy)
Classification: LCC BD431 .L975 2019 | DDC 814/.54—dc23
LC record available at https://lccn.loc.gov/2019032130

W. W. Norton & Company, Inc., 500 Fifth Avenue, New York, N.Y. 10110
www.wwnorton.com

W. W. Norton & Company Ltd., 15 Carlisle Street, London W1D 3BS

1 2 3 4 5 6 7 8 9 0

Contents

Foreword

When I was thirteen, my older sister was killed in a car accident. She was driving me to a piano lesson, and at a blind intersection she pulled out in front of a speeding car which slammed into the driver's door of our 1970 Ford Pinto. She was killed instantly. I emerged without a scratch. Well, physically.

On that day life irrevocably changed for me, split into Before and After. Now I knew. Death exists. It happens. Like many people, I would spend the next many years doing whatever the hell I could to distract myself from that inconvenient truth.

Almost thirty years later, HBO executive Carolyn Strauss pitched me the idea of a television show set in a family-run funeral home. I remembered time I had spent in funeral homes growing up—for my sister, a grandfather, a great-aunt, a grandmother, and finally my dad—and the sticky, surreal dreamlike feel of those times, and something in my head just said *yes.*

Carolyn had mentioned a book called *The American Way of Death* by Jessica Mitford she had read, so I bought a copy to do my writerly research. It turned out to be a kind of screed against the funeral industry—or, as it prefers to be known, the Death Care Industry. Mitford seemed shocked by the mechanics of embalming bodies and offended by the fact that services and products were actually marked up for profit. But she saved her greatest ire, her most righteous indignation, for the idea of salesmen selling to people in their most vulnerable moments, when they might equate the amount of money spent on a casket with the amount of love felt for the person *in* that casket. As if every other industry in the world would not want an advantage like that.

I knew I didn't want to create a show about guys in suits guilting grieving widows out of a few extra dollars. I thought back to the time I had spent in funeral homes and realized I couldn't even remember the presence of funeral directors, they were so silent and unobtrusive. Except for the time my mother broke down at my sister's open casket, and a kindly unthreatening man glided in from nowhere and took her behind a curtain to give her privacy.

I still didn't know how to tell the story of the people we pay to face death for us. And then I discovered Thomas Lynch and his lovely, profound work.

I think a lot of people, maybe most people, who have been touched by death live either in existential terror of it or in complete denial that death happens. Thomas Lynch walks a razor-thin edge in between those polarities. He cannot deny death, he sees it every day, he works with it, he holds it in his hands. Nor is he terrified by something so ubiquitous, by something that is such a fundamental part of life.

Reading Thomas's work is to suddenly be able to see what it's like to be comfortable with mortality. To respect it but not fear it. To see both the absurdity and the beauty of death, sometimes simultaneously. To know that living in the constant presence of death (which we all do, whether we admit it or not) is most importantly *living*, facing and navigating the harsh truths and the unexpected joys, the grief and the gratitude, all with an unblinking humorous and poetic eye.

I will always be grateful to Thomas for his wit and generosity and his gorgeous writing, for helping me see what the soul of *Six Feet Under* could be, and for helping me grow a little in my own complicated and omnipresent awareness of mortality. For reminding me again and again of the immutable truth of life and death and the necessity of being able to shrug it off while still staring it straight in the face. What else are you going to do? Life goes on.

Until it doesn't.

Alan Ball

from

THE UNDERTAKING

Life Studies from the Dismal Trade

THE UNDERTAKING

Every year I bury a couple hundred of my townspeople. Another two or three dozen I take to the crematory to be burned. I sell caskets, burial vaults, and urns for the ashes. I have a sideline in headstones and monuments. I do flowers on commission.

Apart from the tangibles, I sell the use of my building: eleven thousand square feet, furnished and fixtured with an abundance of pastel and chair rail and crown moldings. The whole lash-up is mortgaged and remortgaged well into the next century. My rolling stock includes a hearse, two Fleetwoods, and a minivan with darkened windows our pricelist calls a service vehicle and everyone in town calls the Dead Wagon.

I used to use the *unit pricing method*—the old package deal. It meant that you had only one number to look at. It was a large number. Now everything is itemized. It's the law. So now there is a long list of items and numbers and italicized disclaimers, something like a menu or the Sears Roebuck Wish Book, and sometimes the federally-mandated options begin to look like cruise control or rear-window defrost. I wear black most of the time, to keep folks in mind of the fact we're not talking Buicks here. At the bottom of the list there is still a large number.

In a good year the gross is close to a million, five percent of which we hope to call profit. I am the only undertaker in this town. I have a corner on the market.

The market, such as it is, is figured on what is called *the crude death rate*—the number of deaths every year out of every thousand persons.

Here is how it works.

Imagine a large room into which you coax one thousand people. You slam the doors in January, leaving them plenty of food and drink, color TVs, magazines, and condoms. Your sample should have an age distribution heavy on baby boomers and their children—1.2 children per boomer. Every seventh adult is an old-timer, who, if he or she wasn't in this big room, would probably be in Florida or Arizona or a nursing home. You get the idea. The group will include fifteen lawyers, one faith healer, three dozen real-estate agents, a video technician, several licensed counselors, and a Tupperware distributor. The rest will be between jobs, middle managers, ne'er-do-wells, or retired.

Now for the magic part—come late December when you throw open the doors, only 991.6, give or take, will shuffle out upright. Two hundred and sixty will now be selling Tupperware. The other 8.4 have become the crude death rate.

Here's another stat.

Of the 8.4 corpses, two-thirds will have been old-timers, five percent will be children, and the rest (slightly less than 2.5 corpses) will be boomers—realtors and attorneys likely—one of whom was, no doubt, elected to public office during the year. What's more, three will have died of cerebral-vascular or coronary difficulties, two of cancer, one each of vehicular mayhem, diabetes, and domestic violence. The spare change will be by act of God or suicide—most likely the faith healer.

The figure most often and most conspicuously missing from the insurance charts and demographics is the one I call The Big One, which refers to the number of people out of every hundred born who will die. Over the long haul, The Big One hovers right around . . . well, dead nuts on one hundred percent. If this were on the charts, they'd call it *death expectancy* and no one would buy futures of any kind. But it is a useful number and has its lessons. Maybe you will want to figure out what to do with your life. Maybe it will make you feel a certain kinship with the rest of us. Maybe it will make you hysterical. Whatever the implications of a one hundred percent death expectancy, you can calculate how big a town this is and why it produces for me a steady if unpredictable labor.

THEY DIE AROUND the clock here, without apparent preference for a day of the week, month of the year; there is no clear favorite in the way of season. Nor does the alignment of the stars, fullness of moon, or liturgical calendar have very much to do with it. The whereabouts are neither here nor there. They go off upright or horizontally in Chevrolets and nursing homes, in bathtubs, on the interstates, in ERs, ORs, BMWs. And while it may be that we assign more equipment or more importance to deaths that create themselves in places marked by initials—ICU being somehow better than Greenbriar Convalescent Home—it is also true that the dead don't care. In this way, the dead I bury and burn are like the dead before them, for whom time and space have become mortally unimportant. This loss of interest is, in fact, one of the first sure signs that something serious is about to happen. The next thing is they quit breathing. At this point, to be sure, a *gunshot wound to the chest* or *shock and trauma* will get more ink than a CVA or ASHD, but no cause of death is any less permanent than the other. Any one will do. The dead don't care.

Nor does *who* much matter, either. To say, "I'm OK, you're OK, and by the way, he's dead!" is, for the living, a kind of comfort.

It is why we drag rivers and comb plane wrecks and bomb sites.

It is why MIA is more painful than DOA.

It is why we have open caskets and all read the obits.

Knowing is better than not knowing, and knowing it is you is terrifically better than knowing it is me. Because once I'm the dead guy, whether you're OK or he's OK won't much interest me. You can all go bag your asses, because the dead don't care.

Of course, the living, bound by their adverbs and their actuarials, still do. Now, there is the difference and why I'm in business. The living are careful and oftentimes caring. The dead are careless, or maybe it's care-less. Either way, they don't care. These are unremarkable and verifiable truths.

MY FORMER MOTHER-IN-LAW, herself an unremarkable and verifiable truth, was always fond of holding forth with Cagney-esque bravado—to wit: "When I'm dead, just throw me in a box and throw me in a hole." But whenever I would remind her that we did substantially that with everyone, the woman would grow sullen and a little cranky.

Later, over meatloaf and green beans, she would invariably give out with: "When I'm dead just cremate me and scatter the ashes."

My former mother-in-law was trying to make carelessness sound like fearlessness. The kids would stop eating and look at each other. The kids' mother would plead, "Oh Mom, don't talk like that." I'd take out my lighter and begin to play with it.

In the same way, the priest that married me to this woman's daughter—a man who loved golf and gold ciboria and vestments made of Irish linen; a man who drove a great black sedan with a wine-red interior and who always had his eye on the cardinal's job—this same fellow, leaving the cemetery one day, felt called upon to instruct me thus: "No bronze coffin for me. No sir! No orchids or roses or limousines. The plain pine box is the one I want, a quiet Low Mass and the pauper's grave. No pomp and circumstance."

He wanted, he explained, to be an example of simplicity, of prudence, of piety and austerity—all priestly and, apparently, Christian virtues. When I told him that he needn't wait, that he could begin his ministry of good example even today, that he could quit the country club and do his hacking at the public links and trade his brougham for a used Chevette; that free of his Florsheims and cashmeres and prime ribs, free of his bingo nights and building funds, he could become, for Christ's sake, the very incarnation of Francis himself, or Anthony of Padua; when I said, in fact, that I would be willing to assist him in this, that I would gladly distribute his savings and credit cards among the worthy poor of the parish, and that I would, when the sad duty called, bury him for free in the manner he would have, by then, become accustomed to; when I told your man these things, he said nothing at all, but turned his wild eye on me in the way that the cleric must have looked on Sweeney years ago, before he cursed him, irreversibly, into a bird.

What I was trying to tell the fellow was, of course, that being a dead saint is no more worthwhile than being a dead philodendron or a dead angelfish. Living is the rub, and always has been. Living saints still feel the flames and stigmata of this vale of tears, the ache of chastity and the pangs of conscience. Once dead, they let their relics do the legwork, because, as I was trying to tell this priest, the dead don't care.

Only the living care.

And I am sorry to be repeating myself, but this is the central fact of my business—that there is nothing, once you are dead, that can be done *to you* or *for you* or *with you* or *about you* that will do you any good or any harm; that any damage or decency we do accrues to the living, to whom your death happens, if it really happens to anyone. The living have to live with it. You don't. Theirs is the grief or gladness your death brings. Theirs is the loss or gain of it. Theirs is the pain and the pleasure of memory. Theirs is the invoice for services rendered and theirs is the check in the mail for its payment.

And there is the truth, abundantly self-evident, that seems, now that I think of it, the one most elusive to the old in-laws, the parish priest, and to perfect strangers who are forever accosting me in barber-shops and cocktail parties and parent-teacher conferences, hell-bent or duty-bound to let me in on what it is they want done with them when they are dead.

Give it a rest is the thing I say.

Once you are dead, put your feet up, call it a day, and let the husband or the missus or the kids or a sibling decide whether you are to be buried or burned or blown out of a cannon or left to dry out in a ditch somewhere. It's not your day to watch it, because the dead don't care.

ANOTHER REASON PEOPLE are always rehearsing their obsequies with me has to do with the fear of death that anyone in their right mind has. It is healthy. It keeps us from playing in traffic. I say it's a thing we should pass on to the kids.

There is a belief—widespread among the women I've dated, local Rotarians, and friends of my children—that I, being the undertaker here, have some irregular fascination with, special interest in, inside information about, even attachment to, *the dead.* They assume, these people, some perhaps for defensible reasons, that I want their bodies.

It is an interesting concept.

But here is the truth.

Being dead is one—the worst, the last—but only one in a series of calamities that afflicts our own and several other species. The list may include, but is not limited to, gingivitis, bowel obstruction, contested divorce, tax audit, spiritual vexation, cash flow problems, political upheaval, and on and on and on some more. There is no shortage of misery. And I am no more attracted to the dead than the dentist is to your bad gums, the doctor to your rotten innards, or the accountant to your sloppy expense records. I have no more stomach for misery that the banker or the lawyer, the pastor or the politico—because misery is careless and is everywhere. Misery is the bad check, the ex-spouse, the mob in the street, and the IRS—who, like the dead, feel nothing and, like the dead, *don't care.*

WHICH IS NOT to say that the dead do not matter.

They do. They do. Of course they do.

Last Monday morning Milo Hornsby died. Mrs. Hornsby called at 2 A.M. to say that Milo had *expired* and would I take care of it, as if his condition were like any other that could be renewed or somehow improved upon. At 2 A.M., yanked from my REM sleep, I am thinking, put a quarter into Milo and call me in the morning. But Milo is dead. In a moment, in a twinkling, Milo has slipped irretrievably out of our reach, beyond Mrs. Hornsby and the children, beyond the women at the laundromat he owned, beyond his comrades at the Legion Hall, the Grand Master of the Masonic Lodge, his pastor at First Baptist, beyond the mailman, zoning board, town council, and Chamber of Commerce; beyond us all, and any treachery or any kindness we had in mind for him.

Milo is dead.

X's on his eyes, lights out, curtains.

Helpless, harmless.

Milo's dead.

Which is why I do not haul to my senses, coffee and quick shave, Homburg and great coat, warm up the Dead Wagon, and make for the freeway in the early o'clock for Milo's sake. Milo doesn't have any sake anymore. I go for her—for she who has become, in the same moment and the same twinkling, like water to ice, the Widow Hornsby. I go for her—because she still can cry and care and pray and pay my bill.

THE HOSPITAL THAT Milo died in is state-of-the-art. There are signs on every door declaring a part or a process or bodily function. I like to think that, taken together, the words would add up to The Human Condition, but they never do. What's left of Milo, the remains, are in the basement, between SHIPPING & RECEIVING and LAUNDRY ROOM. Milo would like that if he were still liking things. Milo's room is called PATHOLOGY.

The medical-technical parlance of death emphasizes disorder.

We are forever dying of failures, of anomalies, of insufficiencies, of dysfunctions, arrests, accidents. These are either chronic or acute. The language of death certificates—Milo's says "Cardiopulmonary Failure"—is like the language of weakness. Likewise, Mrs. Hornsby, in her grief, will be said to be breaking down or falling apart or going to pieces, as if there were something structurally awry with her. It is as if death and grief were not part of The Order of Things, as if Milo's failure and his widow's weeping were, or ought to be, sources of embarrassment. "Doing well" for Mrs. Hornsby would mean that she is bearing up, weathering the storm, or being strong for the children. We have willing pharmacists to help her with this. Of course, for Milo, doing well would mean he was back upstairs, holding his own, keeping the meters and monitors bleeping.

But Milo is downstairs, between SHIPPING & RECEIVING and LAUNDRY ROOM, in a stainless-steel drawer, wrapped in white plastic top to toe, and—because of his small head, wide shoulders, ponderous belly, and skinny legs, and the trailing white binding cord from his ankles and toe tag—he looks, for all the world, like a larger than life-size sperm.

I sign for him and get him out of there. At some level, I am still thinking Milo gives a shit, which by now, of course, we all know he doesn't—because the dead don't care.

Back at the funeral home, upstairs in the embalming room, behind a door marked PRIVATE, Milo Hornsby is floating on a porcelain table under florescent lights. Unwrapped, outstretched, Milo is beginning to look a little more like himself—eyes wide open, mouth agape, returning to our gravity. I shave him, close his eyes, his mouth. We call this *setting the features.* These are the features—eyes and mouth—that will never look the way they would have looked in life when they were always opening, closing, focusing, signaling, telling us something. In death, what they tell us is that they will not be doing anything anymore. The last detail to be managed is Milo's hands—one folded over the other, over the umbilicus, in an attitude of ease, of repose, of retirement.

They will not be doing anything anymore, either.

I wash his hands before positioning them.

When my wife moved out some years ago, the children stayed here, as did the dirty laundry. It was big news in a small town. There was the gossip and the goodwill that places like this are famous for. And while there was plenty of talk, no one knew exactly what to say to me. They felt helpless, I suppose. So they brought casseroles and beef stews, took the kids out to the movies or canoeing, brought their younger sisters around to visit me. What Milo did was send his laundry van around twice a week for two months, until I found a housekeeper. Milo would pick up five loads in the morning and return them by lunchtime, fresh and folded. I never asked him to do this. I hardly knew him. I had never been in his home or his laundromat. His wife had never known my wife. His children were too old to play with my children.

After my housekeeper was installed, I went to thank Milo and pay the bill. The invoices detailed the number of loads, the washers and the dryers, detergent, bleaches, fabric softeners. I think the total came to sixty dollars. When I asked Milo what the charges were for pick-up and delivery, for stacking and folding and sorting by size, for saving my life and the lives of my children, for keeping us in clean clothes and towels and bed linen, "Never mind that" is what Milo said. "One hand washes the other."

I place Milo's right hand over his left hand, then try the other way. Then back again. Then I decide that it doesn't matter. One hand washes the other either way.

The embalming takes me about two hours.

It is daylight by the time I am done.

Every Monday morning, Ernest Fuller comes to my office. He was damaged in some profound way in Korea. The details of his damage are unknown to the locals. Ernest Fuller has no limp or anything missing so everyone thinks it was something he saw in Korea that left him a little simple, occasionally perplexed, the type to draw rein abruptly in his day-long walks, to consider the meaning of litter, pausing over bottle caps and gum wrappers. Ernest Fuller has a nervous smile and a dead-fish handshake. He wears a baseball cap and thick eyeglasses. Every Sunday night Ernest goes to the supermarket and buys up the tabloids at the checkout stands with headlines that usually involve Siamese twins or movie stars or UFOs. Ernest is a speed reader and a math whiz but because of his damage, he has never held a job and never applied for one. Every Monday morning, Ernest brings me clippings of stories under headlines like: 601 LB MAN FALLS THRU COFFIN—A GRAVE SITUATION or EMBALMER FOR THE STARS SAYS ELVIS IS FOREVER. The Monday morning Milo Hornsby died, Ernest's clipping had to do with an urn full of ashes, somewhere in East Anglia, that made grunting and groaning noises, that whistled sometimes, and that was expected to begin talking. Certain scientists in England could make no sense of it. They had run several tests. The ashes' widow, however, left with nine children and no estate, is convinced that her dearly beloved and greatly reduced husband is trying to give her winning numbers for the lottery. "Jacky would never leave us without good prospects," she says. "He loved his family more than anything." There is a picture of the two of them, the widow and the urn, the living and the dead, flesh and bronze, the Victrola and the Victrola's dog. She has her ear cocked, waiting.

We are always waiting. Waiting for some good word or the winning numbers. Waiting for a sign or wonder, some signal from our dear dead that the dead still care. We are gladdened when they do outstanding things, when they arise from their graves or fall through their caskets or speak to us in our waking dreams. It pleases us no end, as if the dead still cared, had agendas, were yet alive.

But the sad and well-known fact of the matter is that most of us will stay in our caskets and be dead a long time, and that our urns and graves will never make a sound. Our reason and requiems, our headstones or High Masses, will neither get us in nor keep us out of heaven. The meaning of our lives, and the memories of them, belong to the living, just as our funerals do. Whatever being the dead have now, they have by the living's faith alone.

We heat graves here for winter burials, as a kind of foreplay before digging in, to loosen the frost's hold on the ground before the sexton and his backhoe do the opening. We buried Milo in the ground on Wednesday. The mercy is that what we buried there, in an oak casket, just under the frost line, had ceased to be Milo. Milo had become the idea of himself, a permanent fixture of the third person and past tense, his widow's loss of appetite and trouble sleeping, the absence in places where we look for him, our habits of him breaking, our phantom limb, our one hand washing the other.

GLADSTONE

The undertakers are over on the other island. They are there for what is called their Midwinter Conference: the name they give to the week in February every year when funeral directors from Michigan find some warm place in the Lesser Antilles to discuss the pressing issues of their trade. The names for the workshops and seminars are borderline: "The Future of Funeral Service," "What Folks Want in a Casket," "Coping with the Cremation Crowd"—things like that. The resorts must have room service, hot tubs, good beaches, and shopping on site or nearby. No doubt it is the same for orthodontists and trial lawyers.

And I'm here on the neighboring island—a smaller place with a harbor too shallow for cruise ships and no airport. I'm a ferryboat ride from the undertakers from my home state. But I've timed my relief from the Michigan winter with theirs in case I want to register for a meeting and write off my travel. It is legal and sensible and would reduce the ultimate cost of funerals in my town where I am the funeral director and have been for nearly twenty-five years now.

But I just can't work up any enthusiasm for spending any portion of the fortnight discussing business. It's not that they aren't a great bunch, chatty and amiable as stockbrokers or insurance types; and, out of their hometowns, incognito, hell-bent on a good time, they can be downright fun, if a little bingy. It's just that it seems I've been on a Midwinter Conference of my own for a long time. Enough is enough. I need to walk on the beach now and contemplate my next move.

My father was a funeral director and three of my five brothers are funeral directors; two of my three sisters work pre-need and bookkeeping in one of the four funeral homes around the metro area that bear our name, our father's name. It is an odd arithmetic—a kind of family farm, working the back forty of the emotional register, our livelihood depending on the deaths of others in the way that medicos depend on sickness, lawyers on crime, the clergy on the fear of God.

I can remember my mother and father going off on these Midwinter Conferences and coming back all sunburned and full of ideas and gossip about what my father insisted we call our "colleagues" rather than the "competition." He said it made us sound like doctors and lawyers, you know, professionals—people you could call in the middle of the night if there was trouble, people whose being had begun to meld with their doing, who were what they did.

Our thing—who we are, what we do—has always been about death and dying and grief and bereavement: the vulnerable underbelly of the hardier nouns: life, liberty, the pursuit of . . . well, you know. We traffic in leavetakings, goodbyes, final respects. "The last ones to let you down," my father would joke with the friends he most trusted. "Dignified Service" is what he put on the giveaway matchbooks and plastic combs and rain bonnets. And he loved to quote Gladstone, the great Victorian Liberal who sounded like a New Age Republican when he wrote that he could measure with mathematical precision a people's respect for the laws of the land by the way they cared for their dead. Of course, Gladstone inhabited a century and an England in which funerals were public and sex was private and, though the British were robbing the graves of infidels all over the world for the British Museum, they did so, by all accounts, in a mannerly fashion. I think my father first heard about Gladstone at one of these Midwinter Conferences and lately I've been thinking how right they were—Gladstone, my father.

MY FATHER DIED three years ago tomorrow on an island off the Gulf Coast of Florida. He wasn't exactly on a Midwinter Conference. He'd quit going to those years before, after my mother had died. But he was sharing a condo with a woman friend who always overestimated the remedial powers of sexual aerobics. Or maybe she only underestimated the progress of his heart disease. We all knew it was coming. In the first year of his widowhood, he sat in his chair, heartsore, waiting for the other shoe to drop. Then he started going out with women. The brothers were glad for him. The sisters rolled their eyes a lot. I think they call these "gender issues." In the two years of consortium that followed, he'd had a major—which is to say a chest ripping, down for the count—heart attack every six months like clockwork. He survived all but one. "Three out of four" I can hear him saying. "You're still dead when its over." He'd had enough. Even now I think of that final scene in David Lean's old film when Zhivago's heart is described as "paper thin." He thinks he sees Lara turning a corner in Moscow. He struggles to get off the bus, loosens his tie, finally makes it to the sidewalk where, after two steps, he drops dead. Dead chasing love, the thing we would die for. That was my father—stepping not off a bus but out of a shower in his timeshare condo, not in Moscow but on Boca Grande, but chasing, just as certainly, love. Chasing it to death.

When we got the call from his woman friend, we knew what to do. My brother and I had done the drill in our heads before. We had a travelling kit of embalming supplies: gloves, fluids, needles, odds and ends. We had to explain to the security people at the airlines who scrutinized the contents of the bag, wondering how we might make a bomb out of Dodge Permaglo or overtake the cabin crew with a box marked "Slaughter Surgical Supplies" full of stainless steel oddities they'd never seen before. When we got to the funeral home they had taken him to, taken his body to, the undertaker there asked if we were sure we wanted to do this—our own father, after all?—he'd be happy to call in one of his own embalmers. We assured him it would be OK. He showed us into the prep room, that familiar decor of porcelain and tile and florescent light—a tidy scientific venue for the witless horror of mortality, for how easily we slip from is to isn't.

It was something we had always promised him, though I can't now, for the life of me, remember the context in which it was made—the promise that when he died his sons would embalm him, dress him, pick out a casket, lay him out, prepare the obits, contact the priests, manage the flowers, the casseroles, the wake and procession, the Mass and burial. Maybe it was just understood. His was a funeral he would not have to direct. It was ours to do; and though he'd directed thousands of them, he had never made mention of his own preferences. Whenever he was pressed on the matter he would only say, "You'll know what to do." We did.

There's this "just a shell" theory of how we ought to relate to dead bodies. You hear a lot of it from young clergy, old family friends, well-intentioned in-laws—folks who are unsettled by the fresh grief of others. You hear it when you bring a mother and a father in for the first sight of their dead daughter, killed in a car wreck or left out to rot by some mannish violence. It is proffered as comfort in the teeth of what is a comfortless situation, consolation to the inconsolable. Right between the inhale and exhale of the bonewracking sob such hurts produce, some frightened and well-meaning ignoramus is bound to give out with "It's OK, that's not her, it's just a shell." I once saw an Episcopalian deacon nearly decked by the swift slap of the mother of a teenager, dead of leukemia, to whom he'd tendered this counsel. "I'll tell you when *it's* 'just a shell,'" the woman said. "For now and until I tell you otherwise, *she's* my daughter." She was asserting the longstanding right of the living to declare the dead dead. Just as we declare the living alive through baptisms, lovers in love by nuptials, funerals are the way we close the gap between the death that happens and the death that matters. It's how we assign meaning to our little remarkable histories.

And the rituals we devise to conduct the living and beloved and the dead from one status to another have less to do with *performance* than with *meaning*. In a world where "dysfunctional" has become the operative adjective, a body that has ceased to work has, it would seem, few useful applications—its dysfunction more manifest than the sexual and familial forms that fill our tabloids and talk shows. But a body that doesn't work is, in the early going, the evidence we have of a person who has ceased to be. And a person who has ceased to be is as compelling a prospect as it was when the Neanderthal first dug holes for his dead, shaping the questions we still shape in the face of death: "Is that all there is?" "What does it mean?" "Why is it cold?" "Can it happen to me?"

So to suggest in the early going of grief that the dead body is "just" anything rings as tinny in its attempt to minimalize as it would if we were to say it was "just" a bad hair day when the girl went bald from her chemotherapy. Or that our hope for heaven on her behalf was based on the belief that Christ raised "just" a body from dead. What if, rather than crucifixion, he'd opted for suffering low self-esteem for the remission of sins? What if, rather than "just a shell," he'd raised his personality, say, or The Idea of Himself? Do you think they'd have changed the calendar for that? Done the Crusades? Burned witches? Easter was a body and blood thing, no symbols, no euphemisms, no half measures. If he'd raised anything less, of course, as Paul points out, the deacon and several others of us would be out of business or back to Saturday sabbaths, a sensible diet, and no more Christmases.

The bodies of the newly dead are not debris nor remnant, nor are they entirely icon or essence. They are, rather, changelings, incubates, hatchlings of a new reality that bear our names and dates, our image and likenesses, as surely in the eyes and ears of our children and grandchildren as did word of our birth in the ears of our parents and their parents. It is wise to treat such new things tenderly, carefully, with honor.

I HAD SEEN my father horizontal before. At the end it had been ICUs mostly, after his coronaries and bypasses. He'd been helpless, done unto. But before that there had been the man stretched out on the living room floor tossing one or the other of my younger siblings in the air; or napping in his office at the first funeral home in full uniform, black three-piece suit, striped tie, wingtips, clean shave; or in the bathtub singing "from the halls of Montezuma to the shores of Tripoli." He had outbreaks of the malaria he'd gotten in the South Pacific. In my childhood he was, like every father on the block, invincible. That he would die had been a fiction in my teens, a fear in my twenties, a specter in my thirties and, in my forties, a fact.

But seeing him, outstretched on the embalming table of the Anderson Mortuary in Ft. Myers with the cardiac blue in his ears and fingertips and along his distal regions, shoulders and lower ribs and buttocks and heels, I thought, *this is what my father will look like when he's dead.* And then, like a door slammed shut behind you, the tense of it all shifted into the inescapable present of *this is my father, dead.* My brother and I hugged each other, wept with each other and for each other and for our sisters and brothers home in Michigan. Then I kissed my father's forehead, not yet a shell. Then we went to work in the way our father had trained us.

He was a cooperative body. Despite the arteriosclerosis, his circulatory system made the embalming easy. And having just stepped from the shower into his doom, he was clean and cleanly shaven. He hadn't been sick, in the hospice or intensive care sense of the word. So there were none of the bruises on him or tubes in him that medical science can inflict and install. He'd gotten the death he wanted, caught in full stride, quick and cleanly after a day strolling the beach picking sea shells for the grandchildren and maybe after a little bone bouncing with his condo-mate, though she never said and we never asked and can only hope. And massaging his legs, his hands, his arms, to effect the proper distribution of fluid and drainage, watching the blue clear from his fingertips and heels as the fluid that would preserve him long enough for us to take our leave of him worked its way around his body, I had the sense that I was doing something for him even though, now dead, he was beyond my kindnesses or anyone's. Likewise, his body bore a kind of history: the tattoo with my mother's name on it he'd had done as an eighteen-year-old marine during World War II, the perfectly trimmed mustache I used to watch him darken with my mother's mascara when he was younger than I am and I was younger than my children are. The scars from his quintuple bypass surgery, the A.A. medallion he never removed, and the signet ring my mother gave him for his fortieth birthday, all of us saving money in a jar until fifty dollars was accumulated. Also there were the graying chest hairs, the hairless ankles, the male pattern baldness I see on the heads of men in the first-class section of airplanes and in the double mirrors in the barber's shop. Embalming my father I was reminded of how we bury our dead and then become them. In the end I had to say that maybe *this is what I'm going to look like dead.*

Maybe it was at a Midwinter Conference my father first thought about what he did and why he did it. He always told us that embalming got to be, forgive me, *de rigueur* during the Civil War when, for the first time in our history, lots of people—mostly men, mostly soldiers—were dying far from home and the families that grieved them. Dismal traders worked in tents on the edge of the battlefields charging, one reckons, what the traffic would bear to disinfect, preserve, and "restore" dead bodies—which is to say they closed mouths, sutured bullet holes, stitched limbs or parts of limbs back on, and sent the dead back home to wives and mothers, fathers and sons. All of this bother and expense was predicated on the notion that the dead need to be at their obsequies, or, more correctly, that the living need the dead to be there, so that the living can consign them to the field or fire after commending them to God or the gods or Whatever Is Out There. The presence and participation of the dead human body at its funeral is, as my father told it, every bit as important as the bride's being at her wedding, the baby at its baptism.

And so we brought our dead man home. Flew his body back, faxed the obits to the local papers, called the priests, the sexton, the florists and stonecutter. We act out things we cannot put in words.

Back in '63, I can remember my father saying that the reason we have funerals and open caskets was so that we might confront what he called "the reality of death." I think he'd heard that at one of these conferences. Jessica Mitford had just sold a million copies of *The American Way of Death*, Evelyn Waugh had already weighed in with *The Loved One*, and talk had turned at cocktail parties to "barbaric rituals" and "morbid curiosities." The mortuary associations were scrambling for some cover. Clergy and educators and psychologists—the new clergy—were assembled to say it served some purpose, after all, was emotionally efficient, psychologically correct, to do what we'd been doing all along. The track record was pretty good on this. We'd been doing—the species, not the undertakers—more or less the same thing for millennia: looking up while digging down, trying to make some sense of all of it, disposing of our dead with sufficient pause to say they'd lived in ways different from rocks and rhododendrons and even orangutans and that those lives were worth mentioning and remembering.

Then Kennedy was shot dead and then Lee Harvey Oswald and we spent the end of November that year burying them—the first deaths in our lives that took for most of us boomers. All the other TV types got shot on *Gunsmoke* on a Friday and turned up on *Bonanza*, looking fit by Sunday night. But Kennedy was one of those realities of death my father must have been talking about and though we saw his casket and cortege and little John John saluting and the widow in her sunglasses, we never saw Kennedy dead, most of us, until years later when pictures of the autopsy were released and we all went off to the movies to see what really happened. In the interim, rumors circulated about Kennedy not being dead at all but hooked to some secret and expensive hardware, brainless but breathing. And when the Zapruder film convinced us that he must have died, still we lionized the man beyond belief. Of course, once we saw him dead in the pictures, his face, his body, he became human again: lovable and imperfect, memorable and dead.

AND AS I watch my generation labor to give their teenagers and young adults some "family values" between courses of pizza and Big Macs, I think maybe Gladstone had it right. I think my father did. They understood that the meaning of life is connected, inextricably, to the meaning of death; that mourning is a romance in reverse, and if you love, you grieve and there are no exceptions—only those who do it well and those who don't. And if death is regarded as an embarrassment or an inconvenience, if the dead are regarded as a nuisance from whom we seek a hurried riddance, then life and the living are in for like treatment. McFunerals, McFamilies, McMarriage, McValues. This is the mathematical precision the old Britisher was talking about and what my father was talking about when he said we'd know what to do.

Thus tending to his death, his dead body, had for me the same importance as being present for the births of my sons, my daughter. Some expert on *Oprah* might call this "healing." Another on *Donahue* might say "cathartic." Over on *Geraldo* it might have "scarred him for life." And Sally Jesse Whatshername might mention "making good choices." As if they were talking about men who cut umbilical cords and change diapers or women who confront their self-esteem issues or their date rapists.

It is not about choices or functions or psychological correctness. A dead body has had its options limited, its choices narrowed. It is an old thing in the teeth of which we do what has been done because it is the thing to do. We needn't reinvent the wheel or make the case for it, though my generation always seems determined to.

And they are at it over on the other island. Trying to reinvent the funeral as "a vehicle for the healthy expression of grief," which, of course, it is; or as "a brief therapy for the acutely bereaved," which, of course, it is. There will be talk of "stages," "steps," "recovery." Someone will mention "aftercare," "post-funeral service follow-up," Widow to Widow programs, Mourners Anonymous? And in the afternoons they'll play nine holes, or go snorkeling or start cocktails too early and after dinner they'll go dancing then call home to check in with their offices just before they go to bed, to check on the gross sales, to see who among their townspeople has died.

Maybe I'll take the boat over tomorrow. Maybe some of the old timers are there—men of my father's generation, men you could call in the middle of the night if there was trouble. They remind me of my father and of Gladstone. Maybe they'll say I remind them of him.

CRAPPER

Death and the sun are not to be looked at in the face.

—*La Rochefoucauld,* MAXIMS

Don Paterson and I were crossing the Wolfe Tone Bridge in Galway contemplating Thomas Crapper. This was at early o'clock in the morning on our way back from an awful curry at the only Indian restaurant open in Galway in the wee hours. The night was mild, and our thoughts drifted toward talk of Crapper as the air behind us burned with the elemental fire of flatulence. It was an awful curry.

Why else would two internationally unknown poets, in Galway to recite our internationally unheard of poems, the guests of the Cuirt Festival of Literature, be talking about the implications of the invention of the flush toilet and about its inventor, that dismal man whose name shall forever be associated with shit? Why else?

Here, after all, was an opportunity to tender vengeance toward the man who'd damned, by faint praise, my most recent book of poems—in the *TLS* for chrissakes! Indeed, given Don's fairly damaged condition—a night of drink, the aforementioned curry—I could have pitched him headlong into the Corrib and watched him bob up and down out to Galway Bay humming like Bing Crosby, an odd and gaseous swan gone belly-up from bad food and good riddance. But really the review wasn't as bad as it was, well, "fair" and any ink is better than no ink, after all. And I like Don. He's an amiable Scot, a Dundonian, and a crackerjack poet if, like myself, not exactly a household name. It could be worse, I tell myself. We could be Crappers. And he still drinks well, in a way I never did, allowing excess to be its own reward—a little change from the teetotal life I live back in Michigan, where I haven't had a drink in years, suffering as I do from all of the "F" words: I'm fortyish, a father of four, a funeral director, and full of fear for what might happen if I go back on the Black Bush. So I don't.

The first time I was ever in Ireland was twenty-seven years ago. Driven by curiosity about my family and my affection for the poetry of William Butler Yeats—an internationally known poet—I saved up a hundred dollars beyond the cost of a one-way ticket and lit out, twenty and cocksure, for Ireland. Several of my generation were going off to Vietnam at the time but I'd drawn high numbers in the Nixon lotto so I was free to go. What made me so cocksure was the faith that my parents would bail me out if I got too deep into trouble. So I wasn't exactly like Kerouac or Woody Guthrie but I was, nonetheless, on the road. Or more precisely, flying the friendly skies.

When I located my cousins Tommy and Nora Lynch—brother and sister, bachelor and spinster—they lived in a thatched house on the west coast of Clare, in the townland of Moveen, with flagstone floors, two light sockets, a hot plate and open hearth, and no plumbing. Water existed five fields down the land, bubbling up in a miracle of springwater, clear and cold and clean. I soon learned to grab the bucket and a bit of the *Clare Champion* and on my way down for the precious water, I'd squat to my duties and wipe my ass with the obits or want ads or the local news. It was my first taste of Liberty—to crap out in the open air on the acreage of my ancestors, whilst listening to the sounds of morning: an aubade of birdwhistle and windsong.

Tommy and Nora kept cows, saved hay, went to the creamery and, as any farmer knows, dung is a large part of that bargain. It greens the grass that feeds the cow that makes the milk and shits again: a paradigm for the internal combustion engine, a closed system, efficient as an old Ford. And so the addition of my little bits of excrement to the vast dung-covered acreage was hardly noticeable, like personal grief among paid wailers, it gets lost in the shuffle and becomes anonymous and safe. This is the model for the food chain: the elements of feed, cowshit and what-have-ye, get lost in the shuffle by the time we sit down to the Delmonico or t-bone, likewise we are blind to the copulation of chickens and the habits of pigs when we sit down to the bacon and the eggs. The process blurs—dead fish make onions grow, manure turns into hamburger and tossed salad.

It was a good life. After nights of song and stories and poetry, common in the country in those years before televisions replaced the fire on the floor as the thing stared at and into, I would step out the back door of the cottage and take my stance amid the whitethorn trees my great-great-grandfather had planted years ago as saplings brought home from a horse fair in Kilrush. And looking up into the bright firmament I'd piss the porter out—I was young, I drank too much—and in the midst of this deliverance I'd look up into the vast firmament, as bright in its heaven as the dark was black, and think thoughts of Liberty and be thankful to be alive.

YEARS AFTER, I would try to replicate these reveries when I found myself living in a large old house on Liberty Boulevard in a small town in Michigan. I lived next door to my funeral home and, returning in the early mornings from embalming one of my townspeople, I'd stop near the mock-orange tree by the back door of my home and look up into the heavens and relieve myself. Some nights I would espy Orion or the Pleiades and think of mythologies blurred in my remembrance of them and be thankful for the life of the body and the mind.

Such was the firmament this night in Galway. Don and I had stood shoulder to shoulder before the famous green storefront of Kenny's Bookshop in High Street, swooning and stuporous to see our books, our faces, and bold notice of our readings there in the window among the stars. And despite the flatus, harbinger of impending disaster, Don and I were glad to be alive. Glad for the soft air of springtime, somehow sweeter in Galway than Dundee or Michigan. And glad to be paid for giving out with poems when so few can say they were ever paid for the inner workings of their souls. And glad, I daresay, for the rooms provided for us at the Atlanta Hotel in Dominick Street by the Festival Committee—rooms with solid beds and flush toilets toward which we made our gaseous ways that mild Marchy night in the City of the Tribes.

I still have the house in West Clare. Tommy died and Nora outlived him by twenty-one years, living alone by the fire. Then Nora died, just shy of her ninetieth birthday, a tidy jaundiced corpse, made little and green by pancreatic cancer. She left the house to me. I was her family. I kept coming back to West Clare after that first time, year after year, though the visits were shortened by the building of my business and the making of babies.

When her brother Tommy died, in 1971, she rode the bike into town and called from the post office. I flew over in time for the wake and funeral. I think that was when she began to count me as her next of kin—the one she could call and be sure I'd come. I think that's when she began to trust me with her own obsequies, mention of which was never made until the week before she died.

Of course, first among the several changes I made was the addition of a toilet and shower. I added on a room out the back door and put in a bathroom like a French bordello, all tile and glowing fixtures. I had a septic tank sunk in the back haggard and declared the place all the more habitable for the trouble. I let it to writers when I'm not there.

But for every luxury there is a loss. Just as the installation of a phone when Nora was eighty cost her the excitement of letters coming up the road with John Willie McGrath, the postman on his bike, and the installation of a television when she was eighty-five meant that her friends gave up their twisting relations in favor of *Dallas* reruns, so the introduction of modern toiletry removed from Moveen forever the liberty of walking out into the night air or the morning mist with a full bowel or bladder and having at the landscape in ways that can only be called "close to nature."

THE THING ABOUT the new toilet is that it removes the evidence in such a hurry. The flush toilet, more than any single invention, has "civilized" us in a way that religion and law could never accomplish. No more the morning office of the chamber pot or outhouse, where sights and sounds and odors reminded us of the corruptibility of flesh. Since Crapper's marvelous invention, we need only pull the lever behind us and the evidence disappears, a kind of rapture that removes the nuisance. This dynamic is what the sociologist, Phillip Slater, called "The Toilet Assumption," back in the seventies in a book called *The Pursuit of Loneliness.* He was right: having lost the regular necessity of dealing with unpleasantries, we have lost the ability to do so when the need arises. And we have lost the community well versed in these calamities. In short, when shit happens, we feel alone.

It is the same with our dead. We are embarrassed by them in the way that we are embarrassed by a toilet that overflows the night that company comes. It is an emergency. We call the plumber.

I SOMETIMES THINK the only firms that put their names on what they do anymore are firms that make toilets and direct funerals. In both cases there seems to be an effort to sound trustworthy, stable, established, honest. Twyford's Adamant, Armitage Shanks, Moen

& Moen, Kohler come to mind. Most other enterprises seem hidden behind some "assumed name" someone is "Doing Business As." Drugstores and real estate agents have given up the surnames of their owners for the more dodgy corporate identities of BuyRite or PayLess or Real Estate One. Doctors and lawyers have followed, taking in their shingles and putting out neon with murky identities and corporate cover. Drygoods and greengrocers, furniture merchants, saloons and restaurants—all gone now to malls and marts and supermarkets with meaningless or fictional monikers. But funeral homes and water-closets still stubbornly proclaim the name of the ones you'll be doing business with. Lynch & Sons is the name of ours. Is it ego or identity crisis? I sometimes ask myself.

The house I live in here on Liberty was built in 1880. It had no plumbing at first. It had a cistern in the cellar to collect rainwater and likely had a pump in the kitchen and an outhouse in the backyard surrounded by lilacs. Next to the kitchen was a birthing room where agreeable women of that age had their babies. It was next to the kitchen because, as everyone knows, the having of babies and the boiling of water were gerundives forever linked in the common wisdom of the day. And after the babies were born and showed good signs of living (no sure thing then—more than half of the deaths in 1900 were children under twelve), they were christened, often in a room up front, the priest or parson standing between the aunts and uncles and grandparents that populated the households of that era, where everybody looked liked the Waltons with their John-Boys and Susans and goodnight Grampaws. These were big families, made large by the lovemaking of parents before the mercy of birth control turned families into Mommy and Daddy and 2.34 Johnnies and Sues and the modern welfare state turned households into Mommy and babies and a phantom man—like the "bull brought in a suitcase" to dairy cows in West Clare.

The homes were large to house multiple births and generations. These were households in which, just as babies were being birthed, grandparents were aging upstairs with chicken soup and doctors' home visits until, alas, they died and were taken downstairs to the same room the babies were christened in to get what was called then, "laid out." Between the births and deaths were the courtships—sparkings and spoonings between boys and girls just barely out of their teens, overseen by a maiden aunt who traded her talents for childcare and housekeeping for her place in the household. The smitten young people would sit on a "love seat"—large enough to look into each other's eyes and hold hands, small enough to prevent them getting horizontal. The aunt would appear at strategic intervals to ask about lemonade, teas, room temperatures, the young man's family. Decorum was maintained. The children married, often in the same room—the room with large pocket doors drawn for privacy and access. The room in which grandparents were waked and new babies were baptized and love was proffered and contracted—the parlor.

Half a century, two world wars, and the New Deal later, homes got smaller and garages got bigger as we moved these big events out of the house. The emphasis shifted from stability to mobility. The architecture of the family and the homes they lived in changed forever by invention and intervention and by the niggling sense that such things didn't belong in the house. At the same time, the birthing room became the downstairs "bath"—emphasis upon the cleanly function of indoor plumbing. Births were managed in the sparkling wards of hospitals, or for real romance, on the way, in cars. A common fiction had some hapless civil servant or taxi man birthing a baby in the backseat of a squad car or Buick. The same backseat, it was often assumed, where the baby was invented—sparking and spooning under the supervision of Aunt Cecilia having given way to "parking" under the patrol of Officer Mahoney. Like most important things, courtship was done en route, in transit, on the lam, in a car. Retirees were deported to Sun City. Elders grew aged and sickly not upstairs in their own beds, but in a series of institutional venues: rest homes, nursing homes, hospital wards, sanitoria. Which is where they died: the chance, in 1960, of dying in your own bed: less than one in ten.

And having lived their lives and died their deaths outside the home, they were taken to be laid out, not in the family parlor but to the *funeral* parlor, where the building was outfitted to look like the family parlors gone forever, busy with overstuffed furniture, fern stands, knickknacks, draperies, and the dead.

This is how my business came to be.

Just about the time we were bringing the making of water and the movement of bowels into the house, we were pushing the birthing and marriage and sickness and dying out. And if the family that prayed together stayed together in accordance with the churchy bromide, the one that shits together rarely sticks together.

We have no parlors anymore, no hearthsides. We have, rather, our family rooms in which light flickers from the widescreen multichannel TV on which we watch reruns of a life we are not familiar with. Kitchens are not cooked in, dining rooms go dusty. Living rooms are a kind of mausolea reserved for "company" that seldom comes. Lovemaking is done on those "getaway" weekends at the Hyatt or the Holidome. New homes are built with fewer bedrooms and more full baths. (Note how a half bath is not called a whole crapper.) And everyone has their "personal space," their privacy. The babies are in daycare, the elders are in Arizona or Florida or a nursing home with people their own age, and mom and dad are busting ass to pay for their "dream house" or the remodeled "master suite" where nothing much happens anymore of any consequence.

THIS IS ALSO why the funerals held in my funeral parlor lack an essential manifest—the connection of the baby born to the marriage made to the deaths we grieve in the life of a family. I have no weddings or baptisms in the funeral home and the folks that pay me have maybe lost sight of the obvious connections between the life and the death of us. And how the rituals by which we mark the things that only happen to us once, birth and death, or maybe twice in the case of marriage, carry the same emotional mail—a message of loss and gain, love and grief, things changed utterly.

And just as bringing the crapper indoors has made feces an embarrassment, pushing the dead and dying out has made death one. Often I am asked to deal with the late uncle in the same way that Don Paterson and I were about to ask Armitage Shanks to deal with the bad curry—out of sight out of mind. Make it go away, disappear. Push the button, pull the chain, get on with life. The trouble is, of course, that life, as any fifteen-year-old can tell you, is full of shit and has but one death. And to ignore our excrement might be good form, while to ignore our mortality creates an "imbalance," a kind of spiritual irregularity, psychic impaction, a bunging up of our humanity, a denial of our very nature.

WHEN NORA LYNCH got sick they called. The doctor at the hospital in Ennis mentioned weeks, a month at most, there might be pain. I landed in Shannon on Ash Wednesday morning and on the way to the hospital stopped at the Cathedral in Ennis where school children and townies were getting their ashes before going off to their duties. The nurses at the hospital said I was holier than any one of them—to have flown over and gotten the smudge on my forehead and it not 9 A.M. yet in West Clare. Nora was happy to see me. I asked her what she thought we ought to do. She said she wanted to go home to Moveen. I told her the doctors all thought she was dying. "What harm . . . ," says she. "Aren't we all?" She fixed her bright eyes on the spot in my forehead. I asked the doctors for a day to make arrangements for her homecoming—a visiting nurse from the county health office would make daily calls, the local medico would manage pain with morphine, I laid in some soups and porridges and ice creams, some adult diapers, a portable commode.

The next day I drove back to Ennis to get her, buckled her into the front seat of the rental car, and made for the west along the same road I'd been driving toward her all those years since my first landing in Shannon—an hour from Ennis to Kilrush to Kilkee then five miles out the coast road to Moveen, the townland narrowing between the River Shannon's mouth and North Atlantic, on the westernmost peninsula of County Clare. It was the second day of Lent in Ireland, the green returning to the fields wracked by winter, the morning teetering between showers and sunlight. And all the way home on the road she sang, "The Cliffs of Moveen," "The Rose of Tralee," "The Boys of Kilmichael," "Amazing Grace."

"Nora," I said to her between verses, "no one would know you are dying to hear you singing now."

"Whatever happens," she said, "I'm going home."

SHE WAS DEAD before Easter. Those last days spent by the fire in ever shortening audiences with neighbors and priests and Ann Murray, a neighbor woman I hired to "attend" her when I wasn't there. Two powerful unmarried women, sixty years between them, talking farming and missed chances, unwilling to have their lives defined for them by men. Or deaths.

And I noticed how she stopped eating at all and wondered what the reason for that was.

WHEN I FIRST was in Ireland, that winter and spring a quarter century ago, Nora and I bicycled down to the Regan's farm in Donoughby. Mrs. Regan had had a heart attack. We were vaguely related. We'd have to go. The body was laid out in her bedroom, mass cards strewn at the foot of the bed. Candles were lit. Holy water shook. Women knelt in the room saying rosaries. Men stood out in the yard talking prices, weather, smoking cigarettes. A young Yank,

I was consigned to the women. In the room where Mrs. Regan's body was, despite the candles and the flowers and the February chill—a good thing in townlands where no embalming is done—there was the terrible odor of gastrointestinal distress. Beneath the fine linens, Mrs. Regan's belly seemed bulbous, almost pregnant, almost growing. Between decades of the rosary, neighbor women shot anxious glances among one another. Later I heard, in the hushed din of gossip, that Mrs. Regan, a lighthearted woman unopposed to parties, had made her dinner the day before on boiled cabbage and onions and ham and later followed with several half-pints of lager at Hickie's in Kilkee. And these forgivable excesses, while they may not have caused her death, were directly responsible for the heavy air inside the room she was waked in and the "bad form" Nora called it when the requiems had to be moved up a day and a perfectly enjoyable wake foreshortened by the misbehavior of Mrs. Regan's body.

AT NIGHT NORA would crawl into bed, take the medicine for pain, and sleep. "Collins is our man," she told me toward the end, meaning the undertaker in Carrigaholt who could be counted on for coffins and hearses and grave openings at Moyarta where all our people were, back to our common man, Patrick Lynch. She turned over the bankbook with my name on it, added, she said, after her brother had died all those years ago. "Be sure there's plenty of sandwiches and porter and wine, sherry wine, something sweet. And whiskey for the ones that dig the grave."

Nora Lynch was a tidy corpse, quiet and continent, only a little jaundiced, which never showed in the half light of the room she died in, the room she was born in, the room she was waked in. She never stirred. And we waked her for three full days and nights in late March before taking her to church in Carrigaholt. Then buried her on a Monday in the same vaulted grave as her father and her father's father and her twin brother, dead in infancy, near ninety years before.

We gave whiskey to the gravediggers and had a stone cut with her name and dates on it to overlook her grave and the River Shannon.

There was money enough for all of that. She'd saved. Enough for the priests and the best coffin Collins had and for pipers and tinwhistlers and something for the choir; and to take the entourage to the Long Dock afterward and fill them with food and stout and trade memories and tunes. It was a grand wake and funeral. We wept and laughed and sang and wept some more.

And afterward there was enough left over to build the room that housed the toilet and the shower and haul that ancient cottage—a wedding gift to my great-great-grandfather, my inheritance—into the twentieth century in the nick of time.

Still, there are nights now in West Clare and nights in Michigan when I eschew the porcelain and plumbing in favor of the dark comforts of the yard, the whitethorn or lilac or the mock-orange, the stars in their heaven, the liberty of it; and the drift my thoughts invariably take toward the dead and the living and the ones I love whenever I am at the duties of my toilet.

I think of Nora Lynch and of Mrs. Regan and of the blessings of their lives among us. And lately I've been thinking thoughts of Don Paterson who made it back to the Atlanta Hotel—he to his room and me to mine. And maybe it was the drink or curry or the talk of toilets, or all of it together that made him kneel and hug the bowl and look into the maelstrom as we all have once or more than once, adding to the list of things not to be looked at in the face, the godawful name of Crapper.

THE RIGHT HAND OF THE FATHER

I had an uneventful childhood. Added to my mother's conviction that her children were precious was my father's terrible wariness. He saw peril in everything, disaster was ever at hand. Some mayhem with our name on it lurked around the edges of our neighborhood waiting for a lapse of parental oversight to spirit us away. In the most innocent of enterprises, he saw danger. In every football game he saw the ruptured spleen, the death by drowning in every backyard pool, leukemia in every bruise, broken necks on trampolines, the deadly pox or fever in every rash or bug bite.

It was, of course, the undertaking.

As a funeral director, he was accustomed to random and unreasonable damage. He had learned to fear.

My mother left big things to God. Of her nine children, she was fond of informing us, she had only "planned" one. The rest of us, though not entirely a surprise—she knew what caused it—were gifts from God to be treated accordingly. Likewise, she figured on God's protection and, I firmly believe, she believed in the assignment of guardian angels whose job it was to keep us all out of harm's way.

But my father had seen, in the dead bodies of infants and children and young men and women, evidence that God lived by the Laws of Nature, and obeyed its statutes, however brutal. Kids died of gravity and physics and biology and natural selection. Car wrecks and measles and knives stuck in toasters, household poisons, guns left loaded, kidnappers, serial killers, burst appendices, bee stings, hard-candy chokings, croups untreated—he'd seen too many instances of His unwillingness to overrule the natural order, which included, along with hurricanes and meteorites and other Acts of God, the aberrant disasters of childhood.

So whenever I or one of my siblings would ask to go here or there or do this or that, my father's first response was almost always "No!" He had just buried someone doing that very thing.

He had just buried some boy who had toyed with matches, or played baseball without a helmet on, or went fishing without a life preserver, or ate the candy that a stranger gave him. And what the boys did that led to their fatalities matured as my brothers and sisters and I matured, the causes of their death becoming subtly interpersonal rather than cataclysmic as we aged. The stories of children struck by lightning were replaced by narratives of unrequited love gone suicidal, teenagers killed by speed and drink or overdosed on drugs, and hordes of the careless but otherwise blameless dead who'd found themselves *in the wrong place at the wrong time.*

My mother, who had more faith in the power of prayer and her own careful parenting, would often override his prohibitions. "Oh, Ed," she would argue over dinner, "Leave them be! They've got to learn some things for themselves." Once she told him "Don't be ridiculous, Ed," when he'd refused me permission to spend the night at a friend's house across the street. "What!" she scolded him, "Did you just bury someone who died of a night spent at Jimmy Shryock's house?"

He regarded my mother's interventions not as contrarieties, but as the voice of reason in a world gone mad. It was simply the occasional triumph of her faith over his fear. And when she stepped into the fray with her powerful testimony, he reacted as the drunken man does to the cold water and hot coffee, as if to say, *Thanks, I needed that.*

But his fear was genuine and not unfounded. Even for suburban children who were loved, wanted, protected, doted over, there were no guarantees. The neighborhood was infested with rabid dogs, malarial mosquitoes, weirdoes disguised as mailmen and teachers. The worst seemed always on the brink of happening, as his daily rounds informed him. For my father, even the butterflies were suspect.

So while my mother said her prayers and slept the sound sleep of a child of God; my father was ever wakeful, ever vigilant, ever in earshot of a phone—in case the funeral home should call in the middle of the night—and a radio that monitored police and fire calls. In my childhood I can recall no day he was not up and waiting for me and my siblings to awaken. Nor can I remember any night I lived at home, until I was nineteen, when he was not awake and waiting for our arrival home.

Every morning brought fresh news of overnight catastrophes he'd heard on the radio. And every night brought stories of the obsequies, sad and deliberate, which he directed. Our breakfasts and dinners were populated by the widowed and heartsore, the wretched and bereft, among them the parents permanently damaged by the death of a child. My mother would roll her eyes a little bit and dole out liberties against his worry. Eventually we were allowed to play hardball, go camping, fish alone, drive cars, date, ski, open checking accounts, and run the other ordinary developmental risks—her faith moving mountains his fear created.

"Let go," she would say. "Let God."

Once she even successfully argued on behalf of my older brother, Dan, getting a BBGun, a weapon which he promptly turned against his younger siblings, outfitting us in helmet and leather jacket and instructing us to run across Eaton Park while he practiced his marksmanship. Today he is a colonel in the army and the rest of us are gun-shy.

Far from indifferent, my mother left the business of Life and Death to God in His heaven. This freed her to tend to the day-to-day concerns of making sure we lived up to our potential. She was concerned with "character," "integrity," "our contribution to society," and "the salvation of our souls." She made no secret of her belief that God would hold her personally accountable for the souls of her children—a radical notion today—so that her heaven depended on our good conduct.

For my father, what we did, who we became, were incidental to the tenuous fact of our being: That We Were seemed sufficient for the poor worried man. The rest, he would say, was gravy.

There were, of course, near misses. After the usual flues, poxes, and measles, we entered our teen years in the sixties and seventies. Pat was sucker-punched in a bar fight by a man who broke a beer bottle over his head. Eddie drove off a bridge, crashed his car into the riverbank, and walked away unscathed. He told our parents that another car, apparently driven by an intoxicant, had run him off the road. We called it "Eddie's Chappaquiddick" privy as only siblings are to our brother's taste for beer and cocaine. Julie Ann went through the windshield of a friend's car when the friend drove into a tree and, except for some scalpline lacerations and scars, lived to tell about it. Brigid took too many pills one night in combination with strong drink and what her motivation was remained a mystery for years, known only to my mother. For my part, I fell off a third-story fire-escape in my third year of college, broke several Latin-sounding bones, fractured my pelvis, and compressed three vertebrae but never lost consciousness. My English professor and mentor, the poet Michael Heffernan, was first downstairs and out the door to where I had landed. I must have appeared somewhat dazed and breathless. "Did you hit your head?" he kept asking once he had determined I was alive. "What day is it?" "Who is the president of the United States?" To assure him I had not suffered brain damage, I gave out with "The Love Song of J. Alfred Prufrock"—a moving rendition

I was later told, marred only by my belching through the couplet where your man says, "I grow old . . . I grow old . . . I shall wear the bottoms of my trousers rolled." Then I puked, not from the fall but from the J.W. Dant Bourbon that was credited with saving my life. I had been sufficiently limbered up, it was reasoned, by generous doses of Kentucky sour mash, to have avoided permanent damage.

In the hospital I woke to a look on my father's face I shall always remember—a visage distorted by rage and relief, at war with itself. And by amazement at the menagerie of friends and fellow revelers who accompanied me to hospital. While Professor Heffernan could affect the upright citizen in tweeds and buttondowns, not so Walt Houston, who studied physics and comparative religion and lived most of the school year in a tree somewhere on the edge of the campus and scavenged for food scraps in the student union. Nor Myles Lorentzen, who successfully failed his draft physical after the ingestion of massive doses of caffeine—pot after pot of black coffee followed by the eating whole of a carton of cigarettes. Later, Myles would do hard time in prison for the illegal possession of marijuana. A month after his release they made possession a misdemeanor, punishable by a twenty dollar fine. Worse still, Glenn Wilson, whose only utterance after a six pack of beer was always "Far out, man!" which he would say, for no apparent reason, at the most inappropriate of times. Harmless drunks and ne'er-do-wells, my father looked suspicious of my choice of friends.

My mother thanked God I had not been killed, then fixed her eyes on me in a way it seemed she'd had some practice at—casting the cold eye of the long suffering in the face of a boozy loved one. My father had quit drinking the year before, joined AA, began going to meetings. My brothers and I had been a little surprised by this as we had never seen him drunk before. I had overheard my mother's sister once, complaining aloud about my father's drinking. I must have been six or eight years old. I marched down to Aunt Pat's on the next block and told her outright that my father wasn't a drunk. And once, the Christmas after his father had died, I heard him and my mother come home late. He was raving a little. I thought it must be grief. He insisted the doctor be called. He said he was having a heart attack. The doctor, I think, tried to cover for him, behaved as if there was something wrong other than drink. In any case, by the time I'd taken my dive off the balcony, my father had a year's sobriety under his belt and should have been able to recognize an inebriate when he saw one. But instead of a curse, he saw blessing: his son, somewhat broken but reparable and *alive*.

Now they are both dead and I reckon a fixture in my father's heaven is the absence of any of his children there, and a fixture in my mother's is the intuition that we will all follow, sooner or later but certainly.

WE PARENT THE way we were parented. The year they began to make real sense to me was 1974. In February the first of my children was born. In June we purchased the funeral home in Milford. I was a new parent and the new undertaker in a town where births and deaths are noticed. And one of the things I noticed was the number of stillbirths and fetal deaths we were called upon to handle. There was no nearby hospital twenty years ago; no medical office buildings around town. The prenatal care was not what it should be, and in addition to the hundred adult funerals we handled every year in those days, we would be called upon to take care of the burial of maybe a dozen infants—babies born dead, or born living but soon dead from some anomaly, and several every year from what used to be called crib death and is now called Sudden Infant Death Syndrome.

I WOULD SIT with the moms and dads of these babies—dead of no discernible cause—they simply forgot to breathe, trying to make some sense of all of it. The fathers, used to protecting and paying, felt helpless. The mothers seemed to carry a pain in their innards that made them appear breakable. The overwhelming message on their faces was that nothing mattered anymore, nothing. We would arrange little wakes and graveside services, order in the tiny caskets with the reversible interiors of pink and blue, dust off the "baby bier" on which the casket would rest during the visitation, and shrink all the customs and accouterments to fit this hurt.

When we bury the old, we bury the known past, the past we imagine sometimes better than it was, but the past all the same, a portion of which we inhabited. Memory is the overwhelming theme, the eventual comfort.

But burying infants, we bury the future, unwieldy and unknown, full of promise and possibilities, outcomes punctuated by our rosy hopes. The grief has no borders, no limits, no known ends, and the little infant graves that edge the corners and fencerows of every cemetery are never quite big enough to contain that grief. Some sadnesses are permanent. Dead babies do not give us memories. They give us dreams.

And I remember in those first years as a father and a funeral director, new at making babies and at burying them, I would often wake in the middle of the night, sneak into the rooms where my sons and daughter slept, and bend to their cribsides to hear them breathe. It was enough. I did not need astronauts or presidents or doctors or lawyers. I only wanted them to breathe. Like my father, I had learned to fear.

And, as my children grew, so too the bodies of dead boys and girls I was called upon to bury—infants becoming toddlers, toddlers becoming school children, children becoming adolescents, then teens, then young adults, whose parents I would know from the Little League or Brownies or PTA or Rotary or Chamber of Commerce. Because I would not keep in stock an inventory of children's caskets, I'd order them, as the need arose, in sizes and half sizes from two foot to five foot six, often estimating the size of a dead child, not yet released from the county morgue, by the sizes of my own children, safe and thriving and alive. And the caskets I ordered were invariably "purity and gold" with angels on the corners and shirred crepe interiors of powdery pink or baby blue. And I would never charge more than the wholesale cost of the casket and throw in our services free of charge with the hope in my heart that God would, in turn, spare me the hollowing grief of these parents.

There were exceptions to the "purity and gold." Once a man whose name I remember shot his two children, ages eight and four, while their mother waited tables up in town. Then he shot himself. We laid him out in an 18-gauge steel with the Last Supper on the handles and his daughter and his son in a matching casket together. The bill was never paid. She sold the house, skipped town. I never pursued it.

And one Christmastide twin six-year-olds fell through the ice on the river that divides this town. It ran through their backyard and no one knows if they went in together or one tried to save the other. But the first of the brothers was found the same day and the next one was found two days later, bobbed up downstream after the firemen broke up the ice by the dam. We put them in the one casket with two pillows, foot to foot—identical in their new OshKosh B'Gosh jeans and plaid shirts their mother had mail-ordered from Sears for Christmas. Their father, a young man then, aged overnight and died within five years of nothing so much as sorrow. Their mother got cancer and died after that of grief metastasized. The only one left, the twins' older brother, who must be nearing thirty now, is long gone from this place.

And I remember the poor man with the look of damage on him whose wife strangled their eight-year-old son with a belt. Then she wrote a fourteen-page suicide note, explaining why she felt her son, who had been slow to read, faced a lifetime of ridicule and failure she felt she was freeing him from. Then she took three dozen pills, lay down beside the boy, and died herself. First he selected a cherry casket and laid them out together in it, the boy at rest under his mother's arm. But before the burial, he asked to have the boy removed from the mother's casket and placed in one of his own and buried in his own grave. I did as he instructed and thought it was sensible.

So early on I learned my father's fear. I saw in every move my children made the potentially lethal outcome. We lived in an old house next door to the funeral home. The children grew up playing football in the side yard, roller skating in the parking lot, then skateboarding, riding bikes, then driving cars. When they were ten, nine, six, and four, their mother and I divorced. She moved away. I was "awarded" custody—four badly saddened kids I felt a failure towards. And though I was generally pleased with the riddance that divorce provides—the marriage had become a painful case—I was suddenly aware that single parenting meant, among other things, one pair of eyes to watch out for one's children with. Not two. One pair of ears to keep to the ground. One body to place between them and peril; one mind. There was less conflict and more worry. The house itself was dangerous: poison under every sink, electrocution in every appliance, radon in the basement, contagion in the kitty litter. Having been proclaimed by the courts the more "fit" parent, I was determined to be one.

I would rise early, make the sack lunches while they ate cereal, then drive them to school. I had a housekeeper who came at noon to do the laundry and clean and be there when the youngest came home from kindergarten. I'd be at the office from nine-thirty until four o'clock, then come home to get dinner ready—stews mostly, pastas, chicken and rice. They never ate as much as I prepared. Then there was homework and dance classes and baseball, then bed. And when it was done, when they were in bed and the house was ahum with its appliances, washer and dryer and dishwasher and stereo, I'd pour myself a tumbler of Irish whiskey, sit in a wingback chair and smoke and drink and listen—on guard for whatever it was that would happen next.

Most nights I passed out in the chair, from fatigue or whiskey or from both. I'd crawl up to bed, sleep fitfully, and rise early again.

THE POOR COUSIN of fear is anger.

It is the rage that rises in us when our children do not look both ways before running into busy streets. Or take to heart the free advice we're always serving up to keep them from pitfalls and problems. It is the spanking or tongue lashing, the door slammed, the kicked dog, the clenched fist—the love, Godhelpus, that hurts: the grief. It is the war we wage against those facts of life over which we have no power, none at all. It makes for heroics and histrionics but it is no way to raise children.

And there were mornings I'd awaken heroic and angry, hungover and enraged at the uncontrollable facts of my life: the constant demands of my business, the loneliness of my bed, the damaged goods my children seemed. And though it was anything but them I was really angry at, it was the kids who'd get it three mornings out of every five. I never hit, thank God, or screamed. The words were measured out, meticulous. I seethed. After which I would apologize, pad their allowances, and curry forgiveness the way any drunk does with the ones he loves. Then I stopped drinking, and while the fear did not leave entirely, the anger subsided. I was not "in recovery" so much as I was a drunk who didn't drink and eventually came to understand that I was more grateful than resentful for the deliverance.

BUT FAITH IS, so far as I know it, the only known cure for fear—the sense that someone is in charge here, is checking the ID's and watching the borders. Faith is what my mother said: letting go and letting God—a leap into the unknown where we are not in control but always welcome. Some days it seems like stating the obvious. Some days it feels like we are entirely alone.

Here is a thing that happened. I just buried a young girl whose name was Stephanie, named for St. Stephen; the patron of stonemasons, the first martyr. She died when she was struck by a cemetery marker as she slept in the back seat of her parents' van as the family was driving down the interstate on their way to Georgia. It was the middle of the night. The family had left Michigan that evening to drive to a farm in Georgia where the Blessed Mother was said to appear and speak to the faithful on the thirteenth of every month. As they motored down the highway in the dark through mid-Kentucky, some local boys, half an hour south, were tipping headstones in the local cemetery for something to do. They picked one up that weighed about fourteen pounds—a stone. What they wanted with it is anyone's guess. And as they walked across the overpass of the interstate, they grew tired of carrying their trophy. With not so much malice as mischief, they tossed it over the rail as the lights of southbound traffic blurred below them. It was at this moment that the van that Stephanie's father was driving intersected with the stolen marker from the local cemetery. The stone was falling earthward at thirty-two feet per second, per second. The van was heading south at seventy miles per hour. The stone shattered the windshield, glanced off Stephanie's father's right shoulder, woke her mother riding in the passenger seat and, parting the space between the two front seats, struck Stephanie in the chest as she lay sleeping in the back seat. She had just traded places with her younger brother who cuddled with his two other sisters in the rear seat of the van. It did not kill Stephanie instantly. Her sternum was broken, her heart bruised beyond repair. A trucker stopped to radio for help but at two A.M. in Nowhere, Kentucky, on a Friday morning, such things take time. The family waited by the roadside reciting the rosary as Stephanie gasped for air and moaned. They declared her dead at the hospital two hours later. Stephanie's mother found the stone in the back seat and gave it to the authorities. It said RESERVED FOSTER and was reckoned to be a corner marker from the Foster Lot in Resurrection Cemetery.

SOMETIMES IT SEEMS like multiple choice.

A: It was the Hand of God. God woke up one Friday the 13th and said, "I want Stephanie!" How else to explain the fatal intersection of bizarre events. Say the facts slowly, they sound like God's handiwork. If the outcome were different, we'd call it a miracle.

Or *B*: It wasn't the Hand of God. God knew it, got word of it sooner or later, but didn't lift a hand because He knows how much we've come to count on the Laws of Nature—gravity and objects in motion and at rest—so He doesn't fiddle with the random or deliberate outcomes. He regrets to inform us of this, but surely we must understand His position.

Or *C*: The Devil did it. If faith supports the existence of Goodness, then it supports the probability of Evil. And sometimes, Evil gets the jump on us.

Or *D*: None of the above. Shit happens. That's Life, get over it, get on with it.

Or maybe *E*: All of the above. Mysteries—like decades of the rosary—glorious and sorrowful mysteries.

EACH OF THE answers leaves my inheritance intact—my father's fear, my mother's faith. If God's will, shame on God is what I say. If not, then shame on God. It sounds the same. I keep shaking a fist at the Almighty asking *Where were you on the morning of the thirteenth*? The alibi changes every day.

Of course the answers, the ones that faith does not require, and are not forthcoming, would belong to Stephanie's parents and the hundreds I've known like them over the years.

I'VE PROMISED STEPHANIE'S headstone by Christmas—actually for St. Stephen's Day, December 26th. The day we all remember singing Good King Wenceslaus. Stephen was accused of blasphemy and stoned in 35 A.D.

When I first took Stephanie's parents to the cemetery, to buy a grave for their daughter, her mother stood in the road and pointed to a statue of The Risen Christ. "I want her over there," she said, "at the right hand of Jesus." We walked across the section to an empty, unmarked space underneath the outstretched granite right arm of Christ. "Here," Stephanie's mother said, her wet eyes cast upward into the gray eyes of Christ. Stephanie's father, his eyes growing narrow, was reading the name on the neighboring grave. FOSTER is what it read. It was cut in stone.

THE GOLFATORIUM

Write, read, sing, sigh, keep silence, pray,
bear thy crosses manfully; eternal life
is worthy of all these, and greater combats.

—*Thomas à Kempis*

It came to me high over California. I was flying across the country to read poems in L.A. I had gigs at the Huntington Library, UCLA, San Bernardino, and Pomona College. And between engagements, four days free to wander at will in Southern California. It was a beautiful blue end of September, the year I quit drinking and my mother died. Crisp and cloudless, from my window seat the nation's geography lay below me. The spacious skies, the fruited plane, the purple mountains' majesty.

I was counting my blessings.

To have such a day for my first transcontinental flight, to have someone else paying for the ticket and the expenses and to be proffering stipends I'd gladly pay taxes on, to say that I was the poet and I had the poems that people in California were paying to hear—these were good gifts. My mother was dying back in Michigan, of cancer. She had told the oncologists, "Enough, enough." They had discontinued the chemotherapy. I was running from the implications.

I was scared to death.

From Detroit we first flew over Lake Michigan then the grainy

Midwest and Plains states, then the mountains and valleys of the Great West, and finally the desert west of Vegas and Reno until, in the distance, I could make out the western edges of the San Bernardino Mountains. The Mojave was all dry brown below until, just before the topography began to change from desert to mountain, I saw an irregular rectangle of verdant green. It was the unspeakable green of Co. Kerry or Virgin Gorda purposely transposed to the desert and foothills. I could only hazard a guess at its size—a couple hundred acres I reckoned, though I had no idea what altitude we were flying at. Had we already begun our final descent? The captain had turned on the seat belt sign. All of our seat backs and tray tables were forward.

"MUST BE A golf course," is what I said to myself. I could see geometrically calculated plantings of trees and irregular winding pathways. "Or a cemetery. Hell!" I remember thinking, "This is California, it could be both!"

In the Midwest we think of California as not just another state and time zone but as another state of mind, another zone entirely, having more in common with the Constellation Orion than with Detroit or Cleveland or Illinois.

And then it came to me, the vision. It *could* be both!

I've been working in secret ever since.

It is no especial genius that leads me to the truth that folks in their right minds don't like funerals. I don't think we need a special election or one of those CNN polls on this. Most folks would rather shop dry goods or foodstuffs than caskets and burial vaults. Given the choice, most would choose root canal work over the funeral home. Even that portion of the executive physical where the doctor says, "This may be a little uncomfortable," beats embalming ninety-nine times out of every hundred in the public races. Random samplings of consumer preference almost never turn up "weeping and mourning" as things we want to do on our vacations. Do you think a funeral director could be elected president? Mine was and is and, godhelpus, ever will be The Dismal Trade. We might be trusted (the last ones to let you down my father used to say) or admired (I don't know how you do it!) or tolerated (well, somebody has to do it) and even loved, though our lovers are often a little suspect (how can you stand to have him touch you after . . . ?). But rare is that man or woman who looks forward to funerals with anything even approaching gladness, save perhaps those infrequent but cheerful obsequies for IRS agents or telemarketers or a former spouse's bumptious attorney.

What's worse, all the advertising in the world won't ever make it an expandable market. Mention of our ample parking, clearance prices on bronze and copper, easy credit terms, readiness to serve twenty-four hours a day does little to quicken in any consumer an appetite for funerals in the way that, say, our taste for fast food can be incited to riot by talk of "two all beef patties, special sauce, lettuce, cheese, pickles, onion on a sesame seed bun." How many of us don't salivate, Pavlovian, when someone hums the tune that says, "You deserve a break today"? A drop in the prime rate will send shoppers out in search of the "big ticket" items—homes, cars, and pleasure craft—but never funerals. Chesty teenagers with good muscle tone dressed in their underwear and come-hither looks can sell us more Chevys than we need, more perfume than we need, more Marlboros than we need, more cruises, more computers, more exercise equipment; more and better, and fewer and better and new and improved and faster and cheaper and sexier and bigger and smaller; but the one funeral per customer rule has held for millennia, and we don't really need a study to show us that for most folks even the one and only is the one too many.

Thus we regard funerals and the ones who direct them with the same grim ambivalence as those who deliver us of hemorrhoids and boils and bowel impactions—*Thanks*, we wince or grin at the offer, *but no thanks*!

THERE ARE SOME exceptions to this quite ponderable truth.

As always, the anomalies prove the rule.

Poets, for example, will almost always regard any opportunity to dress up and hold forth in elegiac style as permissible improvement on their usual solitude. If free drink and a buffet featuring Swedish meatballs are figured in the bargain, so much the better. A reviewer of mine quite rightly calls poets the taxidermists of literature, wanting to freeze things in time, always inventing dead aunts and uncles to eulogize in verse. He is right about this. A good laugh, a good cry, a good bowel movement are all the same fellow to those who otherwise spend their days rummaging in the word horde for something to say, or raiding the warehouses of experience for something worth saying something about. And memorable speech like memorable verse calls out for its inscription into stone. Poets know that funerals and gravesides put them in the neighborhood of the memorable. The ears are cocked for answers to the eternal adverbs, the overwhelming questions. "And may these characters remain," we plead with Yeats, in his permanent phrase, "when all is ruin once again."

And there are elements of the reverend clergy who have come to the enlightenment that, better than baptisms or marriages, funerals press the noses of the faithful against the windows of their faith. Vision and insight are often coincidental with demise. Death is the moment when the chips are down. That moment of truth when the truth that we die makes relevant the claims of our prophets and apostles. Faith is not required to sing in the choir, for bake sales or building drives; to usher or deacon or elder or priest. Faith is for the time of our dying and the time of the dying of the ones we love. Those parsons and pastors who are most successful—those who have learned to "minister"—are those who allow their faithful flocks to grieve like humans while believing like Jews or Christians or Muslims or Buddhists or variants of these compatible themes. They affirm the need to weep and dance, to blaspheme and embrace the tenets of our faiths, to upbraid our gods and to thank them.

Uncles find nickels behind our ears. Magicians pulls rabbits from out of hats. Any good talker can preach pie in the sky or break out the warm fuzzies when the time is right. But only by faith do the dead arise and walk among us or speak to us in our soul's dark nights.

So rabbi and preacher, pooh-bah and high priest do well to understand the deadly pretext of their vocation. But for our mortality there'd be no need for churches, mosques, temples, or synagogues. Those clerics who regard funerals as so much fuss and bother, a waste of time better spent in prayer, a waste of money better spent on stained glass or bell towers, should not wonder for whom the bell tolls. They may have heard the call but they've missed the point. The afterlife begins to make the most sense *after life*—when someone we love is dead on the premises. The *bon vivant* abob in his hot tub needs heaven like another belly button. Faith is for the heartbroken, the embittered, the doubting, and the dead. And funerals are the venues at which such folks gather. Some among the clergy have learned to like it. Thus they present themselves at funerals with a good cheer and an unambiguous sympathy that would seem like duplicity in anyone other than a person of faith. I count among the great blessings of my calling that I have known men and women of such bold faith, such powerful witness, that they stand upright between the dead and the living and say, "Behold I tell you a mystery. . . ."

THERE ARE THOSE, too, who are ethnically predisposed in favor of funerals, who recognize among the black drapes and dirges an emotionally potent and spiritually stimulating intersection of the living and the dead. In death and its rituals, they see the leveled playing field so elusive in life. Whether we bury our dead in Wilbert Vaults, leave them in trees to be eaten by birds, burn them or beam them into space; whether choir or cantor, piper or jazz band, casket or coffin or winding sheet, ours is the species that keeps track of our dead and knows that we are always outnumbered by them. Thus immigrant Irish, Jews of the diaspora, Black North Americans, refugees and exiles and prisoners of all persuasions, demonstrate, under the scrutiny of demographers and sociologists, a high tolerance, almost an appetite, for the rites and ceremonies connected to death.

Furthermore, this approval seems predicated on one or more of the following variables: the food, the drink, the music, the shame and guilt, the kisses of aunts and distant cousins, the exultation, the outfits, the heart's hunger for all homecomings.

THE OTHER EXCEPTION to the general abhorrence of funerals is, of course, types of my own stripe whose lives and livelihoods depend on them. What sounds downright oxymoronic to most of the subspecies—a *good* funeral—is, among undertakers, a typical idiom. And though I'll grant some are pulled into the undertaking by big cars and black suits and rumors of riches, the attrition rate is high among those who do not like what they are doing. Unless the novice mortician finds satisfaction in helping others at a time of need, or "serving the living by caring for the dead" as one of our slogans goes, he or she will never stick it. Unless, of course, they make a pile of money early on. But most of us who can afford to send our kids to the orthodontist but not to boarding school, who are tied to our brick and mortar and cash-flow worries, who live with the business phone next to our beds, whose dinners and intimacies are always being interrupted by the needs of others, would not do so unless there were satisfactions beyond the fee schedule. Most of the known world could not be paid enough to embalm a neighbor on Christmas or stand with an old widower at his wife's open casket or talk with a leukemic mother about her fears for her children about to be motherless. The ones who last in this work are the ones who believe what they do is not only good for the business and the bottom line, but good, after everything, for the species.

A man that I work with named Wesley Rice once spent all of one day and all night carefully piecing together the parts of a girl's cranium. She'd been murdered by a madman with a baseball bat after he'd abducted and raped her. The morning of the day it all happened she'd left for school dressed for picture day—a schoolgirl dressed to the nines, waving at her mother, ready for the photographer. The picture was never taken. She was abducted from the bus stop and found a day later in a stand of trees just off the road a township south of here. After he'd raped her and strangled her and stabbed her, he beat her head with a baseball bat, which was found beside the child's body. The details were reported dispassionately in the local media along with the speculations as to which of the wounds was the fatal one—the choking, the knife, or the baseball bat. No doubt these speculations were the focus of the double postmortem the medical examiner performed on her body before signing the death certificate *Multiple Injuries.* Most embalmers, faced with what Wesley Rice was faced with after he'd opened the pouch from the morgue, would have simply said "closed casket," treated the remains enough to control the odor, zipped the pouch, and gone home for cocktails. It would have been easier. The pay was the same. Instead, he started working. Eighteen hours later the girl's mother, who had pleaded to see her, saw her. She was dead, to be sure, and damaged; but her face was hers again, not the madman's version. The hair was hers, not his. The body was hers, not his. Wesley Rice had not raised her from the dead nor hidden the hard facts, but he had retrieved her death from the one who had killed her. He had closed her eyes, her mouth. He'd washed her wounds, sutured her lacerations, pieced her beaten skull together, stitched the incisions from the autopsy, cleaned the dirt from under her fingernails, scrubbed the fingerprint ink from her fingertips, washed her hair, dressed her in jeans and a blue turtleneck, and laid her in a casket beside which her mother stood for two days and sobbed as if something had been pulled from her by force. It was the same when her pastor stood with her and told her "God weeps with you." And the same when they buried the body in the ground. It was then and always will be awful, horrible, unappeasably sad. But the outrage, the horror, the heartbreak belonged, not to the murderer or the media or the morgue, each of whom had staked their claims to it. It belonged to the girl and to her mother. Wesley had given them the body back. "Barbaric" is what Jessica Mitford called this "fussing over the dead body." I say the monster with the baseball bat was barbaric. What Wesley Rice did was a kindness. And, to the extent that it is easier to grieve the loss that we see, than the one we imagine or read about in papers or hear of on the evening news, it was what we undertakers call a good funeral.

It served the living by caring for the dead.

But save this handful of the marginalized—poets and preachers, foreigners and undertakers—few people not under a doctor's care and prescribed powerful medications, really "appreciate" funerals. Safe to say that part of the American Experience, no less the British, or the Japanese or Chinese, has been to turn a blind eye to the "good" in "goodbye," the "sane" in "sadness," the "fun" in "funerals."

THUS, THE CONCEPT of merging the highest and best uses of land, which came to me high over California, seemed an idea whose time had come. The ancient and ongoing duty of the land to receive the dead aligned with the burgeoning craze in the golf business led, by a post-modern devolution, to my vision of a place where one could commemorate their Uncle Larry and work on their short game at the same time—two hundred acres devoted to memories and memorable holes; where tears wept over a missed birdie comingled with those wept over a parent's grave. A *Golfatorium*! It would solve, once and for all, the question of Sundays—what to do before or after or instead of church. The formerly harried husband who always had to promise he'd do the windows "next weekend" in order to get a few holes in during good weather, could now confidently grab his golf shoes and Big Berthas and tell his wife he was going to visit his "family plot." He might let slip some mention of "grief work" or "unfinished business" or "adult-child issues still unresolved." Or say that he was "having dreams" or was feeling "vulnerable." What good wife would keep her mate from such important therapy? What harm if the cure includes a quick nine or eighteen or twenty-seven holes if the weather holds?

So began the dialogue between my selves: the naysayer and the true believer—there's one of each in every one of us. I read my poems in L.A., chatted up the literary set, waxed pithy and beleaguered at the book signings and wine and cheese receptions. But all along I was preoccupied by thoughts of the Golfatorium and my mother dying. When, after the reading at the Huntington Library, I asked the director where would she go if she had four days free in Southern California, she told me "Santa Barbara" and so I went.

THERE ARE ROUGHLY ten acres in every par four. Eighteen of those and you have a golf course. Add twenty acres for practice greens, club house, pool and patio, and parking and two hundred acres is what you'd need. Now divide the usable acres, the hundred and eighty, by the number of burials per acre—one thousand—subtract the greens, the water hazards, and the sand traps, and you still have room for nearly eight thousand burials on the front nine and the same on the back. Let's say, easy, fifteen thousand adult burials for every eighteen holes. Now add back the cremated ashes scattered in sandtraps, the old marines and swabbies tossed overboard in the water hazards and the Italians entombed in the walls of the club house and it doesn't take a genius to come to the conclusion that there's gold in them there hills!

You can laugh all you want, but do the math. Say it costs you ten thousand an acre and as much again in development costs—you know, to turn some beanfield into Roseland Park Golfatorium or Arbordale or Peachtree. I regard as a good omen the interchangeability of the names for golf courses and burial grounds: Glen Eden and Grand Lawn, like Oakland Hills or Pebble Beach could be either one, so why not both? By and large we're talking landscape here. So two million for property and two million for development, the club house, the greens, the watering system. Four million in up-front costs. Now you install an army of telemarketers-slash-memorial counselors to call people during the middle of dinner and sell them lots at an "introductory price" of, say, five hundred a grave—a bargain by any standard—and *cha-ching* you're talking seven point five million. Add in the pre-arranged cremations at a hundred a piece and another hundred for scattering in the memorial sandtraps and you've doubled your money before anyone has bought a tee time or paid a greens fee or bought golf balls or those overpriced hats and accessories from your pro shop. Nor have you sold off the home lots around the edges to those types that want to live on a fairway in Forest Lawn. Building sights at fifty thousand a pop. Clipping coupons is what you'd be. Rich beyond any imagination. And that's not even figuring how much folks would pay to be buried, say, in the same fairway as John Daly or Arnold Palmer. Or to have Jack Nicklaus try to blast out of your sandtrap. And think of the gimmicks—free burial for a hole in one, select tee times for the pre-need market. And the package deals: a condo on the eighteenth hole, six graves on the par-three on the front nine, dinner reservations every Friday night, tennis lessons for the missus, maybe a video package of you and your best foursome for use at your memorial service, to aid in everyone's remembrance of the way you were, your name and dates on the wall of the nineteenth hole where your golf buddies could get a little liquored up and weepy all in your memory. All for one low price, paid in a way that maximized your frequent-flier miles.

THE IMPULSE TO consolidate and conglomerate, to pitch the big tent of goods and services is at the heart of many of this century's success stories. No longer the butcher, the baker, the candlestick maker, we go to supermarkets where we can buy meats, breads, motor oils, pay our light bill, rent a video, and do our banking, all in the one stop. Likewise the corner gas station sells tampons and toothpaste (of course, no one comes out to check your oil, nor can the insomniac behind the glass wall fix your brakes or change your wiper blades). Our churches are no longer little chapels in the pines but crystal cathedrals of human services. Under one roof we get day care and crisis intervention, bible study and columbaria. The great TV ministries of the eighties—the Bakkers and Swaggarts and Falwells—were theme parks and universities and hospital complexes that flung the tax-free safety net of God over as much real estate as could be bought. Perhaps the tendency, manifest in many of today's megachurches, to entertain rather than to inspire, to wow rather than to worship, proceeds from the intelligence, gained generations back, that the big top needed for the tent revival and the three-ring circus was one and the same. Some of these televangelists went to jail, some ran for president, and some rode off into the sunset of oblivion. But they seemed to be selling what the traffic would bear. A kind of one-stop shopping for the soul, where healing, forgiveness, a time-share in the Carolinas, musical ministry, water parks, and pilgrimages to the Holy Land can all be put on one's Visa or Mastercard.

In the same way the Internet is nothing if not an emergent bazaar, a global mall from which one can shop the shelves of a bookstore in Galway, order a pizza or some dim sum, talk dirty to strangers bored with their marriages, and check the demographics of Botswana all without budging from—this would have sounded daft twenty years ago—the "home office."

Thus the paradigm of dual-purpose, high-utility, multitasking applications had taken hold of the market and my imagination.

This had happened to me once before.

Years back before the cremation market really—I can't help this one—heated up, I dreamed a new scheme called "Cremorialization." It was based on the observation that those families who elected to cremate their dead, much as those who buried theirs, felt a need to memorialize them. But unlike earth burial where the memorial took the form of a stone—informative but silent and otherwise useless—those who reduced the dead to ashes and bone fragments seemed to be cheered by the thought that something good might come of something bad, something useful might proceed from what they saw as otherwise useless. Such notions have root in what has been called the Protestant ethic that honors work and utility. The dead, they seemed to be saying, ought to get off their dead ashes and be good for something beyond the simple act of remembrance.

This is the crowd who can always be counted on to say "such a shame" or "what a waste" when they see a room full of flowers at one end of which is a dead human body. The same flowers surrounding a live human body hosting a tea for the visiting professor are, for the most part, "perfectly lovely." Or when the body amid the gladioli is one recovering from triplets, say, or triple bypass surgery, the flowers are reckoned to be "how very thoughtful." But flowers surrounding a casket and corpse are wasteful and shameful—the money better spent on "a good cause." This notion, combined with cremation, which renders the human corpse easily portable—ten to twelve pounds on average—and easily soluble with new age polymers and resins, brought me to the brainstorm years ago of the dead rising from their ashes, doing their part again—Cremorialization. Rather than dumbly occupying an urn, what old hunter wouldn't prefer his ashes to be used to make duck decoys or clay pigeons? The dead fisherman could become a crank-bait or plastic worms, perhaps given, with appropriate ceremony, to a favorite grandson. The minister's wife, ever the quiet and dignified helpmate, could be resurrected as a new tea service for the parsonage, her name etched tastefully into the saucers. Bowlers could be mixed into see-through bowling balls, or bowling pins, or those bags of rosin they are always tossing. Ballroom dancers could be ocarinas, cat lovers could be memorial kitty litter. The possible applications were endless. The ashes of gamblers could become dice and playing chips, car buffs turned into gear shift knobs or hood ornaments or whole families of them into matching hubcaps. After years spent in the kitchen, what gourmand could resist the chance to become a memorial egg-timer, their ashes slipping through the fulcrum in a metaphor of time. Bookends and knickknacks could be made of the otherwise boring and useless dead. And just as the departed would be made more valuable by becoming something, what they became would be more valuable by placing the word "memorial" in front of it.

WE ALWAYS KEPT the ashes in a closet—those that weren't picked up by the family or buried or placed in a niche. After ten years I noticed we'd accumulated several dozen unclaimed boxes of ashes. It seemed as if nobody wanted them. I wondered about the limits of liability. What if there were a fire. I tried to imagine the lawsuits—old family members turning up for "damages." There are, of course, damages that can be done even to a box of ashes. We'd call every year around Christmastime to see if the families of these abandoned ashes had come to any decision about what should be done, but more often than not we'd be left holding the box. One Christmas, my younger brother, Eddie, said we should declare it The Closet of Memories and establish a monthly holding fee, say twenty-five dollars, to be assessed retroactively unless the ashes were picked up in thirty days. Letters were sent out. Calls made. Old cousins and step-children came out of the woodwork. Widows long-since remarried returned. The Closet of Memories was near empty by Easter. Eddie called it a miracle.

What I called it was amazing—the ways we relate to a box of ashes—the remains. And all that winter and spring I'd watch as people called to claim their tiny dead, how exactly it was they "handled" it. Some grinned broadly and talked of the weather, taking up the ashes as one would something from the hardware store or baggage claim, tossing it into the trunk of their car like corn flakes or bird seed. Some received the package—a black plastic box or brown cardboard box with a name and dates on it—as one would old porcelain or First Communion, as if one's hands weren't worthy or able or clean enough to touch it. One elderly woman came to claim the ashes of her younger sister. The younger sister's children could not be bothered, though their aunt valiantly made excuses for them. She carried her sister's ashes to the car. Opened the trunk then closed it up again. Opened the back door of her blue sedan then closed that, too. She finally walked around to the front passenger seat, placed the parcel carefully there, paused momentarily, then put the seat belt around it before getting in and driving away. For several it was a wound reopened. And they were clearly perturbed that we should "hassle" them to take some action or else pay a fee. "What do I want with her ashes?" one woman asked, clearly mindless of the possibility that, however little her dead mother's ashes meant to her, they might mean even less to me.

The only mother who mattered was my own. And she was dying of a cancer that reoccurred a year and a half after the surgery that the doctors assured her had "got it all." They had removed a lung. We'd all put away our worst fears and grabbed the ring the surgeons tossed that said "everything was going to be all right." They were wrong. A cough that started at Thanksgiving and was still there at Valentine's Day sent her to the doctor's at my sister Julie's insistence. The doctors saw "an irregularity" in the x-rays and suggested a season of radiation treatments. I supposed this irregularity must be different than the one for which laxatives and diuretics are prescribed. But by June, her body made dry and purple from the radiation, it still had not occurred to me that she would be dying. Even in August, her voice near a whisper, a pain in her shoulder that never left, I clung to the user-friendly, emotionally neutral lexicon of the oncologist, who kept our focus on the progress of the "irregularity" (read tumor) instead of the woman dying before our eyes, whose pain they called "discomfort"; whose moral terror they called "anxiety"; whose body not only stopped being her friend, it had become her enemy.

I never pursued Cremorialization. The bankers and bean counters couldn't be swayed. One said I was probably ahead of my time. He was right. Strange ads turn up in the trade journals now that promise to turn the cremains into objects of art, which bear a uniform resemblance to those marble eggs that were all the rage a few years ago. Oh, once I dumped a fellow's ashes into a clear whiskey bottle that his wife had wired to work as a desk lamp. "He always said I really turned him on," she says and still signs her Christmas cards *Bev and Mel*. Likewise the widow of a man I fished with brought back his ashes after she remarried and asked me to scatter them on the Pere Marquette—the river where we'd fished the salmon run for years. She'd put them in a thermos bottle, one of those big pricey Stanley ones, and said it would be less conspicuous in the canoe than the urn I'd sold her. "Camouflage" she called it and smiled the smile of loss well grieved. But once I got him downstream to one of our favorite holes, I couldn't let him go that way. I buried him, thermos bottle and all, under a birch tree up from the riverbank. I piled stones there and wrote his name and dates on paper, which I put in a fly-box and hid among the stones. I wanted a place that stood still to remember him at in case his son and daughter, hardly more than toddlers when he died, ever took up fishing or came asking about him.

The world is full of odd alliances. Cable companies buy phone companies, softwares buy hardwares. Before you know it we're talking to the TV. Other combinations are no less a stretch: the "motor home," "medicide." By comparison, a cemetery-golf course combo—a Golfatorium—seems, fetched only as far as, you will excuse, a nine iron.

Furthermore, cemeteries have always been widely and mistakenly regarded as land wasted on the dead. A frequent argument one hears in favor of cremation relies on the notion, an outright fiction, that we are running out of land. But no one complains about the proliferation of golf courses. We've had three open in Milford the last year alone. And no one in public office or private conversation has said that folks should take up contract bridge or ping pong or other less land-needy, acreage-intensive pasttimes and dedicate the land, instead, to low-cost housing or co-op organic gardens. No, the development of a golf course is good news to the real estate and construction trades, reason for rejoicing among the hoteliers, restaurateurs, clothiers, and adjoining industries who have found that our species is quite willing to spend money on pleasure when the pleasure is theirs. Land dedicated to the memorialization of the dead is always suspect in a way that land used for the recreation of the living seldom is. There seems to be, in my lifetime, an inverse relationship between the size of the TV screen and the space we allow for the dead in our lives and landscapes. With the pyramids maybe representing one end of the continuum, and the memorial pendant—in which ashes of your late and greatly reduced spouse are kept dangling tastefully from anklet or bracelet or necklace or keychain—representing the other, we seem to give ground grudgingly to the departed. We've flattened the tombstones, shortened the services, opted for more and more cremation to keep from running out of land better used for amusement parks, off-street parking, go-cart tracks, and golf courses. A graveyard gains favor when we combine it with a nature walk or historical tour, as if the nature and history of our mortality were not lesson enough on any given day. We keep looking for community events to have in them—band concerts, birdwatchings—meanwhile, the community events they are supposed to involve, namely funerals and burials, have become more and more private spectacles. It is not enough for it to be only the repository of our dead and the memories we keep of them, or safe harbor for the often noisome and untidy feelings grief includes; comfort and serenity are not enough. We want our parks, our memorial parks, to entertain us a little, to have some use beyond the obvious. Less, we seem to be telling the dead, is more; while for the living, enough is never quite enough.

So the combination of golf and good grieving seems a natural, each divisible by the requirement for large tracts of green grass, a concentration on holes, and the need for someone to carry the bags—caddies or pallbearers.

There will of course be practical arguments—when are you going to actually "do" the burials? Can people play through a graveside service? What is the protocol? Is there a dress code? What about headstones, decoration day, perpetual care? And what, godhelpus, about handicaps? What will the hearse look like? Must we all begin to dress like Gary Player?

When my mother was dying I hated God. Some days when I think of her, dead at sixty-five, I think of how my father said, "These were supposed to be the Golden Years." She bore and birthed and raised nine children because the teachings or the technologies of her generation did not offer reliable "choice." The daughter of a music teacher, she understood everything but "rhythm." It is the strength in numbers I'm the beneficiary of now. The God of my anger was the God she knew—the fellow with the beard and archangels and the abandonment issues. The practical joker with a mean streak, pulling the chair out from under us, squirting us with the boutonniere, shaking our hands with the lightning-bolt joy buzzer and then wondering why we don't "get it"; can't we "take a joke"?

My mother, a Bing Crosby and Ingrid Bergman Catholic, had her heaven furnished with familiar pieces: her own parents, her sister, friends of her youth. Her vision was precise, down to the doilies.

So checking into the Miramar—an old oceanfront hotel south of Santa Barbara, with blue roof tiles over white clapboard, I wanted to hide, for four days only, from the facts of the matter. I remember waking to the sound of pelicans, gulls, and cormorants diving into the blue water, the listless lapping of the waves. The Pacific was pacific.

I needed peace. I sat on the deck overlooking the beach. Taut bodies jogged by in primary colors or walked with their designer dogs in the morning light. No one was dying in Santa Barbara. I began to make notes about the golf course-cemetery combo. Would calling it "St. Andrews" be too bold? Would people pay more to be buried on the greens? Would a bad divot be desecration? What about headstones? They'd have to go. But what to replace them with? Memorial balls? These and other questions like them quarreled like children for my attention. I ordered coffee. A grilled cheese sandwich. I avoided the temptation to float in the water. The undulent ocean glistened with metaphor. To sit and watch the sea was good. Everything was going to be all right. By sunset I was transfixed by the beauty. I'd worked out the details of my plan—the location, the capitalization, the ad campaign, the board of directors. Why shouldn't our cemeteries be used for fun and fitness? Pleasure and pain were soluble. Laughing and crying are the same release. I didn't know which I should do next, laugh or weep.

My mother believed in redemptive suffering. The paradigm for this was the crucifixion of Christ, an emblem of which she kept in most rooms of our house. This was the bad day against which all others were measured. She was a student of the fifteenth-century mystic Thomas à Kempis whose *Imitation of Christ* she read daily. "Offer it up for the suffering souls," is what she would say when we'd commence our carping over some lapse in creature comforts. I think it was a Catholic variation on the Protestant work ethic. If you're going to be miserable, her logic held, you may as well be miserable for a good cause.

Who were these suffering souls? I'd ask myself.

Likewise, people of the Irish persuasion have a special knack or affliction for searching out the blessing in every badness. "Happy is the grave the rain falls on," they say as they stand ankle deep in mud, burying their dead, finding the good omen in the bad weather. Thus, in a country where it rains every day, they have proclaimed the downpour a blessed thing. "Could be worse," they say in the face of disaster or "The devil you know's better than the one you don't," or when all else fails "Just passing through life." Invasion and famine and occupation have taught them these things. They have a mindset that tolerates, perhaps to a fault, God's little jokes on the likes of us.

So when, as a child, I'd find myself hungry or angry or lonely or tired or brutalized by one of the brothers, among my mother's several comforts was the subtle spiritual dictum to "offer it up for the suffering souls." By patient acceptance of pain I could assist in the universal business of salvation. The currency of hurt became the currency of holiness the way you'd change pounds sterling to greenback dollars. God was the celestial bank teller who kept track of the debits and credits to our accounts. Those who died in arrears went to Purgatory—a kind of bump-and-paint shop for the soul, where the dents and dings and rust of life on earth could be fixed before going on to Heaven. Hell was a Purgatory that never ended, reserved for the true deadbeats who not only didn't pay their tolls but didn't figure they owed anyone anything. Purgatory was for rehabilitation. Hell was for punishment, perpetual, eternal, cruel and unusual. The chief instrument of both locales was fire—the cleansing, if painful, flames of purgatorio, the fire and brimstone recompense, for pleasures ill-got and self-indulgent, of the inferno.

I think sometimes that this is why, for most of the last two millennia, the western Church has avoided cremation—because fire was punitive. When you were in trouble with God you went to hell where you burned. Perhaps this created in us feelings about fire that were largely negative. We burned the trash and buried the treasure. This is why, faced with life's first lessons in mortality—the dead kitten or bunny rabbit, or dead bird fallen from its nest on high—good parents search out shoe boxes and shovels instead of kindling wood or barbecues. It is also why we might witness burials, but cremation, like capital punishment, is hidden from us. Of course, Eastern thought has always favored fire as a purifier, as the element that reunites us with our elements and origins. Hence the great public pyres of Calcutta and Bombay, where dead bodies blacken the skies with smoke from their burning.

My mother did not believe this part. Her children needed neither punishment or purification beyond that which she supplied. We were the children of God and her own best efforts. Salvation was a gift of God. Her gift to us was how to claim it. And when, after the Second Vatican Council, they got rid of Limbo and Purgatory, she fashioned it a kind of enlightenment. Still, life had sufferings enough to go around and she wanted us to use them well. It was part of Nature.

"All grievous things are to be endured for eternal life," is how my mother was instructed by Thomas à Kempis. Suffering was thereby imbued with meaning, purpose, value, and reason. Nature passed suffering out in big doses, random and irreverent, but faith and grace made suffering a part of the way by which we make our journey back to God. Atonement meant to be "at one." And this return, this reunion in heaven, this salvation, was the one true reason for our being, according to my mother. This opinion put her, of course, at odds with everything the culture told us about "feeling good about ourselves" or "taking care of numero uno" or the secular trophies of "happiness" and "validation" and "self-esteem." Hers was a voice crying in the suburban wilderness that we were all given crosses to bear—it was our imitation of Christ—and we should offer it up for the suffering souls.

THAT IS HOW she turned it into prayer—the "irregularity," the cancer, the tumor that moved from her remaining lung up her esophagus, leapt to her spinal cord, and then made for her brain. This was what the doctors said was happening, preferring a discussion of parts failing to persons dying. But for her husband and children what was happening was that her voice was growing more and more quiet, her breath was getting shorter and shorter, her balance was lost to the advance of cancer. My mother was making it work for her, placing the pain and the fear and the grief of it into that account with God she'd kept, by which what was happening to her body became only one of several things that were happening to her. Her body, painful and tumorous, was turning on her and she was dying. I'm sure she was ready to be rid of it. She said her heart was overwhelmed with grief and excitement. Grief at the going from us—her husband of forty-three years, her sons and daughters, grandchildren born and unborn, her sister and brother, her friends. Excitement at the going "home." But as the voice inside her body hushed, her soul's voice seemed to shout out loud, almost to sing. She could see things none of us could see. She refused the morphine and remained lucid and visionary. She spoke words of comfort to each of us—at one point saying we must learn to let go, not only grudgingly, but as an act of praise. I say this not because I understand it but because I witnessed it. I'm not certain that it works—only certain that it worked for her.

Once you've made the leap it's easy. Once you've seen huge tracts of greensward put to seemingly conflicting uses, the world becomes a different place. If golf courses can be graveyards, surely football fields, and soccer pitches, ball diamonds and tennis courts. And what about ski slopes? What folks don't want to be buried on a mountain? Boot Hill we could call it. Listen up, the possible applications are endless. The thrill of victory, the agony of defeat. Life is like that—death is, too.

My mother's funeral was a sadness and a celebration. We wept and laughed, thanked God and cursed God, and asked God to make good on the promises our mother's faith laid claim to in her death. It was Halloween the day we buried her—the eve of All Saints, then All Souls, all suffering souls.

Eddie and I have been looking for acreage. He's a golfer. I'd rather read and write. He says he'll be the Club Pro and I can be the Brains Behind the Operation. We've worked together for years and years. Our sister Brigid does pre-need and our sister Mary has always done the books—payroll and collections and payables. The women seem to control the money. Revenge they call it for our calling it Lynch & Sons.

Whenever I have business at Holy Sepulchre, I stop in section twenty-four, where my mother and father are buried. He lived on after her for two more years. After he was buried we all decided on a tall Celtic cross in Barre granite with their instruction to "Love One Another" cut into the circle that connects the crossed beams. My father had seen crosses like this when I took him to Ireland the year after my mother died. He'd said he liked the look of them.

Stones like these make golf impossible. They stand their ground. It's hard to play through. Those joggers with their designer dogs on leashes and stereos plugged into their ears are not allowed. A sign by the pond reads "No Fishing/Do Not Feed Ducks." The only nature trail in Holy Sepulchre is the one that takes you by the nature of our species to die and to remember.

I miss them so.

I think it's my sisters who plant the impatiens every spring at the base of the stone.

Sometimes I stand among the stones and wonder. Sometimes I laugh, sometimes I weep. Sometimes nothing at all much happens. Life goes on. The dead are everywhere. Eddie says that's par for the course.

TRACT

Share with us—it will be money
in your pockets.
Go now
I think you are ready.

—*William Carlos Williams,* "TRACT"

I'd rather it be February. Not that it will matter much to me. Not that I'm a stickler for details. But since you're asking—February. The month I first became a father, the month my father died. Yes. Better even than November.

I want it cold. I want the gray to inhabit the air like wood does trees: as an essence not a coincidence. And the hope for springtime, gardens, romance, dulled to a stump by the winter in Michigan.

Yes, February. With the cold behind and the cold before you and the darkness stubborn at the edges of the day. And a wind to make the cold more bitter. So that ever after it might be said, "It was a sad old day we did it after all."

And a good frosthold on the ground so that, for nights before it is dug, the sexton will have had to go up and put a fire down, under the hood that fits the space, to soften the topsoil for the backhoe's toothy bucket.

Wake me. Let those who want to come and look. They have their reasons. You'll have yours. And if someone says, "Doesn't he look natural!" take no offense. They've got it right. For this was always in my nature. It's in yours.

And have the clergy take their part in it. Let them take their best shot. If they're ever going to make sense to you, now's the time. They're looking, same as the rest of us. The questions are more instructive than the answers. Be wary of anyone who knows what to say.

As for music, suit yourselves. I'll be out of earshot, stone deaf. A lot can be said for pipers and tinwhistlers. But consider the difference between a funeral with a few tunes and a concert with a corpse down front. Avoid, for your own sakes, anything you've heard in the dentist's office or the roller rink.

Poems might be said. I've had friends who were poets. Mind you, they tend to go on a bit. Especially around horizontal bodies. Sex and death are their principal studies. It is here where the services of an experienced undertaker are most appreciated. Accustomed to being *personae non grata*, they'll act the worthy editor and tell the bards when it's time to put a sock in it.

On the subject of money: you get what you pay for. Deal with someone whose instincts you trust. If anyone tells you you haven't spent enough, tell them to go piss up a rope. Tell the same thing to anyone who says you spent too much. Tell them to go piss up a rope. It's your money. Do what you want with it. But let me make one thing perfectly clear. You know the type who's always saying "When I'm dead, save your money, spend it on something really useful, do me cheaply"? I'm not one of them. Never was. I've always thought that funerals were useful. So do what suits you. It is yours to do. You're entitled to wholesale on most of it.

As for guilt—it's much overrated. Here are the facts in the case at hand: I've known the love of the ones who have loved me. And I've known that they've known that I've loved them, too. Everything else, in the end, seems irrelevant. But if guilt is the thing, forgive yourself, forgive me. And if a little upgrade in the pomp and circumstance makes you feel better, consider it money wisely spent. Compared to shrinks and pharmaceuticals, bartenders or homeopaths, geographical or ecclesiastical cures, even the priciest funeral is a bargain.

I WANT A mess made in the snow so that the earth looks wounded, forced open, an unwilling participant. Forego the tent. Stand openly to the weather. Get the larger equipment out of sight. It's a distraction. But have the sexton, all dirt and indifference, remain at hand. He and the hearse driver can talk of poker or trade jokes in whispers and straight-face while the clergy tender final commendations. Those who lean on shovels and fill holes, like those who lean on custom and old prayers, are, each of them, experts in the one field.

And you should see it till the very end. Avoid the temptation of tidy leavetaking in a room, a cemetery chapel, at the foot of the altar. None of that. Don't dodge it because of the weather. We've fished and watched football in worse conditions. It won't take long. Go to the hole in the ground. Stand over it. Look into it. Wonder. And be cold. But stay until it's over. Until it is done.

On the subject of pallbearers—my darling sons, my fierce daughter, my grandsons and granddaughters, if I've any. The larger muscles should be involved. The ones we use for the real burdens. If men and their muscles are better at lifting, women and theirs are better at bearing. This is a job for which both may be needed. So work together. It will lighten the load.

Look to my beloved for the best example. She has a mighty heart, a rich internal life, and powerful medicines.

After the words are finished, lower it. Leave the ropes. Toss the gray gloves in on top. Push the dirt in and be done. Watch each other's ankles, stamp your feet in the cold, let your heads sink between your shoulders, keep looking down. That's where what is happening is happening. And when you're done, look up and leave. But not until you're done.

So, if you opt for burning, stand and watch. If you cannot watch it, perhaps you should reconsider. Stand in earshot of the sizzle and the pop. Try to get a whiff of the goings on. Warm your hands to the fire. This might be a good time for a song. Bury the ashes, cinders, and bones. The bits of the box that did not burn.

Put them in something.

Mark the spot.

Feed the hungry. It's good form. Feed them well. This business works up an appetite, like going to the seaside, walking the cliff road. After that, be sober.

THIS IS NONE of my business. I won't be there. But if you're asking, here is free advice. You know the part where everybody is always saying that you should have a party now? How the dead guy always insisted he wanted everyone to have a good time and toss a few back and laugh and be happy? I'm not one of them. I think the old teacher is right about this one. There *is* a time to dance. And it just may be this isn't one of them. The dead can't tell the living what to feel.

They used to have this year of mourning. Folks wore armbands, black clothes, played no music in the house. Black wreathes were hung at the front doors. The damaged were identified. For a full year you were allowed your grief—the dreams and sleeplessness, the sadness, the rage. The weeping and giggling in all the wrong places. The catch in your breath at the sound of the name. After a year, you would be back to normal. "Time heals" is what was said to explain this. If not, of course, you were pronounced some version of "crazy" and in need of some professional help.

Whatever's there to feel, feel it—the riddance, the relief, the fright and freedom, the fear of forgetting, the dull ache of your own mortality. Go home in pairs. Warm to the flesh that warms you still. Get with someone you can trust with tears, with anger, and wonderment and utter silence. Get that part done—the sooner the better. The only way around these things is through them.

I know I shouldn't be going on like this.

I've had this problem all my life. Directing funerals.

It's yours to do—my funeral—not mine. The death is yours to live with once I'm dead.

So here is a coupon good for Disregard. And here is another marked My Approval. Ignore, with my blessings, whatever I've said beyond Love One Another.

Live Forever.

ALL I REALLY wanted was a witness. To say I was. To say, daft as it still sounds, maybe I *am*.

To say, if they ask you, it was a sad day after all. It was a cold, gray day.

February.

OF COURSE, ANY other month you're on your own. Have no fear—you'll know what to do. Go now, I think you are ready.

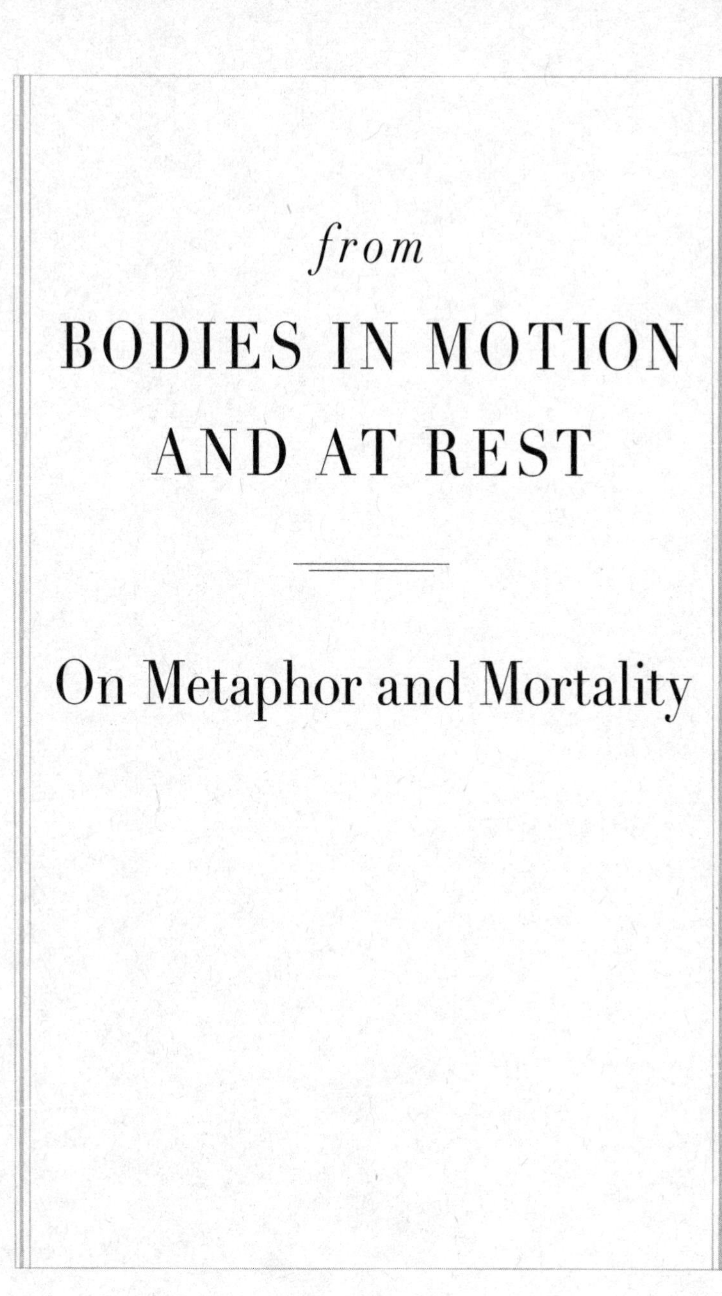

from

BODIES IN MOTION AND AT REST

On Metaphor and Mortality

INTRODUCTION

People sometimes ask me why I write. Because, I tell them, I don't golf. This gives me two or three days a week—five or six the way my brother was doing it before he had a midlife crisis and took up rollerblades. But a couple of days every week at least, with a few hours in them in which to read or write. It's all the same thing to me, reading and writing, twins of the one conversation. We're either speaking or are spoken to. And I don't drink. I did, of course, and plenty of it, but had to quit for the usual reasons. It got to where I was spilling so much of it. This gave me two or three nights a week—five or six the way I was doing it at the end—with a few hours in them when things weren't blurry. With some of those hours I would read or write. And I am married to an Italian woman with some French sensibilities and five brothers, so I am home most nights, and when I'm not, I call. I sleep well, rise early, and since I don't do Tae Bo or day trading, I read or write a few hours each morning. Then I take a walk. Out there on Shank's mare, I think about what I'm reading or writing, which is one of the things I really like—it's portable. You don't need a caddy or a designated driver or a bag full of cameras.

All you need's a little peace and quiet and the words will come to you—your own or the other's. Your own voice or the voice of God. Perspiration, inspiration. It feels like a gift.

Years ago I was watching a woman undress. The room was lit only by the light of the moon coming through an easterly window. Everything about this moment was careless and beautiful except for the sound of a sick boy in the next room coughing and croupy, unable to sleep. He had his medicine. The VapoRub and steam were bubbling away. I was drowsing with the sounds and darkening images, half dreaming of Venice, the Lido and the Zattere, the tall windows of a room I stayed in once, awash in moonlight and shadows, longing for the woman I loved madly then. It was that sweet moment between wake and sleep when the dream has only a foot in the door that the day and its duties have left ajar. I wanted always to remember that sweetness, that moment, and knew I could not rise to write the details down—the sick child, the woman's beauty, the moonlight, the steam bubbling, the balance between the dream and duty, between the romance and the ordinary times—because the slumber was tightening around me. And I was searching for a word, one word that I could keep and remember till the morning; one word only: a key, a password by which I could return to this moment just long enough to make a poem, a purse made of words to keep the treasure of it in. And I was fading quickly, my eyes were closed, my last bit of consciousness was clinging to words then bits of words and finally only bits of noises, the woman beside me, the boy's labored but even breathing, the bubbling of the *vaporizer*, which became in my dream the *vaporetti* idling in the Grand Canal, because it was the key—*vaporetti*—the password, the outright gift of sound whose bubbling and whose syllables sound near enough the same as the *vaporizer* in the next room to let me traffic back and forth at will between the bedroom in Michigan and the bedroom in Venice and the moonlight and the beauty and the moment awash in ivory and shimmering images. I slept with the word. I woke with it. I rose and wrote the poem down. The women are gone. The boy is grown. The poem sits on the shelf in a book. I come and go to Venice as I please. The language is alive and well.

So this is why I write and read. Because I don't golf, and I don't drink, and I'm married to an Italian, and every day I sit down to it, there's the chance that I might get another *vaporetti*, another gift, another of what Hemingway calls the "one true word" that will make some sense out of what we're doing here. That part about Hemingway I heard on the radio. Keep your ears tuned. Words are everywhere.

Today, for example—it is September, the last late summer of the century. Planes have fallen from the sky. Trains are colliding. There's trouble in the Balkans. Farmers are worried about drought and prices. Earthquakes in Turkey. Hurricanes off the Carolinas. Death tolls are rising. Tax cuts and national debt are in the news. The political soap opera carries on. The day is already full of words. I'm listening.

What, as St. Paul asked famously, are we to say to these things? What is the one true word today? What is the word that becomes flesh? The gospel? The good word, the good news? The truth, the whole truth? The will of God? What's a man of my age and my times to make of it all on any given day if he doesn't golf or drink or gallivant? Is bearing a little witness the best I can do?

This morning I was reading the letters of Paul. The one to the Romans is about circumcision, about faith and works, about sin and the law. No wonder he seems to go in circles a bit.

He's telling the Romans that they don't have to become Jews to become Christians. The earliest Christians were Jews, of course, including, it is worth repeating, Jesus Himself or himself, depending on your particulars. Guilt and shame are ecumenical and have always worked for observant Christians and observant Jews.

Specifically, Paul is telling the Romans that they needn't be circumcised. This is good news on any given day, at least to the men of the congregation. There's a concept they can get behind. Then, as now, women were given to wonder about the things men worry about. The laws about diet and fashions and the keeping of feasts are easy enough and all in line with the rules of good living. But circumcision is a deal breaker and Paul knows it. So he's trying to tell them it's not all that important after all. He's floating this option of "spiritual circumcision." It's a talking point and the numbers look good. Then, too, he doesn't want to offend the brethren back in the Promised Land, who are, it is well known, his kinsmen and the Chosen People. If he devalues the old deal made between God and Abraham, the Old Testament, that early covenant of blood, he's going to lose the very ones who have bought into his take on the Nazarene—the part about Him being the Son of God. Try telling some coreligionist who just had his foreskin removed that it really wasn't necessary and see what happens. This is where the faith and works come in, the part that is so important to Luther fifteen centuries later when the Reformation begins. By deconstructing that section of Genesis where God and Abraham cut their deal, Paul is able to coax both Gentile and Jew in the direction of his version of things. Here is a man who is able to make both those with foreskins and those without feel good about themselves. It's a bit like watching a game of Twister, but it is a deft little exercise in the use of language.

Language, some right thinker said, is a dialect with a navy. Much the same can be said for religions—whatever the word is, they need a navy or an army to spread it. Paul is Christianity's navy. He has some impressive character flaws—he's pompous, opinionated, opportunistic, misogynistic, vexed by sexuality in general and, like any true believer, a dangerous man. Before he came to his senses he was slaughtering Christians with enthusiasm. Still, no one can say he's not willing to travel, to "take it to them" in our latter-day parlance, to walk the walk that goes with the talk. No doubt he'll remind you of someone you know. Maybe your husband or father or brother-in-law. Today he'd be a radio talk-show host or TV preacher, prime minister or lately retired Speaker of the House. Women would be uniformly offended by and attracted to him, each for reasons unique to themselves, none of which would have to do with circumcision. All the same it should be said that Time, such as we know it, would be nothing without the travels of Paul and his letters. We would not all be hovering over the changing of millennia, fretting about disasters and apocalypse and computer glitches. We would not have divided Time into B.C. and A.D., because whether C(hrist) was D(omine) was pretty much up for grabs until Paul got knocked off his horse and saw the light. But for that today would be just another day in the year of some pagan deity.

So today neither dialects nor religions need navies or armies or missionaries as much as they need Web sites and wideband space and a lobbyist. Maybe Paul looks a little obsolete, with his horse and epistles and his true belief. And if the business of foreskins isn't what it once was, still, the deals that are cut between blood and belief, tribe and creed, dialect and sect, color and kind, define every age before Paul and since. Then, as now, the haves and the have-nots are badly divided.

So maybe the word today isn't *circumcision.*

Maybe it's *faith* or *works.* Or *sin* and *the law.* Those chicken-and-egg games that Paul rolls out for us to kick around the yard for the rest of history. Did God give Abraham a son in old age and make him the father of nations because of his faith or because of what he was willing to do to prove his faith? If there were no law, would there be no sin? Can ignorance be bliss if not a defense? Your man argues all sides of these and related issues in his letters. The true words are in there blinking, but I cannot find them. Not today. Today I'll have to get by on faith.

Maybe it's not the word today at all. Maybe it's a number. The language is full of them. You could start counting now and never finish. Like words, they've got us, well, outnumbered. All you can do is hunt and peck for the good word, the lucky number, the truth of the matter.

My father's lucky number was thirteen. He was born on the thirteenth and wore number thirteen on his jersey in high school and signed his best deals on the thirteenth of the month and died in a condo that was number thirteen. He always said that thirteen was his number. Who could blame him? So I'm looking at the thirteenth verse of the thirteenth chapter of Paul's letter to the Romans because my wife is Italian and I'm not drinking this morning and no one's coming to take me golfing and here's what it says there, word for word: "Let us live honorably as in the day, not in reveling and drunkenness, not in debauchery and licentiousness, not in quarreling and jealousy." Now, that mightn't make the hairs stand on the back of your neck, but the Romans were done no harm when they heard it and for me it sounds like the voice of my father. Not that he talked like that, mind you, but still it's a concept he could get behind. Because he was the kind of guy who wasn't looking for all the answers. Just enough to get him through the day. Just one little something that rang true enough that he could hang his hat on it when he came home and find it still there in the morning. Unlike Abraham, he didn't want to be the father of a nation. Unlike Paul, he didn't want to save the world. He just wanted his children to outlive him, his wife to love him and everything to work out in the end. It did.

Same for me. Just enough good word to get through the day. It's liable to turn up anywhere—a good book, the Good Book, the bumper of a car, something on the radio, something your daughter says, something that comes to you in a dream, like "Eat more fruit, Adam," or "Say your prayers," which is what my sainted mother frequently says when I dream of her. Or maybe it is something your true love says, like the time mine said, "Everything is going to be all right." I believed her then, I believe her now. Or, let's say you're standing in the shower, counting syllables, when it comes to you that *nine thousand, nine hundred, ninety-nine* has exactly nine syllables in it and is exactly the number of dollars you can deposit in cash without the tax man getting involved, or line those nines up, all four in a row, and they look like the day and the month and the year you're thinking this. Who invented wonders like that? Or maybe it hits you like a bolt of lightning, like *preaching to bishops is like farting at skunks.* What disgruntled cleric first told me that? These are words to live by? I don't know. What if Paul had written them to the Romans? Maybe they'd have learned to lighten up. Maybe they wouldn't have gotten so schismatic after all.

Or maybe you go looking for the one true word, like last fall in Barcelona when I climbed to the top of those towering spires in Gaudi's cathedral, La Sagrada Família. It's a hundred years in the making and not done yet. Maybe they should declare it a shopping mall and finish the thing. Maybe they just like it as a work in progress. Anyway, I'm climbing to the very top of the steeple, overlooking the city like any good pilgrim, and at the top I say "Here I am Lord" and the wind is howling in my ears like Moses on the mountain. "Give me the Good Word, God! I'll cut it in stone." And the city out before me and I'm whispering so that none of the other pilgrims will hear me, but I'm saying it out loud: "Show me a sign and I'll write it down!" And you know what the sign said, the one I first saw when I turned to make my way down from the heights? It said, WATCH YOUR STEP. In Catalan and in English and in Japanese, which is, I suppose, a sign that God speaks in all our tongues. Maybe next time I'll go looking in Venice. Maybe next time I'll take the gondola. Maybe I don't have to go looking at all. Maybe it will come to me. On its own. When I least expect it.

So what are we to make of these things?

You want to get some good words like these? I say don't golf, don't drink, marry an Italian—it could happen to you.

But maybe you'll make a different deal with God. There's other things you want? Instead of words? A scratch game, a good Beaujolais, a date with a shepherd from the Hebrides? That's fine. God knows your heart. God knows you want your children to outlive you, your beloved to love you, everything to work out in the end.

Work hard. Have faith. It will.

One last thing. A word to the wise. Like with me and my father, like with Peter and Paul, like with Moses and Abraham—when dealing with God, or rabbis and bishops, any of that crowd—a thing well worth knowing is where to cut.

—TL

MILFORD, MICHIGAN

BODIES IN MOTION AND AT REST

So I'm over at the Hortons' with my stretcher and minivan and my able apprentice, young Matt Sheffler, because they found old George, the cemetery sexton, dead in bed this Thursday morning in ordinary time. And the police have been in to rule out foul play and the EMS team to run a tape so some ER doctor wired to the world can declare him dead at a safe distance. And now it's ours to do—Matt's and mine—to ease George from the bed to the stretcher, negotiate the sharp turn at the top of the stairs, and go out the front door to the dead wagon idling in the driveway and back to the funeral home from whence he'll take his leave—waked and well remembered—a Saturday service in the middle of April, his death observed, his taxes due.

We are bodies in motion and at rest—there in George's master bedroom, in the gray light of the midmorning, an hour or so after his daughter found him because he didn't answer when she called this morning, and he always answers, and she always calls, so she got in the car and drove over and found him exactly as we find him here: breathless, unfettered, perfectly still, manifestly indifferent to all this hubbub. And he is here, assembled on his bed as if nothing had happened, still propped on his left shoulder, his left ear buried in his pillow, his right leg hitched up over the left one, his right hand tucked up under the far pillow his ex-wife used to sleep on, before she left him twenty years ago, and under the former Mrs. Horton's pillow, I lift to show Matt, is a little pearl-handled .22 caliber that George always slept with since he has slept alone. "Security," he called it. He said it helped him sleep.

And really there is nothing out of order, no sign of panic or struggle or pain, and except for the cardiac-blue tinting around his ears, the faint odor of body heat and a little early rigor in his limbs, which makes the moving of him easier, one'd never guess George wasn't just sleeping in this morning—catching the twenty extra winks—because maybe he'd been up late playing poker with the boys, or maybe he'd had a late dinner with his woman friend, or maybe he was just a little tired from digging graves and filling them, and anyway, he hadn't a grave to open this morning for one of the locals who was really dead.

But this morning George Horton is really dead and he's really being removed from his premises by Matt and me after we swaddle him in his own bed linens, sidle him on to the stretcher, tip the stretcher up to make the tight turn at the top of the stairs and carefully ease it down, trying to keep the wheels from thumping each time the heavier head end of the enterprise takes a step. And it's really a shame, all things considered, because here's George, more or less in his prime, just south of sixty, his kids raised, his house paid off, a girlfriend still in her thirties with whom he maintained twice-weekly relations—"catch as catch can," he liked to say. And he's a scratch golfer and a small business owner with reliable employees and frequent flier miles that he spends on trips to Vegas twice a year, where he lets himself get a little crazy with the crap tables and showgirls. And he has his money tucked into rental homes and mutual funds, and a host of friends who'd only say good things about him, and a daughter about to make him a grandfather for the first time, and really old George seemed to have it made, and except for our moving him feet first down the stairs this morning, he has everything to live for, everything.

And it is there, on the landing of the first floor, only a few feet from the front door out, that his very pregnant daughter waits in her warmup suit to tender her good-byes to the grandfather of her baby, not yet born. And Matt's face is flushed with the lifting, the huffing and puffing, or the weight of it all, or the sad beauty of the woman as she runs her hand along her father's cheek, and she is catching her breath and her eyes are red and wet and she lifts her face to ask me, "Why?"

"His heart, Nancy . . ." is what I tell her. "It looks like he just slept away. He never felt a thing." These are all the well-tested comforts one learns after twenty-five years of doing these things.

"But *why*?" she asks me, and now it is clear that *how* it happened is not good enough. And here I'm thinking all the usual suspects: the cheeseburgers, the whiskey, the Lucky Strikes, the thirty extra pounds we, some of us, carry, the walks we didn't take, the preventive medicines we all ignore, the work and the worry and the tax man, the luck of the draw, the nature of the beast, the way of the world, the shit that happens because it happens.

But Nancy is not asking for particulars. She wants to know why in the much larger, Overwhelming Question sense: why we don't just live forever. Why are we all eventually orphaned and heartbroken? Why we human beings cease to be. Why our nature won't leave well enough alone. Why we are not all immortal. Why this morning? Why George Horton? Why oh why oh why?

No few times in my life as a funeral director have I been asked this. Schoolchildren, the newly widowed, musing clergy, fellow pilgrims—maybe they think it was my idea. Maybe they just like to see me squirm contemplating a world in which folks wouldn't need caskets and hearses and the likes of me always ready and willing and at their service. Or maybe, like me, sometimes they really wonder.

"Do the math" is what George Horton would say. Or "Bottom line." Or "It's par for the course." Or "It's Biblical." If none of these wisdoms seemed to suit, then "Not my day to watch it" is what he'd say. Pressed on the vast adverbials that come to mind whilst opening or closing graves, George could be counted for tidy answers. Self-schooled in the Ways of the World, he confined his reading to the King James Bible, *The Wall Street Journal, Golf Digest,* the *Victoria's Secret* catalog and the Big Book of Alcoholics Anonymous. He watched C-SPAN, The Home Shopping Network and The Weather Channel. Most afternoons he'd doze off watching Oprah, with whom he was, quite helplessly, in love. On quiet days he'd surf the Web or check his portfolio on-line. On Sundays he watched talking heads and went to dinner and the movies with his woman friend. Weekday mornings he had coffee with the guys at the Summit Café before making the rounds of the half dozen cemeteries he was in charge of. Wednesdays and Saturdays he'd mostly golf.

"Do the math" I heard him give out with once from the cab of his backhoe for no apparent reason. He was backfilling a grave in Milford Memorial. "You gonna make babies, you've gotta make some room; it's Biblical."

Or once, leaning on a shovel, waiting for the priest to finish: "Copulation, population, inspiration, expiration. It's all arithmetic—addition, multiplication, subtraction and long division. That's all we're doing here, just the math. Bottom line, we're buried a thousand per acre, or burned into two quarts of ashes, give or take."

There was no telling when such wisdoms would come to him.

BUT IT CAME to me, embalming George later that morning, that the comfort in numbers is that they all add up. There is a balm in the known quantities, however finite. Any given year at this end of the millennium, 2.3 million Americans will die. Ten percent of pregnancies will be unintended. There'll be 60 million common colds.

These are numbers you can take to the bank. Give or take, 3.9 million babies will be born. It's Biblical. They'll get a little more or a little less of their 76 years of life expectancy. The boys will grow to just over 69 inches, the girls to just under 64. Of them, 25 percent will be cremated, 35 percent will be overweight, 52 percent will drink. Every year 2 million will get divorced, 4 million will get married and there'll be 30,000 suicides. A few will win the lotto, a few will run for public office, a few will be struck by lightning. And any given day, par for the course, 6,300 of our fellow citizens, just like George, will get breathless and outstretched and spoken of in the past tense; and most will be dressed up the way I dress up George, in his good blue suit, and put him in a casket with Matt Sheffler's help, and assemble the 2 or 3 dozen floral tributes and the 100 or 200 family and friends and the 60 or 70 cars that will follow in the 15 mile per hour procession down through town to grave 4 of lot 17 of section C in Milford Memorial, which will become, in the parlance of our trade, his final resting place, over which a 24-by-12-by-4-inch Barre granite stone will be placed, into which we will have sandblasted his name and dates, one of which, subtracted from the other, will amount, more or less, to his life and times. The corruptible, according to the officiating clergy, will have put on incorruption, the mortal will have put on immortality. "Not my day to watch it" will be among the things we'll never hear George Horton say again.

Nor can we see clearly now, looking into his daughter Nancy's eyes, the blue morning at the end of this coming May when she'll stand, upright as any walking wound, holding her newborn at the graveside of the man, her one and only father, for whom her baby will be named. Nor can we hear the promises she makes to keep him alive, to always remember, forever and ever, in her heart of hearts. Nor is there any math or bottom line or Bible verse that adds or subtracts or in any way accounts for the moment or the mystery she holds there.

FISH STORIES

I taught my son to fish when he was four. It was a pond in Westchester County, New York. We'd gone there from Michigan to visit his mother's family. I brought a bass rod with an ultralight spinning reel, hooks and sinkers and bobbers. We dug worms. I cast out the line and handed him the pole and launched into the usual preachments on Patience. I hadn't ten words out of my mouth when the red-and-white bobber started popping, the line tightened and the pole shook and Tommy, without further instruction, set the hook and reeled in a bluegill the size of my hand. My first son's first fish.

He held the thing, still hooked, both of them round-eyed and gaping in amazement, both of them gulping the blue air in each other's face. He was hooked. He wanted to take it and show his mother.

I said if he took it to show his mother it would die and we would eat it. Or we could put it back in the pond and it could go see its own fish mother and tell her about the boy it'd caught and it would live to get bigger and bigger and bigger. "No, Dad," he said, he'd just go show his mother. He didn't want to eat it. He'd just go show his mother and come right back and send it back to its mother and everything would be right with the world. But I told him the fish couldn't live out of the water. It couldn't breathe out of the water. It would die out of the water. It was in its nature.

He wanted to keep it. And he didn't want it to die. And I could see in his bright blue eyes the recognition that these aims were at cross-purposes. This was a game he couldn't play for "keeps." He was crying when he put it back in the water. Catch and release, like love and grief, are difficult notions. We've been fishing together ever since.

I know you're thinking that's cute enough to make you puke. I know you're thinking to yourself, Oh, sure, I'll bet—bluegill, blue eyes, the blue day in Westchester County. But it's true. He was hooked.

After that it was carp fishing on Sunday mornings at the secret spot south of town. We'd pack soggy Raisin Bran around big treble hooks and heave it out and let it sit on the bottom until some old carp would come and suck it up. Tommy was a carp-killing boy. And long after I learned to sleep in on Sundays, he'd bike out to the secret spot and kill carp all spring and summer and bring them home to plant them in the garden, where now, near twenty years since, the perennials grow thick and hardy and fishy. Once I remember him golden among a dozen shorter admirers returning from fishing with a carp the size of a small child hanging from his handlebars, blood and creamy milt oozing from it, its tail dragging in the dust and all of his amazed compatriots poking it and holding their noses and putting forth a frenzy of questions. "What kind? How big? How long the fight? Was it dead?" And even the one some noisy boyo advanced about the white substance proceeding from the dead carp's lower parts, to which Tommy replied, as if he knew what it meant, "Spawning." They took him at his word. In just such ways young boys get attached to trophies.

Then he got crazy for bass and pike and all the other pan fish that habited the inland lakes around our town. Arbogast Bug-eyes, and Fat Rapallas and plastic worms in every flavor filled his tackle box. He'd fish mornings before school and afternoons after school and show up at home shortly after dark smelly and content. He never excelled at his studies much.

When he was nine I took him to the Pere Marquette—the long river in western Michigan named for the French Jesuit who died in its estuary. It was early March. It was freezing. But the river, working its ninety-mile way west from Baldwin to its eventual spillage into Lake Michigan at Ludington, never slowed enough to ice over. We hiked in, in Red Ball waders and snowmobile suits, through the snow and frozen swamp. I remember holding him up, afloat, his left hand high in my right hand, like dancers, to keep him from dipping his waders through deeper spots in the river bottom. The place we fished was called Gus's Hole because the man who showed me the spot some years before had called it that. We drifted spawn bags on long light leaders below split shot through gravel runs and a deep sandy hole for winter-run steelhead and resident browns. It was here Tommy learned to distinguish the tick of the tiny sinkers moving through stones from the bite of fish. It was here the topography of the riverbed began to make sense to him. He could close his eyes and see the bottom, its undulant waterscape of runs and pools and holes and flats, the pockets of curling water, the structure of tree stumps and rock forms, the gravel beds where fish would hold, the shaded and the sunlit water. The only fish caught that day was an eighteen-inch brown trout, beautifully speckled. All fathers pray for their sons to outfish them. My prayers were answered and have been answered ever since.

That September we went back to the Pere Marquette to fish the salmon run. I explained, I suppose, how they went upstream to spawn and die—how everything in nature replicates itself then disappears. I thought he might have further questions on this theme and figured the river was a good place to discuss them. But he was more concerned with the relative attractions of Mepps spinners, Little Cleos and the assortment of streamers and flies he had brought with him. He caught two beauties, two big fresh males, fishing deep gravel between two sunken logs at Gleeson's Landing.

I have a picture of his boyhood in my mind that shows him standing upright between these two huge fish he is trying to hold aloft that weigh near half as much as he does. Half-wince, half-grin, his face is all effort and capability. Behind him it is late September—scrub pines, cedar and winter oak—the air is golden with possibilities, the river is silver, the smell of leaf fall and blood sport is everywhere and he is happy because we are taking his trophies home to show his mother. And I must be nearby holding the camera, trying to keep this moment permanent, in tact, coaxing him always "Smile, Tommy, smile!"

I used to think that it was trying to replicate this moment, this very picture, there between his trophies, that has kept him fishing ever since. That perfect autumn before his mother and father were divorced, the river thick with chinook and coho, his grandparents still alive, there in the bronze light of that September, still years before a girl he loved in school would grow into a woman and leave town and marry someone else, there in his waders, nine and smiling, the blissful ignorance of a boyhood undisturbed by love and grief, sex and death, the heart's divisions between catch and release.

But I was wrong. It was not my son who was trying to save it. It was me. It was my image of his childhood—that innocence—my hopeless efforts to spare him heartache, my own stupidity, my own daft fears of this life's opposites. He was never afraid of these things. Like everything in nature, he was laboring to know them better.

I am the age my father was when I was my son's age. Figure that: halfway between the middle half-century between those two. Sometimes it seems that we repeat ourselves. Time seems a constant game of catch and release. Dream and vision, memory and reflection—each is an effort to hold life still, like paintings of fruit and flowers on a table. There is no still life. My son's youth, my age, my father's death—each is a marvel of time and motion. Each becomes the other, endlessly.

And, like everything in nature, salmon bear their share of existential lessons. In the autumn all they do is spawn and die. They return to the exact water of their own making undistracted by the smaller details. They do not feed. It is not hunger that makes them crush a caddis or stone fly in their bony jaw; it is rage.

"Imagine," Tom once told me, "you're getting it on with the one true love of your life, your one and only. And this is quite literally the one you will die for, and you're making progress and someone keeps ringing the doorbell with a pizza you never even ordered, and you're trying to stay focused because you've come a long way to do this and you've never had any practice and you're only going to get this one shot and then it's curtains and the goddamn doorbell keeps ringing and someone shouting at you 'Pizza's here!' and all you can think of is how you're not hungry and didn't order anything and you're busy at the moment with the meaning of life and now this asshole's banging on the door shouting 'Pizza!' and you'd do anything to make him disappear because you've really got important things to do here and he keeps on ringing and banging and shouting until all you can think of to do is kill him. I tie my flies," he said, "not to look like pizza, but to look like the delivery guy."

Such wisdoms as these ought not be forgotten.

The hens find home gravel, fanning it clean with their huge tails before they deposit their abundant roe among the stones. The bucks find spawning hens, behind whom they hold in the current waiting for the moment of their ejaculation. The hens' dance makes the bucks dance wildly until, crazy with the kind of blind desire young men relate to and old men remember, they spend themselves entirely. By this point in the process, they have begun to die. Their fins whiten, their bodies darken, they get toothy and tired and make for the slow backwater pools and shallows.

The English poet laureate Ted Hughes, who died himself one recent October, and knew some things about death and desire, wrote it well when he wrote in "October Salmon" thus:

That holds him so steady in his wounds, so loyal to his doom,
so patient
In the machinery of heaven.

Boys, of course, know sex when they see it. So do girls. And they know death. And standing in the Pere Marquette, my son has seen a lot of each. The river in October is full of the sweet air of desire and putrefaction—silver fish, full of life's aching, making their fierce way upriver. Dark fish, their duties spent, float belly-up downstream, lodge in the log jams, rotting, dead.

We must all be steady in our wounds, loyal to our doom, patient in the machinery of heaven.

Having taught him to fish, now he teaches me. He rows me down the river, through the deep holes and gravel runs, and shows me what to cast and where to cast it.

He works the river for a living now. He has a drift boat, a regular clientele and hard-won expertise. He ties his own flies, packs shore lunches for his customers, ties their knots and nets their fish, and coaches them, as he still coaches me, on the intricacies of pattern and presentation and the river bottom, on the structure of currents that can't be seen, the epic poise, and on the catching of salmon and their release.

Y2KAT

By the time you read this the cat will be dead.

So long have I longed for the truth of that utterance that I have grown mad-anxious with the longing for it. But the sweet odor of truth is in it now, oozing from the little pores of the sentence like frankincense. *By the time you read this the cat will be dead.* Can you smell the truth and beauty of it there?

Though the cat is not presently dead, here in the exact moment of these contemplations, in the coincidence of my writing such matters down, consigning the details of my dark hopes to a text, as it were; nonetheless, by the time you read this the fact will have bloomed, fully fledged in the corpse of a cat who will be dead, as I said, by the time you read this. It has been, as final, finished details always are, cut in stone.

About which more, alas, anon.

For now let me say, simply and for the record, that I've hated the cat. And that I hate the cat. Furthermore, I am, at this very moment, hating the cat and tomorrow will be hating the cat some more. There is no tense or participle or variation of the verb *to hate* that does not apply to my relations with the cat.

By this time next week I will have been hating the cat for all but a few months of all but a few years of the last two decades of the last century of the second millennium. It is the only century my dear dead parents lived in, the only one that several loyal dogs of my acquaintance took breath from, the only millennium that Joyce or Yeats or Edna St. Vincent Millay were alive in. Ted Hughes did not outlive it or Frank Sinatra or Mother Teresa. They're all dead. John Lennon, Roy Rogers, Roy Orbison, Princess Di. Remembered quite rightly but nonetheless dead.

And the cat, as I write this, is still alive? Is there no one else out there to share my outrage? That a much-despised gray angora should occupy two millennia whilst Mohandas Gandhi and Martin Luther King, Jr. only one? Either way, if, by the grace of God and the luck of the actuarial draw, I am allowed to draw breath in the new millennium, to be, as it were, a citizen of the Old Age and the New One, I have made it my duty to vouchsafe the cat does not. It is the least I can do—a self-imposed debt to history and the future. You can take it to the bank, bet the ranch, let it ride—if I'm alive for a few more months, by the time you read this the cat will be dead.

SOME FELLOW WITH too much time on his hands once opined that the world is divided into those who hate cats and those who love them. Would that things were just so simple. We could quit the Balkans and Belfast and other border wars. All the imbroglios of distrust and distemper that infect the planet could be flushed into history if all that divided the species were cats. But let me say from the get-go that my hatred for the cat is not so simple as that. It is not the *feline* in general but this cat in particular that I hate (have hated, am hating, will hate, etc.). That it is a cat is only incidental to the fact that it is hateful. The ability of our species to abhor particular members of a subspecies whilst otherwise approving of the sort at large is well established. The point is also worth making that my hatred for the cat is in no way tied to species elitism, or animal harassment, or any all-encompassing prejudice against four-legged sorts. Nothing like that. Why, only last month (and I have witnesses), whilst visiting my cottage in West Clare, I was caught frying rashers and black pudding for a stray cat that visited every morning during our stay there. I set out fresh bacon and fresh milk and a bit of cheese and, in the evenings, a bit of fresh mackerel from the several dozen of same I'd liberate from the sea every day, as is my habit and custom there. I even began to call the cat by little familiar gender-indifferent names the way my late cousin Nora, from whom I'd inherited the house, was known to call her mousers. "Tippins" and "Blackie" and "Pookie" and such noises as that, because a hungry cat around a country house is no bad thing, especially near the changing of seasons, when the local rodentia are enthused about establishing cushy quarters behind the old cooker and fridge and in the press, where the back boiler keeps the bedclothes and linens warm.

So it can be said outright that I approve of the feline in the larger sense and only hate this one fat, old, lazy, gray she-cat; this one and only good-for-nothing beast that has, for lo! these past two decades now, refused to call it quits of my house. It will not die or run away or get lost like any normal cat would do.

Which is why I hate *this* cat. Though my hating of this cat neither increases nor decreases the statistical likelihood of my hating another cat, or loving another cat. My hatred for this cat in particular is unrelated to my associations, whatever they may be, with cats in general.

And maybe I belabor this point, but I want it on the record once and for all that I don't hate cats. I want the record clear on this because once I wrote a passionately unflattering poem about a former spouse, the mother of my children, in the months that followed our divorce years ago. However well crafted, this malediction, which appeared in my first slim volume of poems, was the reason for a damning little comment from at least one reviewer to the effect that "Mr. Lynch apparently does not like women."

Nothing, I want the record to show, could be further from the truth. Must one's distemper with one woman mark him or her ever as a Woman Hater? Remember the cat we are after talking about?

THE SPIRIT OF the thing was, to be sure, unfortunate. These were bad old times for all of us.

There I was, dumped in my mid-thirties when my wife fell in love with a man from her video-production class at the community college. It is, I suppose, fair to say that before falling in love with him she fell out of love with me, with the idea of being the wife and homemaker—two thankless jobs, then as now—with the whole *Leave It to Beaver*, Love Conquers All, early Joni Mitchell vision of things that had brought us together twelve years before. Gone were the dreams of suburban bliss, secure income, a family and a social life. Gone were the satisfactions of safe and certain, albeit predictable, sex.

She wanted something "more."

There'd been signs I'd chosen mostly to ignore, distracting myself with work and writing, playing with the kids, while she seemed to be growing distant from us. She flew east to visit a woman friend and ended up in the island home of an older man she'd had a crush on as a girl. There were more trips east. Phone bills inflated. Afraid of the answers, I didn't ask questions. By the time the fellow from the community college started calling, I was really the last to know.

In the parsing of intimacies fashionable then, she loved me but was no longer, and furthermore maybe never really had been, *in love* with me. It was all a mistake she'd rushed into, she was sorry. She really didn't want to hurt me, but I was like a weight around her neck dragging her down, keeping her from realizing her full potential. There was talk of "spreading her wings," and she really reckoned she had just "outgrown" me and the marriage. It sounded like the cover copy on *Cosmopolitan*. I said I thought for the sake of the children we ought to seek counseling, what with four little lives hanging in the balance.

We found a husband-and-wife team in the university town nearby. They'd written a book and came highly recommended. There were personality assessments and lots of multiple-choice tests. We had a few joint sessions that mostly ended with her stomping out. "Sabotage," the shrinks called it. We persevered. It wasn't that I'd done anything wrong, it was just that I was fairly boring. I paid the bills, helped with the kids, was sexually attentive, but too routine. I didn't hit or scream or bully or sleep around. Neither did I excite or inspire or make her weak with desire the way the fellow from the community college did. She was spending more and more time on the phone, out late with "friends," ever busy with "lab projects" at school.

We divided into individual sessions. She talked with the wife. I talked with the husband. We did more questionnaires. He told me that she was already "psychologically divorced" and that I shouldn't hold out much hope for repair. He told me that there were women out there who would give anything for the kind of love and loyalty I offered. I didn't believe him. I felt like shit.

There's this memory I have of working on a sonnet while she sat at the table in the next room cursing at an overdraft notice from the bank. She'd established a separate checking account so that what was mine was ours and what was hers was hers. Hers was apparently overdrawn. She was badmouthing the checkbook and punching the calculator and seemed to be trying to tell me something. She was sometimes violent with animate and inanimate things.

"If you want help with that, all you need do is ask me," I said. Weeks with the shrink had taught me to talk like this.

"It's all here if you want to help," she said.

I said that I didn't really want to help. I had the checkbook at the office and the checkbook for the Rotary Club and the checkbook of our household accounts to keep balanced, so that I really didn't want or need another set of books to juggle.

"But if you want help," I told her, "all you have to say is, 'Please, help me,' and, of course, I will."

"Okay, fine, then, please," she said, and I went to take a look.

She had added something instead of subtracting. The miscalculation amounted to seventy-five dollars and overdraft fees. When I pointed this out to her she looked at me with cool contempt. I had found the problem. Now what was I going to do about it? What was clear to me then was that if I bailed her out, if I gave her the money, I'd be the asshole who did. If I didn't, then I'd be the asshole who didn't. Either way I was going to be the asshole.

By midsummer things had gone from bad to worse. We agreed to go on a long-planned family vacation. We'd paid the deposit and reserved the cottage on the lake the year before, when we'd been happy there. Bad as things were, I still held out hope.

One night, after the kids had gone to bed all sunburned and ignorant of what was looming, I told her that her relationship with her "friend" really hurt me, that it was making me crazy, and that if we were going to work on the marriage, at the least we should not confuse matters with other liaisons. I told her that I could abide playing the cuckold but I couldn't abide having to play the fool as well.

When she left the next afternoon after preening all morning, ready and willing and perfumed, I knew she had arranged to meet her lover. I sat on a log on the beach with the children, watching the lake and knowing it was finished. I got a sinker from my tackle box and, with a bit of shoelace, fashioned it into a kind of necklace. When she returned from her assignation, I asked her to walk with me down the beach. I gave her the little necklace and said she'd convinced me. I told her that I would think of our marriage as dead and always think of us in the past tense and that I'd never weigh her down again. The next day we assembled the children in the cottage and told them all the ordinary lies failed marrieds must tell the ones they've failed the most—how everything was going to be all right and that even though Mommy and Daddy didn't love each other anymore we both loved them more than anything in the world and how it wasn't "about" them, and everything would be all right, and they wouldn't have to move and of course Mommy and Daddy still "liked" each other and everything would be all right.

They were ten, nine, six and four when it happened. The day sits like a lump of coal in their lives, sometimes smoldering, sometimes dark and cool, but always there, always ready to be reddened by forces still out of our control.

In the end, after the lawyers and shrinks, after all the hateful ballyhoo of tearing sheets, after all the sadness and the sundering, I borrowed enough to write her a check for her half of the much-mortgaged "marital home." She left with her clothes, half the furnishings, high hopes for a new life, the cash, the cat and her visitation rights.

"Good riddance" is the thing I said.

I found myself the court-awarded custodial parent of four minor children, crazy with bag lunches and laundry, feeling the failure, seething quietly at the cruel twists of fate.

Poetry is not therapy. Got a problem? I say call a priest, see a shrink, have at one of those 900 numbers, take up macramé or marathons. But don't, for God's sake, think that you can write yourself into or out of good mental hygiene. It's not going to happen. Trust me on this.

So I called the priest. He brought by forms for an annulment. He said I was a young man and would want to marry again and this would allow me to do it in church. All that was required was a fairly comprehensive history of my former wife's business and my own. When I told him I wouldn't be sending the intimate details of my failed married life downtown to the chancery for a panel of celibates to "consider," he warned that without an annulment I could get only a "civil" marriage if I ever wed again. I said I thought that would be an improvement on the last one. I couldn't imagine being married again.

As for shrinks, I'm afraid I had lost my faith. Oh, I was taking the kids, once a week. And it was good for them. But the bills were getting prohibitive and I really didn't want to "get in touch with my feelings." That was an altogether frightening prospect. A large dose of Irish every night kept me a safe distance from myself and helped me sleep and kept my anger keen.

I don't run or do crafts, the more's the pity.

And that's how the unfortunate poem came to be.

"For the Ex-Wife on the Occasion of Her Birthday" gave voice to my unspeakable rage—a rage that simmered for a year before finding its way into carefully crafted lines, seventy or so of them—a kind of bitter litany, in loose blank verse, of all the things I claimed *not* to wish on her, venom done up as carefully off-rhymed birthday greetings, to wit:

> . . . tumors or loose stools
> blood in your urine, oozing from any orifice
> the list is endless of those ills I do not pray befall you.
> Night sweats, occasional itching, PMS,
> fits, starts, ticks, boils, bad vibes, vaginal odors,
> emotional upheavals or hormonal disorders;
> green discharges, lumps, growths, nor tell-tale signs of gray;
> dry heaves, hiccups, heartbreaks, fallen ovaries
> nor cramps—before, during or after. I pray you only
> laughter in the face of your mortality . . .

There was more, of course. Plenty more: mention of her mother, her "donkey lovers," her "whining discontent" and "all those hapless duties husbanding a woman of [her] disenchantments came to be." It finished with an allusion to the ancient Irish epic about Mad

Sweeney, who was cursed into a bird and made "to nest among the mounds of dung" back in the good old days when "all that ever came with age was wisdom." It was abusive, excessive, full of the half-rhymes and whole truths that make poems memorable.

The first time I aired it at a reading, some men cheered, some women hissed, but mostly everyone roared with laughter. The feel of the words in my mouth was a kind of balm. It made me feel better than any therapy. And though poetry is not therapy, every time I read it I felt better and better. Because every time I read it I felt more in control of a life that was still spinning out of control, with drink and house duties and a business to run and the lives of my children in constant danger. I feared my anger and I feared its opposite.

Once, with my darling daughter in earshot, I was coaxed into reading it to a group of writers at a summer workshop in northern Michigan. It had earned a certain celebrity by now. To my everlasting shame, I never thought how much hearing it would hurt her. And by the time I saw the pain and confusion in her face, I was too far into it to turn around. Or I was having too good a time being the center of attention. Later, I tried to tell her that the poem was really not *about* her mother, but *about* my anger, and that as a poet, I had artistic rights and license in the matter, that I was entitled to my feelings and their free expression. To her credit she did not believe me.

Once, at the University of Cincinnati, the poet and critic Richard Howard did me the honor of attending a reading of mine. At the end he was all praise, mentioning this poem and that poem, quoting me to me. It was an honor to have the great man saying such things. Then he said, "The poem for the ex-wife is really remarkable. You should probably never read it again."

It was hard to make out what it was he meant. Was he trying to save me from the PC police that patrolled the universities? Or was he trying to save me from my own dark habits, which he recognized this poem was an emblem of?

It was strange counsel from a wise man and I took it. I've never read the poem to an audience since. The book is now out of print. The few thousand copies it sold are mostly in libraries or used-book stores now. The poem has never been anthologized. It and the rage it gave voice to are gone.

NOT LONG THEREAFTER I began hating the cat.

SOME POP-PSYCHERS ARE maybe saying now, sure, the cat and the ex-wife are in some way connected. Maybe you're throwing around words like *transference* or *surrogate* or *scapegoat* or such. The dear knows I wish they *were* connected. The truth is they deserve each other. I was pleased when the one left with the other.

At the time I did not hate the cat. I could have gone either way on the thing. Still, I figured my hands were full enough of living, breathing things to care for. Every other weekend she would take the kids, some Tuesdays, some Thursdays, depending on her schedule. The exercise of her visitation rights was always "optional," "contingent," "flexible," ever subject to the frequently shifting realities of her life and times. New housing, new romance, new jobs, new deals—the multiple variables made for a variable schedule. No plans could be made because nothing was certain. We would sit waiting in a kind of expectant limbo, for "Saturday at noon" or "Thursday by dinnertime"—the kids kept from straying too far from the yard, in case she'd come. Then the call would come—she was running a little late—twenty minutes, two hours, a day, a week. Or there'd be "rain checks" or "makeups" or "tomorrow, for sure." It was years before we learned not to work our lives around her ever-changing schedule.

So in the early going I counted as a comfort that, though the children and the dog and the mortgage were my daily duties, the cat was hers, and a good riddance to it. I did not hate the cat then. I had no cause to.

For reasons best known to my former spouse, not six months after she'd moved out with the cat, back it came with its bowl and box of Tender Vittles and pan full of used kitty litter. It seems it was not working out with the new lifestyle or living space.

This pleased the children, especially my middle son, whose fondness for the cat owed, I supposed, to the sweetness in him, his gentle habits and the fact that he and the cat were about the same age—both of them going on seven that year. His brothers and sister, to be sure, all fed the thing and let it in and out the door and ranged between endearments and indifference in their dealings with it, but Michael's attachment to the cat seemed primal. They understood each other's eyes and sounds and moods and needs.

Because I loved the boy I could abide the cat's return. Whilst marketing I'd find my way to the pet-foods aisle for little tinned delicacies, bags of kitty litter, even those little pastel-colored fishy-scented treats with which to curry the cat's favor. At a church rummage sale I paid good money for one of those cushy little oval-shaped affairs in which the cat never learned to sleep next to Mike's bed, preferring, instead, to curl itself in the corner by the pillow on which my darling golden boy himself would slumber.

I even tried to pet it once. It rose and walked out of the room, sneezing as it went, as if it were allergic to me. Its indifference I could tolerate. All cats—it is well known—can take or leave their humans. But the cat seemed to bear toward me a malice quite inexplicable considering that I housed it, fed it, paid for its vaccinations and grooming, observed the little regimens to prevent distemper, diarrhea, hangnails and heartworms. It not only was disinterested in my life, it seemed disturbed by my very being. Whatever I'd do, enough was never enough. Whatever I didn't do, it was too much. Damned if I did or if I didn't—the cat's discontent, at least so far as I was concerned, was manifest. It was developing an "attitude" with me. While it was always a bother, it could not, itself, be bothered to catch a mouse, or provide good company. Only Mike could make it purr.

Those few moments in the day not devoted to the office or the menu or the wash-and-wear or livery services, those minutes in which I reserved the right to hear my own self think, were always being interrupted by the cat. It whined, it roared, it needed to go out, come in, be fed or watered or left alone.

I'd get the children bathed, their homework done. I read to them. We'd say their little bedtime prayers and then I'd sneak downstairs to the day's remains—the sink full of dishes, the bathtub ring, the sad facts of the matter. I'd pour whiskey in a glass, assemble myself at my writing desk and take up revisions to a poem, sent back by some "important" literary journal that paid nothing and was read by no one, whose editor hadn't bothered beyond a form-letter version of the same rejection I saw in every aspect of my life. I'd be laboring over some adjective, some verb, some salvation from the word-horde that would make the thing desirable, when the cat would come roaring its late-night hunger or desires. It would not eat unless I watched it eat. It would not leave unless I held the door. In all weathers it would take its time coming and going. Still, for all my efforts, it looked upon me as a necessary evil. Thus were the seeds of my dislike of it sown.

Worse still were the rare nights when the children would be away with their mother. Sometimes a woman friend would spend the night. I'd freshen the bed linens, tidy everything, put the music on and put the cat outdoors. I remember one late December in particular. The children were spending Christmas with their mom. My true love and I had opened our gifts, built a fire, watched old movies on the TV and made our way upstairs, intent on hours of blessed coupling and uncoupling. It was bitter outside, the wind was howling, the snow drifting up and down the darkened streets, and the warmth of our consortium seemed so much more the gift. We were touching each other in that way that lovers do—slowly, deliberate, willing to pleasure the other for one's own pleasure's sake. The candles, the music, the beauty of her body, the quiet in the house—it almost seemed as if

I wasn't trapped and desperate and utterly rejected; it almost seemed as if I would survive.

It was then that I heard the cat outside the bedroom window. I had put it outside in hopes that it would freeze. At first it only meowed. Then it whined, the sound of it driven on the cold wind through the old walls of the house. Then it began to roar. Then it began to scratch at the corner of the window sash. The mood was being broken badly. I rose from our reveries, opened the curtains and saw the evil green eyes looking back at me. It had, apparently, made its way up the magnolia tree I'd planted too near the house some years before—a Valentine's Day gift to the former missus—and onto the little roof outside my bedroom window from whence it sat making known its objections to our privacy and purpose. I opened the window and tried to knock it off the roof with a shoe, but it was too sure-footed. Then I thought I'd coax it in from the cold and that would satisfy it. It approached the open window but would not come in. It roared the louder. My shins were freezing, my passions were shriveling. It paced up and back the roof. The wind and snow were chilling the interior. It would neither come nor go. Not until I lumbered downstairs, naked and cursing, and opened the side door by the bald magnolia and called out the gray cat's name did it deign to come down the magnolia tree, across the snowdrift, up the steps and into the house. By the time I got back upstairs, the room was freezing, the woman sleeping, the candles quenched, the music quieted. I went downstairs to kill the cat with a blunt object but couldn't find it, though I searched for hours, shaking the box full of kitty treats, holding the baseball bat aloft, my eyes wild with murder and mayhem in them.

TO LOATHE SOMETHING your child loves is difficult. To harbor far-from-kindly feelings toward the object of an innocent's affection is cause for secrecy. You cannot speak of the damage you would like to do it for fear of damaging the youngster. Every divorced parent knows these things. To let some loose word slip about one's former spouse's deplorable habits in earshot of the child is bad form. Already divided by divorce, the little self is cleft again by the war of words that puts the heart at odds with its own affections and identity. To object is a betrayal. To agree is a betrayal too. To consent, by silence, festers in the heart.

And knowing this I did my best around the children, to say only positive things about their mother, how she loved them dearly and would always be "there" for them, though where "there" was was often anyone's guess. And failing that, to say nothing at all. And when my hateful poem hurt them all, when it was published in a book for all to see, I resolved never to write about their mother again, or my righteous anger, or my rage.

In my head I knew that what was good for her was good for our children. Her sanity, her security, her safety, her happiness—her well-being inured to the well-being of my sons and daughter. So while a part of me wished for her disappearance from our lives, I adopted, as a form of spiritual exercise, the habit of genuine daily prayer on her behalf.

And praying for the ones that piss you off can make for miracles. Whatever was going on in her life, mine got some better.

I quit drinking. The anger subsided.

I quit writing for fear it might rekindle the rage.

I quit fighting with my former spouse. I quit talking to her altogether.

The sound of a voice I recognized as my own—reason and rhyming and ranting—grew still. I listened for a while. But it was gone.

The children grew in grace and in beauty.

I might've held my peace but for the cat.

BY FORTY I had chest pains and teenagers, a new woman in my life, money in the bank and a cat that was trying to kill me.

My abhorrence of the thing, despite every effort to keep it corked, was beginning to leak into my daily meditations. Behind the glad face I turned toward my sons and daughter in the conduct of my parental duties was the certainty of the malice she bore me, the sense I had of her inherent evil and the worry over the powers she might have. One night she woke me from a deep sleep with her fierce crying. Making my way downstairs to fix what ailed her, I nearly fell to my death at the diabolical sound she made when I stepped on her tail. She had positioned herself halfway up the staircase in the dark, awakened me with her roaring and plotted the fatal fall or infarction to finish me. Only deft footwork and good conditioning saved me that night. I chased the thing around with a hammer in preemptive self-defense but could not catch her. Awakened by the ruckus, Michael came down half-asleep, took her up in his arms and, speaking baby talk to her—"Whazamatter, kiddy? Did that old man wake you up?"—took her up to bed. I stood barefooted on the cold kitchen floor, clenching a hammer, blazing with adrenaline and revulsion. I did not sleep for days.

As they aged, their attachment only grew stronger. He could not see the fiend beneath the fur. He'd rub her and brush her, and speak to her in the voice one saves for one's beloved. He told me once, if she should ever die, he wanted to have her taxidermied. Some mornings I'd say she was looking especially lovely and we could have her stuffed today, thus freezing in time her abundant "beauty," and I would pay for the procedure. Mike wasn't amused. My detestation festered. My heart hurt with it, my head ached with it, my bowel burned with it. Because I could not speak my rage, it spoke to me.

AMONG THE GIFTS I got one Christmas was a vocabulary calendar. Every day of the new year brought a new word to be learned and used and incorporated into the common speech. Along with the news that it was Wednesday 30 June 1990 came *phlegm*: "\'flem\ n 1: thick mucus secreted in abnormal quantity *2a: dull apathetic coldness or indifference b: intrepid coolness or calm fortitude." And, of course, it would be used in a sentence: "*Burt surveyed the accident scene with a lofty phlegm, maintaining the controlled detachment that allowed him to report on such grim events." Better still, on the back of the page was some little-known etymological detail with which you might amaze your friends over dinner, if you had any.

> The ancient Greek physician Hippocrates theorized that human personalities were controlled by four humors: blood (dominant in cheerful, optimistic types), black bile (which rendered a soul gloomy and melancholy), yellow bile (the source of irritable, angry attitudes) and phlegm (ruling cool, unemotional types). Logically, when the Greeks related these humors to their four elements (air, earth, fire and water), phlegm was linked to water. But the word's etymology defies logic: "phlegm" traces back to the Greek verb *phlegein*, which means "to burn."

Oh, how I longed to be like Burt, to exude detachment, to be free of the black bile, rid of the yellow bile, returned to my ordinarily optimistic blood, to achieve "intrepid coolness" and "calm fortitude"; to be the third-person singular masculine subject of a sentence my friends would use in which not too long after the appropriate verb the predicate object would be *phlegm*.

Such was the condition of my life that a new word every day seemed a beatitude, holding forth a bouquet of promise and possibilities.

Some day in May you'd get *ennui*. You'd use it ten times before dinner and folks would say, "My, but he's enjoying the calendar this year." Later there'd be *irrefragable* and *mugwump* and, in November, *penultimate*.

It was in March, a gray day I remember, near the vernal equinox, I first encountered the word *grimalkin*: "\gri-ˋmo(l)-ken\n: a domestic cat; especially: an old female cat." The use in a sentence was unremarkable, but the bit of detail on the back was this:

In the opening scene of *Macbeth*, one of the three witches planning to meet with Macbeth announces, "I come, Graymalkin!" Shakespeare's "graymalkin" literally meant "gray cat" and figuratively referred to the familiar, or spirit servant, of the witch. The "gray" in "graymalkin" is, of course, the color; the "malkin" was a nickname for Mary, Matilda, or Maude that came to be used in dialect as a general name for a cat (or other animal) or an untidy woman. By the 1630s, "graymalkin" had been altered to the modern spelling "grimalkin."

I am a slave to words. I am their servant. The acoustics and meanings, their sounds and sense, sometimes make me shiver—the precision, the liberties, the health and healing in their meanings. Language is the first among God's many gifts. To name and proclaim makes us feel like gods. To define and discern, to clarify and articulate, to affirm—surely this was what our maker had in mind when we were made in that image and likeness. Not the beard or lightning bolts or bluster. It was no big bang. It was a whisper. It was a word made flesh—our Creation. And the real power of Creation is the power of words to guard us like angels, to protect and defend and define us; to incite, and excite, and inspire; to separate us from the grunting, growling, noisome, wordless, worthless meowing things. Thus when I came upon this word *grimalkin*—this "gray cat," this "familiar of a witch," this "untidy woman"—I saw it as the gift of my personal savior. Not, mind you, the accidental kindness of a random god. No, this was a word with my name on it, sent from a heaven where my name was known, by a God who knew the hairs on my head the way the First Baptists have always claimed He (for they think of him as a He) did. By a God who said to Himself, that poor crazy hopeless case down there doesn't need a good word, he needs this good word: *grimalkin*.

I sat at my desk with a blank sheet of paper, filled my best pen with fresh black ink and in my best hand wrote at the top of the page, *GRIMALKIN*.

As all good words do, it incited such a riot in my brainy parts that bits of verse began to spark all over. Of a sudden the world took on a clarity and reason. Everything in Creation began to hum with the sense of it. The divisions in my psyche were made as one. I was speaking in dactyls and iambs and trochees. Things began almost to rhyme. The acoustics of even the most humdrum words took on the vaulted, echoey tone of prayer and incantation. I began at once to write it down.

The cat was working its way across the living room carpet, crying out its customary discontent, strutting the well-known facts of the matter that because I loved the boy who loved her, I had to abide its miseries, its contemptuous green eyes fixed on me with long-established indifference. The first line came to me immediately:

> One of these days she will lie there and be dead.

How had this profound comfort kept itself from me these long, silent years? All I had to do was outlive the thing. How long can a cat live, I asked myself? Nothing that miserable can enjoy a long life—the black bile, the yellow bile, would certainly kill it. And then?

> I'll take her out back in a garbage bag
> and bury her among my son's canaries

Oh, happy thought! Oh, blessed harbingings!

> the ill-fated turtles, a pair of angel fish,
> the tragic and mannerly household pests
> that had the better sense to take their leaves
> before their welcomes or my patience had worn thin.

Michael came in for lemonade and, seeing the strange glee in my eyes, asked, "What are you writing, Dad?"

"A poem about your cat."

"Deep down inside you really love her, don't you, Dad?"

I said nothing.

"Be sure and put my name in it." Mike was jealous of his sister, whose name appeared in the title of my first collection.

For twelve long years I've suffered this damn cat.
While Mike, my darling middle son, himself
twelve years this coming May, has grown into
the tender, if quick-tempered manchild
his breeding blessed and cursed him to become.
And only his affection keeps the cat alive

It was true. Michael, like his brothers and sister, was the making of his mother and his father, blessed and cursed by both of us with talents and tendencies, gifts from God, each one of them. And like all things made by God and humankind, a combination of love and rage, beauty and beastliness and benignity.

though more than once I've threatened violence:
the brick and burlap in the river recompense
for mounds of furballs littering the house
choking the vacuum cleaner, or what's worse
shit in the closets, piss in the planters, mice
that winter indoors safely as she sleeps
curled about a table-leg, vigilant
as any knick-knack in a partial coma.

I hated the cat. And I had good reasons. And saying them out loud, writing them down, giving them voice, made them sound convincing.

But Mike, of course, is blind to all of it—
the gray angora breed of arrogance,
the sluttish roar, the way she disappears for days
sex desperate, once or twice a year,
urgently ripping her way out the screen door
to have her way with everything that moves
while Mike sits up with tuna fish and worry,
crying into the darkness, "Here kitty kitty"
mindless of her whorish treacheries
or of her crimes against upholsteries—

I loved that rhyme, *treacheries, upholsteries.* Such gifts were signs that God was on my side. I wrote as if I had a mission, as if I were the channel of Creation and the Truth.

the sofas, loveseats, wingbacks, easy chairs
she's puked and mauled into dilapidation.
I have this reoccurring dream of driving her
deep into the desert east of town
and dumping her out there with a few days' feed
and water. In the dream, she's always found
by kindly tribespeople who eat her kind
on certain holydays as a form of penance.

Mike came in asking for lunch, but, seeing in my eyes the dull glaze of creation, decided, wisely, not to press the matter. He took up his cat, who looked at me with its own feckless wisdom, and both of them went back outdoors.

God knows, I don't know what he sees in her.
Sometimes he holds her like a child in his arms
rubbing her underside until she sounds
like one of those battery powered vibrators

folks claim to use for the ache in their shoulders.
And under Mike's protection she will fix
her indolent green-eyed gaze on me as if
to say "Whadaya gonna do about it, Slick?
The child loves me and you love the child."

How to loathe something your child loves? How to rid the planet of the thing? How to do the perfect crime? And not get caught?

Truth told I really ought to have her "fixed"
in the old way, with an airtight alibi,
a bag of ready-mix and no eyewitnesses.
But one of these days she will lie there and be dead

Blessed assurance—there in that line—oh, what a foretaste of glory divine! This was my story, this was my song. The miserable cat's life wouldn't be long.

And choking back loud hallelujahs, I'll pretend
a brief bereavement for my Michael's sake,
letting him think, as he has often said
"Deep down inside you really love her don't you Dad?"
I'll even hold some cheerful obsequies
careful to observe God's never failing care
for even these, the least of His creatures,
making some mention of a cat-heaven where
cat-ashes to ashes, cat-dust to dust
and the Lord gives, and the Lord has taken away.

Yes, yes, I'd let Nature take its course! Patience and tolerance would win the day. I could be an example of forbearance to my children—a good father, a good man, good for something, after all!

Thus claiming my innocence to the end,
I'd turn Mike homeward from that wicked little grave
And if he asks, we'll get another one because
all boys need practice in the arts of love
and all their aging fathers in the arts of rage.

The poem was written in a day—a gray spring day gone blue, the buds on the magnolia busting loose, the boys out shooting hoops in the driveway, their sister sleeping in, whilst I was indoors disabusing myself of long years of contained contempt. It became the title poem for my second collection. Its words in my mouth were a kind deliverance from the yellow bile and the black bile and the disabling rage. I could live with the cat, or live without it. I could take or leave the thing and either way I didn't have to like it. And though I was left with the old dilemma—how not to love something your child does—all I needed to preserve was a home in which Michael could love the cat and love me, a thing he'd been managing well enough all along.

The children of divorce learn such divisions. I remember Michael in the first months of his parents' disaffections. We'd be out for groceries or riding down Main Street and he'd always want me to buy his mother flowers, or bring her home a gift, some surprise. He wanted me to woo her, to win her love back, to draw the distance in his little heart the nearer, to return his "selves" to himself by restoring the accord between his creators. Or he would say something really nice about his mother, about how she was the best at this or the best at that, and then he'd wait and watch and listen for my agreement—some hook on which to hang the little hope that we would not destroy the world he occupied. No doubt he did the same things with his mother. And as much as we loved him and his brothers and sister, as much as we would have done anything we could to spare them any hurt, in the end, we could not find a way to love each other anymore.

In the wars of divorce, it is children who pay the piper. Among the whole lies and half-truths my generation tells itself are the ones that say the kids are better off, or the kids will be fine, or that time heals all wounds. The kids are damaged. Some wounds won't heal. They may survive and thrive and learn to love themselves, but the harm that is done them is very, very real. Most divorces are not done to save lives or end abuses, or remedy interminable pain. There are those terrible few tinged by violence and madness, or persistent abuse or neglect, but the garden variety, amicably upmarket, suburban no-fault procedure common to my generation and our times, has less to do with life and death than with love and faith and fear and faithlessness. Most divorces are difficult choices in a world that applauds the exercise of choice, even the bad ones. And to have good reasons for divorce—as I did, as my former spouse would, no doubt, say she did, as we always do—does not make divorcing good. At its best it is the lesser of evils, a way to cut our losses, a way to say we couldn't keep the vows we made but we are still "okay." Whatever else it is, it is a shame that love contracted publicly with drinking and dancing and dressed to the nines is quit so quietly—a paper shuffle in the attorney's office, the grim facts filed with the county clerk, a hush long fallen over the crowd. It is the children who pay, for the two sets of parents and households, holidays and disciplines. However equal and amicable they might be, they are always separate, covertly at odds, subtly competing, quietly instructing in the separate and subversive dialects of love.

And though my former spouse got what she wanted and I got what I wanted, our children got, for the most part, divided between the love of their mother and the love of their father and the promises we made, in front of God and all those people, but did not keep. The parents got what they deserved. The children deserved some better than they got. And though I've heard and read every cheery argument to the contrary, I'd have to say it was like they were hobbled by it, the divorce, a kind of ball and chain they limped along with, then learned to walk with, then learned to run with, then ignored.

Though they learn to live with the damage, the damage done is permanent. It is not that their parents don't love them, it's that their parents do not love each other. Thus the children become beings divided against themselves. One parent's patience, the other's smile; Dad's sense of humor, Mom's sense of style—these incarnations become liabilities in the children of parents who no longer love each other. "You're just like your father" goes from appreciation to disparagement. What good to have your mother's eyes when your father does not love them?

ALL THAT WAS years ago now, the sadness and anger, the love and rage. The boy has grown into a man; his brothers and his sister likewise have grown lovely and capable, out beyond the orbit of their parents' choices. The cat is uglier, untidier, unrepentant as ever. The kids can vote and go to bars and fall in love and get their own credit. They live within the gravity of their own choices now. The cat roars and whines and will not be comforted. My gratitudes so far outnumber any grievances that most days and nights all I say is thanks to whatever God is listening for the safety of my sons and daughter. The cat is curled most days into a kind of fetal slumber between the legs of a table in the living room. It sleeps now more than anything. The boy who loves it most comes and goes. The cat remains.

Last year Mike was petting the cat and noticed some lumps in her hindquarters. "Cancer," I said, perhaps too gleefully, and said to take her to Dr. Clarke, the vet. I reckoned he'd recommend euthanasia. But Mike returned, bearing the cat like a newborn in his arms, saying it was only burrs and fur balls and such. They'd shaved the cat from the midsection back so that it came out looking like the Lion King, its little bald rump a spectacle. It cost $160 to find out the cat was badly groomed and was not dying.

Last spring it was nearly finished. I'd been emailing Mike for weeks at school, telling him about the cat's bad leg, how the arthritis seemed to be especially vexing to her, how her cataracts were becoming more cloudy, her deafness more pronounced, her miseries more noisome, her toilet habits more free-ranging. I told Mike something merciful would have to be considered. He said nothing. It hurt me to think of how it would hurt him. Still, he understood the difficult decisions that were facing him.

I called Dr. Clarke. There followed a highly professional discussion on the nature of pain and palliative care and incapacity. The poor cat, I told him, could hardly move and was puking and oozing from every orifice and that Mike was coming home for the Easter break and that "the right thing would have to be done." Dr. Clarke, ever the empathist, ever the compassionate professional, set an appointment for Saturday at one P.M.

And everything was going more or less according to plan. The cat looked especially haggard. Mike was sad and resolute. It was the doctor's last appointment for the day. It was a good day for the cat to die. I'd ordered in a wee box for the occasion and even had a stone cut with the cat's name and dates—*1978–1999*—a tasteful little twenty-by-ten-by-four-inch memorial in a dense eastern granite, to mark the space already dug in the back garden where all of Mike's more normally mortal pets were buried. The cold granite waited in the garage, the box beside it, everything in readiness. I'd left an eleven o'clock funeral service early to go with Mike. I wanted to "be there" for him, the way that dads are supposed to do. Even the cat seemed resigned to her fate.

And Dr. Clarke, a boon to man and beast alike, was saying all the right things about how "nothing lives forever" and how Mike had been such a "loyal friend" and how he'd have to do the "right thing," however painful, here at the end. And they were both nodding their heads in sad consensus, and the cat's head was nodding too, and I was nodding mine as well, and Mike's brave face was reddening and his eyes were welling up, and maybe it was the sight of this big, abundantly handsome young man holding his cat, holding back the big sob, and one tear working its way down his cheekbone, that was more than even Dr. Clarke and his attendant nurse could handle. I don't know, but whatever it was I heard Dr. Clarke stammer something about "perhaps a shot of cortisone," how maybe that would offer some "relief," how maybe it would give her some "quality of life," and I was thinking that it had better be one massive overdose of cortisone, because inside my head I'm screaming *NO, NO—IT'S NOT QUALITY OF LIFE WE CAME FOR*, because I'm counting on the cat to be dead tonight. I'd all but ordered up the cake and coffee. But Mike, with this little hand of hope extended, was nodding, yes, yes, that would at least give him time to finish the semester at school, you know, and spend more quality time with the cat, and I was still thinking the vet was just kidding about all of this when the nurse returned with Kleenex for Mike and a hypodermic that was given to the cat and the cat didn't die, not then, not since, and, in fact, she has begun to get a little bounce back in her limp and she shits in the kitty litter now and the old toms are appearing at the back door again and she sleeps all day and roars all night and grins at me as if she knew all along that the pardon and reprieve were set.

But here's the thing. The thing she doesn't know. The stone is cut. It is out there in the garage with her name and dates on it, and *1999* is what it says.

And I'm not one to make a liar out of stones.

Which is why if she won't die by natural causes or some household calamity, then, by all that's holy, the last thing I'll do in this millennium is drop that blunt lump of gray granite, all fifty or sixty pounds of it, on that godawful gray cat before the New Year turns. Whether the ball drops in Times Square, planes fall from the sky or lights go out around the globe; whether banks fail, phones fall silent; whether the world ends with a bang or a whimper; whether the earth or sea give up their dead; whatever happens or doesn't happen, call it mercy or murder, call me crazy or Katvorkian, by the first dawn of the New Age the old cat will be out of my life and times forever. I promise. By the time you read this the cat will be dead.

THE WAY WE ARE

I hope my pony knows the way back home.

—Tom Waits

"I want to remember him the way he was."

I GET TOLD this a lot by the ones who love the ones who die. Most times there is a casket involved.

"THIS IS GOING to be a closed casket," they tell me, in the voice we are trained to discuss our options in. Like sunroofs or modems. It's easier to talk about things than people.

"HE WOULDN'T WANT people seeing him like this." As if the dead, safe in whatever heaven or oblivion they inhabit, give a rap about appearances. Maybe he got skinny with AIDS or prostate cancer, or went green with liver failure, or bulbous with renal failure, or flipped his semi on the interstate. Maybe he hanged himself from a basement rafter or drove his snowmobile into the side of a tree, or curled up fetal in the end, a shadow only of his former self.

"IT'S NOT HIM anymore," they say emphatically.

Or "her." These things happen to "hers" as well—the cancers and the cardiac arrests, the lapses of caution that do us in.

"I want to remember him the way he was."

And who could blame them? Who'd want to see someone they love like this? Whatever way they got like this. Dead.

"But remembering him the way he was," I say, slowly, deliberately, as if the listener were breakable, "begins by dealing with the way he is." I'm an apostle of the present tense. After years and years of directing funerals, I've come to the conclusion that seeing is the hardest and most helpful part. The truth, even when it hurts, has a healing in it, better than fiction or fantasy. When someone dies, it is not them we fear seeing, it is them *dead*. It is the death. We fear that seeing will be believing.

We fear not seeing too. We search the wreckage and the ruins, the battle fields and ocean floors. We must find our dead to let the loss be real.

Confrontation, closure, catharsis, denial—these are words I learned in mortuary school. And for going on thirty years, I've stood with bereaved parents, the widowed and heartsore, in front of open caskets and over open graves. And I've waited with the families of abducted children, tornado victims, foreign missionaries, drowned toddlers, Peace Corps volunteers, Vietnam and Gulf War casualties—waited for their precious dead to be found and named and sent back home to them to be buried or burned, mourned and remembered. I've listened while well-meaning but ill-informed clergy, nervous in-laws, neighbors and old friends sought to comfort the living by telling them the body in the box was "just a shell." The operative word in this is *just*.

The effort to minimize the hurt by minimizing the loss, pretending that a dead body has lost its meaning or identity, is another tune we whistle past the graveyard. The sad truths I've been taught by the families of the dead are these: seeing is believing; knowing is better than not knowing; to name the hurt returns a kind of comfort; the grief ignored will never go away. For those whose sons and daughters, husbands, wives, mothers, fathers and friends went off alive and never did return, the worst that can happen has already happened. The light and air of what is known, however difficult, is better than the dark. The facts of death, like the facts of life, are required learning.

But oh, so difficult, the tuition.

I want to remember my son the way he was.

He wouldn't want people seeing him like this.

It's not him anymore.

I want to remember him the way he was—that bright and beaming boy with the blue eyes and the freckles in the photos, holding the walleye on his grandfather's dock, or dressed in his first suit for his sister's grade-school graduation, or sucking his thumb while drawing at the kitchen counter, or playing his first guitar, or posing with the brothers from down the block on his first day of school. I want to remember him in chest waders in the river with his brothers and me, or up at the cottage, those summers of his boyhood, a hero to his younger cousins, the pied piper with plenty of time, or with his stepmother on the roller coaster at Cedar Point, or there—there on the beach beside me before the divorce, it was July in that picture of the two of us his mother took—me on my elbows, him on his knees, me in my thirties, him at three and I'm showing him something in my hand—I can't for the life of me remember—and his mother must have just called his name or said "Smile" because he's smiling, the blue of the sea and the day behind us, that moment there, when everything was well. I have videos too—of talent shows and First Communion, soccer matches and skateboarding in the parking lot next door, or playing drums. God, he was really good on the drums.

And the guitar—really anything with strings. I've some of him on tape—his first songs, his first recordings. I have his first paintings, his first notebooks full of still lifes, figures, portraits, body studies. He has such talents. I want to remember him the way he was.

I want to remember him the way he was, with one grandmother's red hair and the other's eye for shape and color, with his mother's smile and my curiosities, before that first sip, whenever it was, first quickened in him the unquenchable thirst; when his body's chemistry locked and loaded on what it was it had been waiting for all these years, this little bit of giddy oblivion, this alcohol, this sedation.

He wouldn't want people seeing him like this—laid out, cold, pale, dead to the world, a corpse that has forgotten to hold its breath—smelling like so many corpses I've smelled for whom the issue of whether or not they had a drinking problem has become moot. Once they make it to the bright lights, porcelain table, universal precautions stage, when their bagged viscera smell like stale excess and their cranium is wadded with cotton and stitched shut by the morgue, once they make it to my embalming room, whether they are a dead social drinker or a dead alcoholic makes little difference. They are dead.

So if, thanks to guardian angels or maybe his sainted grandmothers' interventions, he's not dead yet, all the same, he wouldn't want people seeing him like this—dead drunk, passed out, half in and half out of his clothes—horizontal on the leather couch, someplace between seizure and coma, dying by doses, dead to the world.

It's not him anymore. It hasn't been for some time now. Not since he was fourteen and the thirst became a sickness. It is the thirst and sickness that has dogged my people in every generation that I remember.

My grandfathers were vaguely bingey men who'd learned to consummate big deals with drink—the wakes and weddings and baptisms, hunting and fishing trips, Fourths of July, Christmases and family crises. My mother's father died young, of a big heart, huffing and puffing to his purple end, before we formed many memories of him. My father's father, when my father went to war, swore off the drink in a deal he made with God for his only son's safe return. And when the young marine came home, my grandfather kept his end of the bargain. I remember going with him to the bars up and down Six Mile Road. "Bumming," he called it—hanging out with his pals, talking local sports and politics, showing off his grandsons—but he'd drink only Vernors ginger ale, and died sober and happy that his son had outlived him.

But World War II and the First Marines taught my father more than fear and killing. They taught him fearlessness and drinking. He came home skinny and malarial, as in the snapshots, our mother's name tattooed on his arm, enrolled in mortuary school, married his sweetheart, moved to the suburbs and began making babies and a future for us. I remember the cases of Stroh's beer on the basement landing, how he and his pals would play cards some nights, or sit out on the porch on a Sunday listening to ball games. They would talk and drink and laugh and be happy.

I don't know when my father's drinking turned on him, when his thirst turned to sickness. I don't know. I saw him drunk only once.

I was sixteen. His father had died eight weeks before of a sudden heart attack. Now it was New Year's. My mother couldn't get him out of the car. He claimed he was having a heart attack. The doctor came and called it "sympathetic pains." My mother wasn't buying "sympathy." Whatever it was for my dad, for my mother that night was enough. She wouldn't cover for him anymore. She wouldn't pretend for him anymore. She wouldn't keep his dinners warm or secrets anymore. It was her threat, if his drinking continued, to send his sons out looking for him, up and down his haunts on Woodward Avenue, that got him to swear off. And swear is what he did. God damn it. He could do it. He would show her. He would show us all. A year or so later, when he missed my youngest brother's birthday party, getting too blurry over a boozy lunch with a casket salesman to get home for the cake and ice cream, the remorse and guilt were more than he could bear.

That night he went to his first AA meeting. I was not quite eighteen, working at the funeral home, when my father told me he was an alcoholic. He could not promise he'd never drink again. But he said he hoped to be sober that day. He asked me to pray for him.

Twenty-five years later we buried him with a bottle of whiskey under each elbow, in case, as he sometimes speculated, maybe in heaven he could drink again. His quarter century's sobriety was a gift.

If most of his sons and daughters inherited his disease, most likewise followed in his sobriety. Whether blind luck or the grace of God kept us from killing ourselves or someone else, hard as we tried to, is hard to say. Either way, we all outlived our father and our mother and found ourselves having to make our own peace with drink and drugs and their afflictions. Whether we were problem drinkers or not, whenever there were problems, we were drinking.

For me it happened after years of successfully ducking punches and dodging disasters. I never liked the beer they were drinking in high school, but learned in college to like whiskey. Marijuana mostly put me to sleep, and I mistrusted the way it turned ignoramuses into philosophers. I tried some uppers when I worked at the state hospital, which made me jumpy, and I got sick on wine, and vodka seemed medicinal, but whiskey was lovely and the drinking of it made me feel mannish and Irish and worthy and numb.

By twenty I'd gotten into fights, fallen off of buildings, driven into ditches, lost my way—mayhems within the "normal," "acceptable" range of youthful dereliction. After I married and the family came along, I became more cautious. With more to lose, I learned how to manage my drinking. I stayed close to home, mostly drinking with poet friends and Rotarians—genius and business providing good cover. I'd get a little tight on Tuesday nights from cocktails at Harold Hansen's house, followed by dinner with the Rotary, followed by afterglow at the local drinkery. About the time I could not feel my jaw, it would be time to drive home, less than a mile, and since the police chief was a fellow Rotarian, his deputies might follow me home for safety's sake, but unless I ran into or over something I was left alone. Weekends I'd binge a little with neighbors and friends, at dinner parties and barbecues, card games now and then. There were a few "episodes," but nothing to panic over. I made only the usual fool of myself. I was your garden-variety suburban boozer, and for the most part it made me happier than sadder. I might look a little stupid, blather on too much, get a little sloppy, but I didn't scream or get into fights or ignore my duties, so what harm? I was functioning. I might've gone on like that forever.

This sickness, this thirst, this alcoholism, I've come to think of as a card that comes in everyone's deck—a joker, maybe—but it is there for sure. When it is going to turn up is anyone's guess. For most, I suppose, they never get to it. It's down at the bottom where it is supposed to be. They don't outlive their possible draws. For some the deck is shuffled differently, maybe by genetics or the luck of the Irish or the star-crossed heavens, who's to know? But they get to the joker that much quicker. It turns up when they're fortyish, fiftyish, sixty or more. Others find it earlier, or it finds them. The more they drink the less good it does them, but the joker keeps winking at them as if everything is fine.

It was after I divorced that it began to turn for me. It was, mind you, a divorce made in heaven. She deserved better. So did I. We agreed on almost nothing—money, religion, the rearing of children. We made beautiful babies and enjoyed doing it, but otherwise we were at odds. I never really much admired her. I could live with her, but I could live without her too. It seems she thought as much of me. When it was over I was left with physical custody of our toddler and preteens, half my estimated life expectancy, a double mortgage on the house, and this low-grade, ever-ready anger at anything that moved. And there was this fear, like a knot always tightening inside me that could be loosened a little by nightly doses of alcohol. The blather began to turn bitter, the foolishness turned calculating, I seethed. My children were caught between my fears for what might happen to them and my anger at what had happened to me. They were damned if they did and if they didn't.

I ruled by guilt and shame and sarcasm. My ever-shifting mood kept them on their toes, always trying to curry favor with me. It was easier than reason or listening to them. I don't know how long we lived like this. Whether it was weeks or months or years—I just don't know. And I don't know if the divorce was coincidental with my drinking going bad, or correlated to it, or the thing that caused it. Like a tumor or infection, it is hard to say when or why drink gets malignant, when the thirst gets terminal. But once it does it no longer matters—what happens or what doesn't happen. I drank because that's what sick drinkers do, whether to celebrate the good day or compensate for the bad one, whether shit happens or doesn't happen. Because it is Friday is reason enough. Because it's November will also do.

But I remember, and pray I always remember, the morning in April, it was a Monday, making bologna sandwiches for the bag lunches and shouting orders to the older boys and their sister about their homework and their school uniforms and how they'd better hurry or we'd be late and I was harried with house duties and hung over from a bottle of Bushmills that I had finished the night before to celebrate nothing in particular and I had to drive them to school and get back and shower and shave and get dressed for a ten o'clock funeral because I was the guy whose name was on the sign and if I didn't do it it wouldn't be done right and here it was Monday and I was already playing catch-up-ball with the office and the carpool and the cash flow and the kids and I'm slamming the apples and cookies in with the bologna sandwiches and cursing my fates and barking out orders and wondering what a guy has to do for a drink around here when I see my darling boy who is nine in this memory sitting at the counter with his bowl of Froot Loops and orange juice in his blue shirt and the look in his eyes as he's looking at me is fear, godhelpus, and he is afraid of me, of my anger and of my fear.

I didn't know if I was an alcoholic. But I knew that I never wanted to see that fear of me again in the eyes of any of my children. So I didn't drink that night, and the next morning, all other things being equal, I was not as angry. And the morning after that was calmer still. And whether or not I was an alcoholic, the removal of alcohol made things some better.

For months I stayed dry for the sake of my children and was feeling like "what a guy," and no wonder the court-appointed shrinks found me the more "stable" parent and the judge had "awarded" me custody, what with my willpower and moral courage and the rest. I was feeling pretty special, kind of like a sacrificial lamb, or local hero, or martyr for the cause; kind of like a guy who gave up his one wee consolation for the kids, kind of like I imagined moms must feel like most of the time.

That October I was traveling through southern California, giving poetry readings at schools and libraries, afraid that I hadn't written a line in months, afraid that my children were three thousand miles back home with my woman friend, afraid that none of my poems would last fifty years, afraid that my mother was dying of lung cancer, afraid of what would happen if I bought a bottle and took the day off, afraid of what would happen if I didn't.

Instead of taking a walk on the beach or writing the great American poem, or staring into the Pacific, I spent the whole day holed up pacing and vexed, wondering about a drink. Not drinking was taking up as much time and energy as drinking would have taken. There had to be an easier way. I found the number in the phone book on the first page of *A*'s. I called and told them where I was. They told me where to go. That's how I got to my first AA meeting—at a church called All Saints on a beach in Santa Barbara. The first time I said that I was an alcoholic, I wasn't really sure. And when I said it—"My name's Tom and I'm an alcoholic"—it felt like diving into cold water on a hot day. Still, the sky didn't fall, the earth didn't quake, the folks at the table responded as if I'd told them Wednesday follows Tuesday or the Yankees play ball. Later, when I told the people I really loved that I thought possibly there was this off chance, one in a million really, that I might be alcoholic, "Oh, really?" they said. "Do tell! What was your first clue?" Neither perfect strangers nor my nearest and dearest were very startled by this intelligence. It seems I was the very last to know.

In time I went from dry to sober. In time it seemed less like giving up something and more like getting something out of the blue. In time the fear gave way to faith, the anger to a kind of gratitude. The shit that still happened did not overwhelm. I didn't have to drink about it.

The conventional wisdom among recovering drunks is that the sickness leaves us three possibilities, like that old game show *Let's Make a Deal.* We get well. We go crazy. Or we die. I keep wishing there was another choice, say, behind Door Number Four, where we can all have a drink and talk it over. But it seems that there are only three. We stop drinking and get sober. Or we keep drinking and spend a lot of time in jail or hospitals or asylums or on the street. Or we keep drinking and spend a lot of time in the cemetery.

Nor is there a cure. We can't be fixed by any surgery or pill that will let us drink or drug like ordinary humans. Even when we are getting better, the disease is getting worse. We can get a lifelong remission, but once the drinking turns ugly there is no return. A pickle can't become a cucumber again.

And I hate that part sometimes—the way they've got these tidy little bromides like that one just now, about the pickle. There's one for every possible contingency. "Fake it till you make it" someone will say, or "One day at a time," or "Stay out of using places and using faces." Give me a break. Here I am a goddamn published poet who has been ignored in several countries in the Western world and translated into Serbo-Croatian and left out of several of the best anthologies and I've got to listen to rhymes like these? "Walk the walk and talk the talk." "The past is history, the future's a mystery." Or some quirky little alliterative like "Let Go Let God." As if we ever let go of anything without leaving claw marks in it. And God? This Higher Power business? Why can't they just settle on a name like any other bunch? Yahweh or Jehovah or Jesus or Steve? And what about these little acronyms, like KISS (Keep It Simple Stupid), or don't get HALT (Hungry Angry Lonely or Tired)! How is a guy who's always been TBBTO (The Brains Behind the Operation) supposed to take such things seriously? Because even when they tell me it's a simple program for complex people, I think there must be more to it than that; more to it than some old-timer grinning at a table and holding up his thumb, saying "Don't take a drink," and then, on his index finger, "Go to meetings." Just two things? That's it? Give me a break. What's a guy who's read Dante and Pushkin need with meetings and head cases, and what does it mean when these nuts begin to make sense to him? And why can't it be like riding a bike—once you've got it you won't ever forget it? Though I've quit drinking like a drunk, I'm still inclined to thinking like one. Hear that little rhyme in there? And there's always this blathering idiot in my ear saying I can toss a few back like any normal guy, like eight out of ten of my fellow citizens, for whom enough is enough. What harm would it do? And the only thing between me and believing that voice and following its instructions are the men and women I meet with regularly who help me to remember the way I was.

Which, godhelpus, maybe is the way my son is now—frightened and angry, stuck between egomania and inferiority complex, sick and tired, dead drunk. If his thirst is like mine he won't be able to talk his way out of it, think his way out of it, read or write or run his way out of it, lie or cheat or buy his way out of it. The only victory is in an admission of defeat. The only weapon is surrender.

Still, the father in me—the take-charge, I'll handle it, you can count on me, master of our destiny fellow—wants to fix it for him.

Protecting and providing, that's what dads do. I've always been pretty good at scripts and I've got one for him with a happy ending if only he'll just learn the lines by heart and do exactly what I tell him to do.

Years back—it was the autumn of his freshman year in high school—when his grades went to hell and his smile disappeared and the music in our house got dark, I took him out of school one morning and said I was taking him to find out what the matter was. I said I thought there must be something very wrong to account for all the changes I could see. Maybe a tumor or a loose screw or maybe, because it ran in our family, drink and drugs and addictions. I told him we wouldn't quit until we found out what accounted for the darkness that had descended on his life and times. No diagnostic stone would be unturned.

So we started with the drug and alcohol assessment, which turned up, unremarkably, positive. He was fourteen and trying anything that came his way. So I explained how it was like diabetes or an allergy and he should know that he was in danger because of his family history. A beer for him, a joint, whatever pills or powders were going round, might do more damage than "experimenting"—which is what we parents tell ourselves our sons and daughters are always doing.

By midwinter things had gone from bad to worse. I tried my best to ignore the obvious—his lackluster grades, the long hours in his room, the distance he began to keep, the smell of alcohol that was always on him. One night he came home besotted and muddy. He had passed out in the park, in a puddle. How he kept from drowning, how he crawled home, remains a mystery. The next morning I took him to a treatment center that one of my brothers had been to before. They took him in for thirteen days, detoxed him, told him that he was alcoholic, and told us he should get long-term care, that his alcoholism was chronic, acute and full-blown. There would be no cure, but with treatment he might get into a pattern of recovery that would allow him to live without using in a using world. We all wept.

Inquiries were made. An adolescent treatment center was found. It was at a hospital on the south side of Cleveland and was named for a saint I'd never heard of before. My son said if I made him go he'd kill himself. There was a calm in his voice that said he wasn't bluffing. I said he was killing himself already. I said I'd buried lots of boys for lots of fathers. I said if I was going to have to be like those poor hollow men, standing in the funeral home with my darling son in a casket, while neighbors and friends and family gathered to say they wished there was something they could say or do, I told him, if he was going to be dead either way, at least he wouldn't die of my denial, my ignorance, my unwillingness to deal with the way we are. I said if he killed himself I would miss him terribly, I would never forget him and always love him and I'd hate to outlive him but I'd survive. And I'd call someone before I'd drink about it.

Calling this bet broke something inside.

Every Friday for three months I'd drive down and get him, bring him home for two nights and take him back Sunday in the afternoon. The turkey vultures and red-tailed hawks hovering over the Ohio Turnpike are all I remember of those travels now. It was a summer lost to our disease. Everywhere I looked was the shadow of death. But he survived it and came home and got a sponsor and started going to AA meetings and the darkness seemed to lift from him. His grades were good, his music improved, he was painting, writing, smiling again. He started dating. For all of a year he went on like this and I got to thinking it had all been worth it, the driving and the money and all the madness, because he was fixed, better, thriving again. He was living the life he was supposed to live. So when the old signs started up again I didn't see them. I didn't want to see them. I'd quit looking. I kept wanting to see him according to the script I'd written in which all these demons were behind him, before he had anything more to lose.

It was halfway through his third year of high school when I told him I couldn't ignore the obvious anymore. I couldn't live with a using alcoholic. It was making me crazy, all the pretense and worry. I asked him to go back into treatment, or take up an outpatient program, or return to his AA meetings, anything besides relapsing again. He refused. I told him I couldn't live with him. He called his mother. She came and got him.

In the best of all cases, he would have had to move to her side of the state, lose his drinking buddies, find a new school and new buyers and suppliers, pay the price for his drinking on demand. Instead, his mother got him an apartment here in town so he could stay in the same school, hang out at the old haunts and have fewer of the parental hoops to jump through.

It is nearly impossible for any divorced parent to bypass the opportunity to save a child from the other parent. Rescue is what parents are good at. And if a son or daughter needs rescuing from the same asshole that you couldn't live with, well, who's to blame them? Of course, the children pay dearly for such second opinions, in discipline avoided, diluted rules, old wars and old divisions redeclared. By the time most parents have evolved beyond such temptations, their children are married and parents on their own.

One night in midwinter I found him passed out in a snowbank on Main Street. He was drunk, frozen, full of remorse, mumbling things like "You shouldn't have to see me like this." I called his mother and said she could come and get him. She took him to the hospital because we didn't know what he might have taken. Or if he had frostbite. Or if his shivering was a seizure. When the emergency room pronounced him out of danger, she called the number my wife had given her. It was another treatment center. She buckled on her courage and took him there.

He spent twelve days in that drunk tank. He came out and returned more or less immediately to his relapse, only this time he tried to "manage" it better. His mother, wanting to be helpful, hopeful, trusting, because she loves him, signed for his driver's license and bought him a car. He got picked up for stealing wine from the grocer's, busted for possession of beer in the park, lost one job and then another, dented the car in a parking lot. Otherwise we saw little of him. The high school gave him a diploma. He lost his driver's license and got a year's probation.

On the strength of his portfolio he got admitted to a posh art school, and because I wanted badly to believe, because I wanted badly to say, in spite of everything I knew to the contrary, maybe talent and promise and art could overcome disease, maybe he had outgrown it, I paid his tuition, room and board, and watched and waited and said my prayers. One weekend he got picked up for driving drunk without a valid license and spent the night in jail. His grades at first were not great and then they disappeared. He spent another weekend in jail for his crimes and got another year's probation.

When he asked to move home this summer from the dormitory at the art school I said I would not live with a using drunk. He said he understood. That's the way we talk. I couldn't say I wouldn't live with him. He couldn't say he wouldn't drink again.

In the space between what we didn't say, my stupid hope and his sickness flourished. I wanted to remember him the way he was. And wanting it so bad, I welcomed him, half-hoping some of the lost months of his lost years would return. But they are gone and the summer has gone from bad to worse. He's tried so hard to keep from being a bother. He tries to come home after we've gone to bed. Some nights he calls and says he's staying with friends and some nights he falls asleep on the couch downstairs. He holds his breath and kisses us. He says he loves us. He really doesn't want me to worry. He doesn't want to bother me with his drinking. He doesn't want to disturb my remembrances and I want to remember the way he was and I know he wouldn't want people seeing him like this because really that's not him anymore, there on the couch, at four-thirty in the early morning, neither sleeping nor dead but somewhere in between with no clear indication of which way he's going.

Putting him out of my house is like sending a child to chemotherapy. It hurts so bad to think I cannot save him, protect him, keep him out of harm's way, shield him from pain. What good are fathers if not for these things? Why can't he be a boy again, safe from these perils and disasters? Lately I'm always on the brink of breaking. But remembering the way he was begins by dealing with the way he is, which is sick, sick to death, with something that tells him he's "not so bad"—that jail and joblessness and loneliness and blackouts are all within the "normal" range. His thirst puts him utterly beyond my protection but never outside the loop of my love. If he is going to die on a couch some night, of alcohol poisoning or from choking on his own puke, or burned up from a cigarette he passed out smoking; or if he drives his car into a bridge abutment or over some edge from which there is no return; or if he gets so crazy with pain and fear he puts a pistol in his mouth, Oh my God, the best I can manage is not my couch, not my car, not my pistol, Oh my God. If I cannot save him, I will not help him die, or welcome his killer in my home.

What I've learned from my sobriety, from the men and women who keep me sober, is how to pray. Blind drunks who get sober get a kind of blind faith—not so much a vision of who God is, but who God isn't, namely me.

When I was a child all of my prayers sounded like "Gimme, Gimme." I wanted a Jerry Mahoney puppet, to fly like Superman, and for my brothers and sisters to be adopted by other kindly parents and leave me and my mother and father alone. I got none of these things. These prayers were never answered.

When I was my son's age, I'd always begin with "Show me, Lord." I wanted a sign. I wanted God to prove Himself or Herself or Itself to me. In this I was a typical youth, full of outrage and arrogance and bravado. Nothing ever happened. I never saw a statue move or lightning strike or heard any voices that I couldn't account for. The ones I prayed to be blighted thrived. The proofs I prayed for never appeared. None of these prayers were ever answered.

For years, twenty of them anyway, as a new husband, new parent, new funeral director in town, as a social drinker and a working poet, I'd pray, albeit infrequently, "Why me, God?" The more I drank, the more I prayed it. Why do I have to work harder, longer, for less thanks or wages? Why does that magazine publish only brunettes or professors or free verse or the famous? Why can't I sleep in or get a break or win the lotto? Why would any woman leave a man like me? And when my inventory of "why me's" was exhausted, I would ask on behalf of my fellow man. Why did cars crash, planes fall out of the sky, bad things happen to good people? Why, if Anyone's in charge, did children die? Or folks go homeless? Or others get away with murder? I was carping daily, a victim of my all too often self-inflicted wounds. The silence out of heaven to these questions was real. Why wasn't God listening? I wanted to know. And before I'd agree to step one foot in heaven, I had a list of things I wanted explanations for.

There's a reason we are given two ears and one mouth.

Someone told me that I should just say "Thanks," and that all my prayers should begin that way and never stray far from the notion that life was a gift to be grateful for. I began by giving thanks for my family, for the blessings to my household, the gifts of my children. Then the daylight and the nightfall and the weather. Then the kindness you could see in humankind, their foibles and their tender mercies. I could even be grateful for the ex-wife, the tax man, the gobshites who run the world and ruin everything. The more I mouthed my thanks for them, the less they bothered me. There's another thing to be thankful for. I could be thankful even for this awful illness—cunning, baffling and powerful—that has taught me to weep and laugh out loud and better and for real. And thankful that, of all the fatal diseases my son might have gotten, he got one for which there is this little sliver of a hope that if he surrenders, he'll survive. Whatever happens, God will take care of him.

And every time I say it, the prayer gets answered. Someone, out of the blue, every day—maybe my wife or someone at the office or the guy in the line at the airport or something in a letter that came in the mail, or something in the lives of my sons or daughter—someone gives out with a sign or wonder in the voice of God, in some other voice than mine, to answer my prayer. Every day, every time, never fails, if I just say "Thanks," I'll get the answer, before the darkness comes—"You're welcome," it says. "You're welcome."

RENO

So I'm sitting in the casino of the Reno Hilton on the twenty-first of June, 1999. It is the summer solstice, the end of the age. And I've lengthened the light of the longest day by boarding a jet and flying westward from Michigan, where this morning I woke up at four o'clock. I've seen the sunup in Milford in Eastern Daylight Time and the sundown from my room on the twenty-fourth floor, dipping below the mountains into the Pacific—nearly twenty hours of blessed light.

Maybe it was the catnap in coach class, or maybe it's the accumulated lag from too many jets, or maybe the certain knowledge that the days will indeed be getting shorter—solstice and equinox, time and light—or maybe it's the coffee. I don't know.

Whatever the reasons, here I am nearing midnight in Reno mindlessly playing the dollar slots in a room full of conventioneers and crazies and insomniacs: strangely expressionless people, neither happy nor sad but more or less numb. And we're, all of us, basking in the manufactured lights of PAYDAY and JACKPOT and MEGA-BUCKS blinking wildly from the banks of machines, the space beaming with chandeliers, neon icons and images everywhere. And there is some nonspecific late-century pop music coming out of the ceiling and the occasional voice-over informing us of the "All-you-can-eat crab-and-shrimp buffet served nightly for only 10.99," and an underdin of oddly comforting bells and whistles and electrical signals all mixing together in a kind of babel. I'm pressing the buttons, the way I'm supposed to, watching the sevens and cherries and double and triple bars twirling round and round, giving and taking away the money. And everything is blinking and blurring and buzzing with bright assurances, like there's no tomorrow, and I should let it ride, and I'm wondering if everyone here is wondering the way I'm wondering now—*what exactly are we doing here?*

THE DAYS ARE getting shorter. It is later than we think.

I'M HERE AT the invite of the California Funeral Directors Association, which has convened its annual meeting here. There's something for everyone in the family. While Dad is doing committee work and inspecting caskets at the exhibit hall, the kids can play downstairs in the nickel arcade and Mom can play blackjack for big bucks or browse in the mall. There are side trips to Tahoe and Virginia City, a golf outing and other organized events. I'm here to deliver the keynote speech in the morning—to tell them what it is exactly that we're doing here.

Last week I was in Rotterdam for the thirtieth annual Poetry International—poets, translators, editors, publishers, from every corner of the spoken word, invited to the Low Countries for a weeklong festival.

And the week before that it was Kentucky for the undertakers, and the week before that, Scotland and Ireland on the poetry biz, and the month before that, a kind of midwestern, Buddy Holly tour of mortuary conventions—five states in six days—and the week before that one, some poetry jobs at Eau Claire and Winona and Williamsburg, Virginia. All of it's a litany now of literary and mortuary confabs that stretch back through the winter and fall of last year—Belfast and Barcelona; Galway and Boston; Glasgow, Manhattan and Amsterdam; Ocean City; Rapid City; Seattle; Atlantic City; Edinburgh; San Francisco; Denver and Atlanta; London and Dundee and Cornwall and Dublin and Portland and Chicago and Philly and D.C.; and Bozeman, Montana; Indianapolis; Minneapolis; Wichita, Kansas; godhelpus—blather and racket until I'm all but struck dumb with it and these blinking lights that are all beginning to blend together now into a kind of blindness. The more of the planet I see, the less I see it.

MAYBE IT IS time to get some sleep.

AMONG MY WRITERLY friends, the hushed talk eventually comes round to the fact that I'm a funeral director. How is it, they want to know, that someone who writes sonnets also embalms, sells caskets, drives a hearse and greets the mourners at the door? It strikes them a strange commingling: the mortuary and literary arts. Why, they wonder, don't I take up a day job teaching grad students something meaningful about dactyls and pentameters at the university?

Among my fellow funeral directors, I am likewise suspect. There are dark rumors about bookish and artistic "types"—a wariness that owes, I suppose, to Mitford and Waugh—a mistrust of wordsmiths and journalists. Why, they wonder, don't I take up golf or the stock market, boating or Web browsing?

Of course, my publishers have made some hay off this, to their advantage and to mine. An "undertaker/poet," like a cop who sings opera or a wrestler turned governor, makes for good copy and easy interviews. Oddity and celebrity are near enough cousins. Ink and airtime—coin of the realm in the info-tainment industry—are easier when you have a quirky angle.

Much the same, the mortuary associations have put me on the "circuit" of state and national conventions, where I'm fresh fodder for the programs and exhibit committees. After years of psycho-babblers and marketing gurus dispensing warm-fuzzies and motivationals, a reading and book signing by a "poet and author and one of our own" has a certain panache.

I charge accordingly, as any dancing bear would do.

BUT HERE'S THE quiet little truth of the matter. Requiems and prosodies, sonnets and obsequies, poems and funerals—they are all the same. The arrangement of flowers and homages, casseroles and sympathies; the arrangement of images and idioms, words on a page—it is all the same—an effort at meaning and metaphor, an exercise in symbol and ritualized speech, the heightened acoustics of language raised against what is reckoned unspeakable—faith and heartbreak, desire and pain, love and grief, the joyous and sorrowful mysteries by which we keep track of our lives and times.

Sometimes I see in the stillness of the dead the blank space between stanzas, the held breath of inspiration, the silence that rhymes with almost anything. The math of each enterprise is imprecise—wholesale, retail, rhyme and meter, the counting of syllables, the tally of charges: all numbers games that end in bottom lines. Still, the words we cut in stone or shape in poems are worth more, somehow, than the usual palaver.

A good funeral, like a good poem, is driven by voices, images, intellections and the permanent. It moves us up and back the cognitive and imaginative and emotive register. The transport seems effortless, inspired, natural as breathing or the loss of it. In the space between what is said and unsaid, in the pause between utterances, whole histories are told; whole galaxies are glimpsed in the margins, if only momentarily. At wakes and in verse, both absence and presence inform the work. What is said and what is unsaid are both instructive. The elegist and eulogist must both attend to the adverbs, be sparing with the adjectives, be mindful of the changing tense of predicates and have a sense of when enough is enough. The fashions in verse-making and leave-taking are always changing while the fundamental witness remains the same. Good poems and good funerals are stories well told.

It is likewise so that we poets and funeral directors have a fondness for black, the keening of pipers, irregular hours, free drink and horizontal bodies. Our children uniformly report that we often seem distracted. Our spouses endure our bouts of passion and distemper, egomania and inferiority. Whether we err on the side of excess or meanness, when we miss the point, we miss it badly.

We are all the same. And no two are alike. Dante's *Commedia*, Grant's Tomb, your child's first quatrain, your one and only mother's death, your father's.

WHENEVER FUNERAL DIRECTORS get together they talk about the fact that no one likes funerals. Whenever poets get together they talk about the fact that no one likes poetry. Co-misery plays a big part in their get-togethers. There are worries over audience interest and the marketplace.

For poetry readings the general rule is that if the poet is outnumbered, it is a success. If outnumbered by a dozen or more, it is a huge success. A crowd like the crowds they turn up in Rotterdam—hundreds to listen to the likes of me or Lorna Goodison from Jamaica or Chen Li from Taiwan or Haji Gora Haji from Zanzibar—such multitudes will be mentioned in our obituaries. "He once filled the Rotterdam City Theatre," it will read, a tasteful dose of hyperbole, "with people hungry for his poems." Lost to literary history will be the three Dubliners who turned out to Bewley's in Grafton Street one Wednesday in October some years ago—my driver, "the events organizer" and one fetching young woman we took to be a discerning reader, but it turned out she was actually lost.

The same rule holds for funerals. Wherever two or three are gathered is enough to outnumber the dead guy. If one of them will stand up and hold forth, you've got all the ingredients you will ever need: someone who agrees to quit breathing, someone who cares, and someone who's trying to make some sense of all of this. Half a dozen and they can carry the dead one to the final resting place. More than a hundred makes it an "exceptional tribute," especially on a weekday when the weather is bad.

And though poetry and funerals have been around for a while, there's the sense that their ancient forms may not be relevant to the postmodern, postindustrial, 24-7 televised news cycle of a deconstructed, digital world where everything is wired and managed by mouse-click and mass-marketed or geared to a niche or a focus group or a poll and anyone who wants to be one of the players better play by the numbers and compete for space and offend no one and appeal to a crowd and hold their attention, keep them entertained enough to keep them from changing channels, or keep them anesthetized enough so that they'll think they're getting something for their money, like these folks here in Reno, there at the two-for-one bar, and here at the sure-bet slots, and there at the all-you-can-eat buffet.

Last week in Rotterdam, for example, Poetry International was opened with a "Defense of Poetry"—a kind of keynote speech—by the Mongolian poet and shaman Galsan Tschinag, a Tuvan tribal chief. His native language having no script, he writes in German, which he learned in Leipzig. He sings in Tuvinian. His defense of poetry ran about an hour. Translations were available in booklets in the lobby afterward. Several dozen copies were given away. Everyone applauded and nodded and smiled.

Perhaps if they shot a poet, or hanged one, or banished one to some hinterland like they used to in the old days when language was dangerous and words were magic and poets weren't tenured but they weren't ignored, the attention and attendance would be better. The poems would reach a broader audience. Dead poets always fare better than live ones. Better yet if one was burned at the stake. At least the media would turn up for the show: the roving reporters, the poetry-cam, the talking heads to tell us what we heard and saw.

AND ONE OF the workshops here in Reno will certainly sound like a "Defense of Funerals." Some Ph.D. or M.D. or M.S.W. will tell the F.D.'s all about the "Value of the Funeral." Maybe if funerals hadn't been so co-opted by the grief therapists and memorial counselors, the pie-in-the-skyers and casket peddlers; maybe if it was about more than our "feelings" or our "salvation" or our disposal. Maybe if funerals were a whole-being enterprise: something for our flesh and fears and faith and for the dead. If we burned them in public or buried them ourselves or bore them through town giving thanks and praise, making peace with the powers of God and Nature in carefully worded lamentations, incantations, benedictions, we would have to defend neither poetry nor funerals. We would simply do them whenever the spirits, the living or the dead ones, moved us to.

When, I wonder, do things become self-evident.

Poetry tunes our senses to the language. Without it how could we bear the Information Age and all its words, its lists of options, its multiple choices, its idiot menus from which we must make our selections? And funerals tune our senses to our mortal nature; like proper punctuation, whether we end with exclamation, questions or full stop, they lend meaning to our lives, our human being. Both press our attention to the existentials, the adverbials, the sensual and overwhelming questions, the mysteries and certainties of life and death.

Maybe it is because we have removed the poems and the corpses from our daily rounds. We are glad to have poets in the way we are glad to have good infrastructure. Smooth roads, clean drinking water, a sestina now and then—we are willing to pay the millage so that we can ignore them. We tuck them into universities with living wages and dental coverage and the captive audience of our sons and daughters. We are glad they are writing poems and gladder still that we needn't read them. We give them grants and sabbaticals, a little airtime on the radio, a little shelf space in the corner of the megastore, and otherwise expect them to be still and disappear into the larger lifescapes of politics, history, events and entertainments, self-help and diet fads.

Much as we want the dead and dying to be still and disappear. Though we are drawn to the movies and the evening news with their murders and virtual blood and gore, and though the mort-cam is always at the ready to hover overhead the latest tragedy or terrorism; though prepackaged, media-approved, commercially viable opportunities abound for "national" mourning, surrogate sadnesses and remote-control grief, our locally dying and our local dead, our real-life family and friends, are, for the most part, disappeared—their bodies quickly hidden or disposed of in the name of efficiency and dignity, privacy and convenience. The actual, palpable, slowly decomposing and tangible facts of the matter are declared irrelevant, like good infrastructure, like poetry.

I REMEMBER THE first poem I ever heard, the first dead human body I ever saw. Neither scarred my psyche but each changed my life. Each gave it meaning by holding forth a mystery.

> Angel of God, my guardian dear,
> to whom God's love commits me here,
> ever this day be at my side
> to light to guard to rule and guide.

My mother taught me to say this poem morning, noon and night. I hadn't a clue what it meant exactly, but the jaunty progress toward its echoes pleased my ear. The sense that its syllables, the saying of them, held powerful medicine and protections proceeded from that pleasure, then as now.

The first dead person I remember seeing was an old man on the table of the embalming room at my father's office. I was ten, I think, or thereabouts. My father had taken me to work with him on a Saturday. The embalming room was at the back of the old funeral home. We entered by the back door off the alley. I wasn't told I was about to see a dead body or that it should do me any damage, or that there were any preparations I should make emotionally. I was only going to work with my father. I knew his work involved the dead as sons of doctors know their parents deal with sickness or the children of clergy have heard of sin, as every child is aware of sex—the idea of the thing but not the thing itself. I remember that the room smelled like the doctor's office and the figure on the table was covered by a sheet except for his head, his face. The sheet was white, the table was white, the face was white and it was quiet. There was a stillness about that body unlike anything I'd witnessed in nature before. His head was bald, his eyes and mouth were closed, his nose was large, as were his earlobes. I asked my father what his name was, what his age was, what he died of and if he had children. And though I can't remember the particulars, I remember that my father gave me answers. He also said that I should say a prayer. I wasn't frightened but I was changed.

And sometimes I wonder what my life would have been if not for dead bodies and dead poets.

"When you are old and gray and full of sleep/and nodding by the fire take down this book . . ." William Butler Yeats wrote in his memorable pentameters to Maud Gonne, whom he loved and who wouldn't have him a century ago. He had, in his youth, the certain sense that these lines and others like them would survive their youth, their age, their century. They have. The great Irish master bridged the nineteenth and twentieth centuries with poetry of such power and appeal that instructions written but months before his death ring true and timely still:

> Irish poets, learn your trade,
> Sing whatever is well made,
> Scorn the sort now growing up
> All out of shape from toe to top . . .

It is the meter and rhyme scheme of Yeats's late poem that W. H. Auden, not quite thirty-two when Yeats died on January 28, 1939, echoed in his famous elegy "In Memory of W. B. Yeats":

> Earth, receive an honored guest;
> William Yeats is laid to rest:
> Let the Irish vessel lie
> Emptied of its poetry.
>
> Time that is intolerant
> Of the brave and innocent,
> And indifferent in a week
> To a beautiful physique,
>
> Worships language and forgives
> Everyone by whom it lives;
> Pardons cowardice, conceit,
> Lays its honours at their feet.

I was among the fortunate hundreds who heard Seamus Heaney—one by whom the language lives—in Galway's Town Hall Theatre a few Aprils ago during the Cuirt Festival of Literature. The Nobel laureate, noting this borrowing of Yeats's meter and rhyme, paraphrased Auden to the effect that "poetry is what we do to break bread with the dead." And extending Auden's metaphor, Heaney added, "If so, then surely rhyme and meter are the table manners." He is, of course, correct.

Poetry is a kind of communion, the chore of ordinary talk made sacramental by the attention to what is memorable, transcendent, permanent, in the language. It is the common tongue by which the species remains connected to the past and bears its witness to the future. Each age offers variations on the themes of love and grief, reason and desire, prayer and homage, epic and elegy and honor. Some things are constantly changing. Some things never do. Poets and their poetry keep track of each.

But before it was a written and read thing, poetry was a spoken and said thing that happened in the ears and mouth before the eyes and intellect were engaged. It belonged to the body as much as the mind. It earned its place by pleasuring the senses. Before there were daily papers and news anchors and talking heads, there were bards who made their way from village to village bearing the news—*Who was king in the next county; who stole whose cow; who slept with whose wife; who slaughtered whose son.* And they were paid, well paid, to praise in verse a comely bride, a valiant warrior, a loyal dog; and paid to curse the blackguard, the enemy and the enemy's gods. And all of this was done out loud—for the sound and sense of it—the way we sing in the shower, practice our proposals and listen for our own voice before we fall asleep at night. Rhyme and meter were tools of the trade, a way of making words memorable and memorizable, a pace tied to the footfall of the poets' journeys.

We are drawn to the acoustic pleasures of poetry by nature and metabolism. Our hearts beat in iambs and trochees night and day. Our breath is caught between inspiration and expiration. Our pulse divided by our breathing equals the five-finger-tapping pentameters of Frost: "The land was ours before we were the land's." And Shakespeare: "From forth the fatal loins of these two foes." And Millay:

"What lips my lips have kissed, and where, and why." Is it any wonder that we know these things by heart?

Our first petitions are learned by rhyme and meter: "Now I lay me down to sleep/and pray the Lord my soul to keep." Our first benedictions: "God is great, God is good/Let us thank Him for our food." Our first mysteries: "Twinkle, twinkle, little star/How I wonder what you are." Our first mastery: "A B C D E F G/H I J K lmno P." Our first formula: "Red sky at morning/Sailor take warning/Red sky at night/Sailor's delight." Our first poem, memorized: "Tyger! Tyger! burning bright/In the forests of the night,/What immortal hand or eye?/Could frame thy fearful symmetry?"

If this meter of William Blake's became Yeats's late instruction to Irish poets, and later Auden's elegy for Yeats, it serves as well for Seamus Heaney's lament for Joseph Brodsky, the Russian exile and fellow Nobel laureate who learned to write in English and died too young on January 28, 1996. Giving his poems in Galway that spring, Heaney took up his place at the table of poets who will outlive their centuries. With impeccable manners and in a well-tested form, he paid his respects to his dead friend, to old masters and to their ancient craft in "Audenesque—In Memory of Joseph Brodsky."

Joseph, yes, you know the beat.
Wystan Auden's metric feet
Marched to it, unstressed and stressed,
Laying William Yeats to rest.

Therefore, Joseph, on this day,
Yeats' anniversary,
(Double-crossed and death-marched date,
January twenty-eight),

Its measured ways I tread again
Quatrain by constrained quatrain,

Meting grief and reason out
As you said a poem ought.

Trochee, trochee, falling: thus
Grief and metre order us.
Repetition is the rule,
Spins on lines we learnt at school.

Heaney's poem, which gathers power and sorrow for another dozen quatrains, will be part, no doubt, of a future collection. It is good to be alive while this man is writing. It is good to hear his voice in two millennia.

But well-made poems outlive their makers and slip the restraints of ordinary time to become confluent with language at its source, all those tributaries of the human voice, in all its dialects, vernaculars and patois; wellsprings that rise to the species' thirst for metaphor.

Last month in a schoolhouse on the edge of the ocean in West Clare a student raised his hand to ask me, "Sir, what age did ye get your poetic license?" His classmates giggled, his kindly teacher grinned and blushed. But the boy himself was dead serious. He knew it was something that gave you privileges and special powers, like driving the tractor or fishing the cliffs, or serving the priest at Sunday Masses. I told him I was born with it. I told him he was too—born with it—and he should never lose it, his poetic license, his voice, his ear for this life's griefs and meters.

I said he would have to exercise it, "use it or lose it" is what I said, and I could see he liked the sound of that, the *oozes* and *its*, the affirmation. I told him to listen closely, to talk to himself, to say it out loud. I told him to read or write something every day, a poem, a paragraph, a letter, and be wary of distractions and diversions.

And every day it seems a game of chance. A clean page, another version, new griefs and meters, a fresh deck of possibilities. In Reno it is played as if there's no tomorrow. We look like robots, humanoids putting tokens in machines, waiting for the payoff, hoping for a sign, or killing time until our time kills us.

But we could all be alive tomorrow and if so we'll need some better answers than these games afford us. After a long night of winning or losing, it's good to have a desert close at hand into which one could do worse than to wander, like holy ones of old, to listen for the voices in the air or to raise up songs of thanks or to curse the luck or praise the name of whatever is out there listening, or isn't.

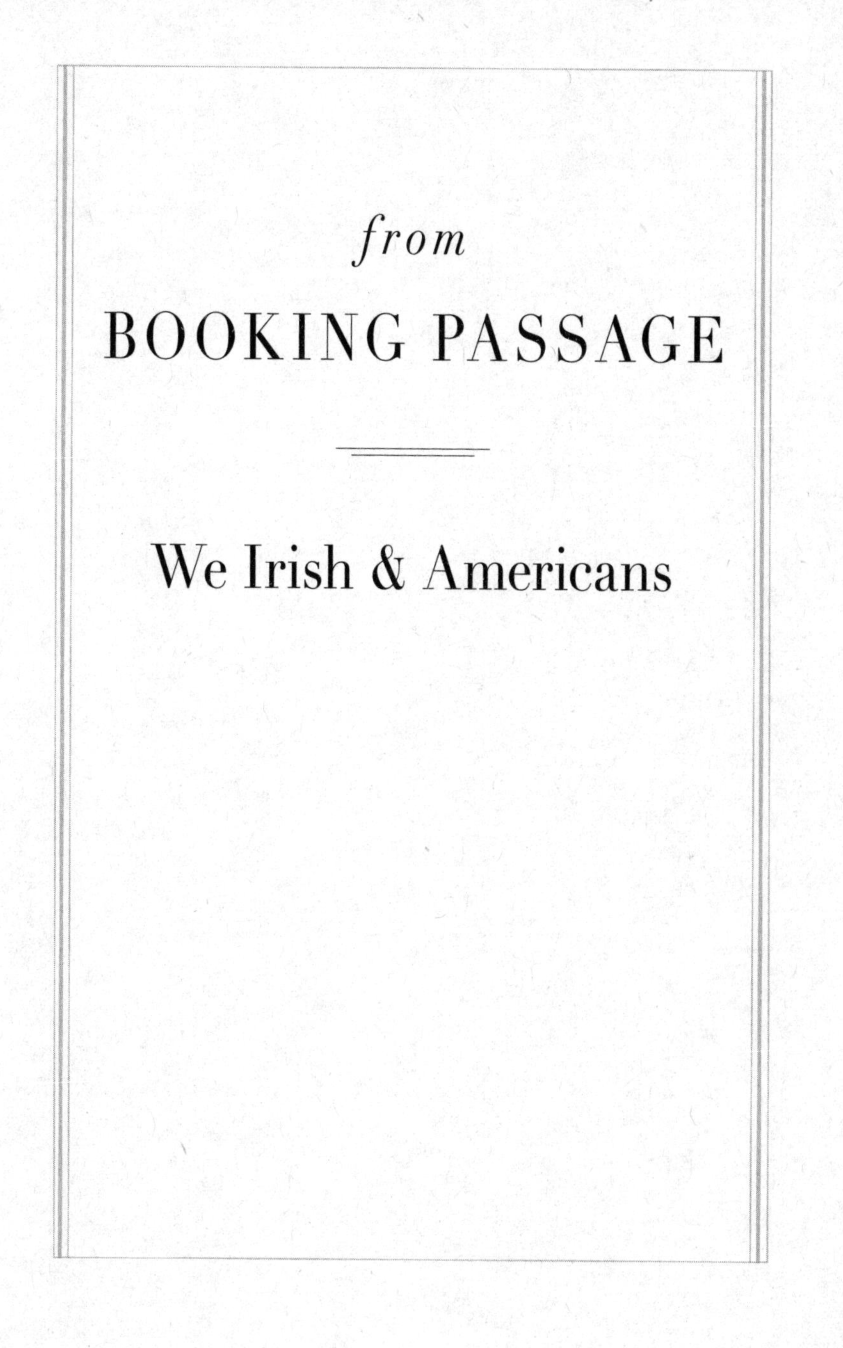

from

BOOKING PASSAGE

We Irish & Americans

INTRODUCTION

The Ethnography of Everyday Life

The center for the Ethnography of Everyday Life at the University of Michigan invited me to present at their recent conference, "Doing Documentary Work: Life, Letters and the Field."

Where I come from, upstream on the Huron from smart Ann Arbor, we rarely offload words like *ethnography* unless we are appearing before the zoning board of appeals or possibly trying to avoid jury duty. All the same, I thanked the organizers and said I would be happy, etc., honored, of course, and marked the dates and times in my diary.

To be on the safe side, I looked it up—*ethnography*—and it says, "The branch of anthropology that deals with the description of various racial and cultural groups of people." And *anthropology*—I looked that up too—is "the study of the origin, the behavior, and the physical, social and cultural development of human beings."

Anthology—"a gathering of literary pieces, a miscellany, an assortment or catalogue"—is on the same page as *anthropology*. It comes from the Greek, as students are told, for "gathering flowers."

As the man in that movie about the big fat wedding says, everything comes from the Greek for something else.

Dictionaries are like that—you go in for a quick hit of ethnography and come out with flowers by the bunch. Two pages east and you've got *Antigone*, "the daughter of Oedipus and Jocasta, in Greek mythology, who performed funeral rites over her brother's body in defiance of the king" at Thebes. That ancient city's on the same page as *theater* and *theatre*, which have several definitions all derived from the Greek "to watch." Think of "the milieu of actors and playwrights." Think Mrs. Patrick Campbell. Think Sophocles.

At the Abbey Theatre in Dublin, just last week, a new version of *Antigone* called *The Burial at Thebes* opened to great reviews in the Irish papers. One commentator claimed that Creon the king was like President George W. Bush, caught in a conflict he'd a hand in making. How's that for ethnography and everyday? How's that for life, letters, and the field?

I avoided the quagmire of *milieu*, suspect as we are lately of anything French, but looked up *human* and *human beings* and got what you'd guess, but came across *humic*, which sent me to *humus*, which has to do with "a layer of soil that comes from the decay of leaves and other vegetation and which contains valuable plant food." It is a twin of the Latin word—because everything in our house came from Latin, except for the *Kyrie*—for soil, earth.

Which put me in mind of a book I'd been reading by Robert Pogue Harrison, *The Dominion of the Dead*, in which he speaks about our "humic density"—we human beings, shaped out of earth, fashioned out of dirt, because we are primally bound to the ground our shelters and buildings and monuments rise out of and our dead are buried in. Everything—architecture, history, religion—"rooted" in the humus of the home place and to the stories and corpses that are buried there.

Thus was I shown, in my first days in West Clare years ago, the house and haggard, hay barn and turf-shed, cow cabins and out-offices, gateposts, stone walls, fields and wells and ditches, forts and gaps, church and grave vault, names and dates in stone—all the works and days of hands that belonged to the people that belonged to me, all dead now, dead and gone back to the ground out of which arose these emblements of humic density.

> The awareness of death that defines human nature is inseparable from—indeed it rises from—our awareness that we are not self-authored, that we follow in the footsteps of the dead. Everywhere one looks across the spectrum of human cultures one finds the foundational authority of the predecessor. . . . Whether we are conscious of it or not we do the will of the ancestors: our commandments come to us from their realm; their precedents are our law; we submit to their dictates, even when we rebel against them. Our diligence, hardihood, rectitude, and heroism, but also our folly, spite, rancor, and pathologies, are so many signatures of the dead on the contracts that seal our identities. We inherit their obsessions; assume their burdens; carry on their causes; promote their mentalities, ideologies, and very often their superstitions; and very often we die trying to vindicate their humiliations. —*The Dominion of the Dead*, pages ix–x, Robert Pogue Harrison

Isn't that just like people? Ethnographically speaking? Or anthropologically? To think of the place where their ancients lived and worked, fought, believed, and are buried as sacred, central to their own identity.

So we're back to burials again—Antigone and Thebes. Creon and Bush. Do you suppose that humus is good for flowers?

Such is the trouble with the everyday—one thing leads to another. You start out with ethnography and end up with flowers, like the paperwhite narcissus my true love grows every Christmas from bulbs she buries in a kitchen pot, or the crocuses that press through the litter of old leaves, pine needles, melting snow, and warming soil every year in April up here at the lake. The everyday, predictable, measurable truth assumes a routine that we think we can study: how the seasons change, the moon runs through its phases, the sun rises earlier every day. "April showers," we say, "red sky at morning." Monday begets Tuesday, which in turn begets . . . well, you get it. We make our plans upon such reliable sciences. "Home by Friday, with the help of God," I tell my darling on the way out the door.

MAYBE YOU WANT to know what I said at the conference?

I said it looked like "a paradigm shift." (They were paying me a handsome honorarium.) I said it looked like a paradigm shift, from a sense of holy ground and grounding, to a kind of rootlessness—spiritually, ethnographically, anthropologically speaking, humanity-wise. At which point in the proceedings I removed from my bag and placed upon the table by the lectern from which I was holding forth, a golf-bag cremation urn. Molded, no doubt, out of some new-age resin or high-grade polymer, it stands about fourteen inches high and looks like everyone's idea of the big nut-brown leather bag with plump pockets and a plush towel and precious memories in which "Dad" or "Grandpa" or "Good Old [insert most recently deceased golf-buddy's nickname]" would have kept his good old golf clubs. The bottom of the golf-bag urn is fashioned to look like the greensward of a well-maintained fairway. So the whole thing looks like a slice of golf heaven. There is even a golf ball resting beside the base of the bag, waiting for the erstwhile golfer to chip it up for an easy putt. The thing is hollow, the better to accommodate the two hundred-some cubic centimeters, give or take, most cremated human beings will amount to.

I confess that the idea of the urn only came to me at the last moment, because I wanted to see the looks on their faces. It's a character flaw, based upon my own lack of scholastic pedigree. Except for an honorary doctorate in humanities from the university I never managed to graduate from—though the Dear knows I paid for many classes—I hold no degree. I'm not bachelor, master, or doctor of anything, and though I was "certified" in mortuary science by a regionally respected university, a battery of state and national board exams, and the completion of a requisite apprenticeship, I'm self-conscious about standing before a room full of serious students and scholars. It is this fear—surely every human has it—of being exposed as a fraud that makes one eager to supply a diversion. Thus the urn: if I could not *earn* their respect, I'd . . . well, never mind.

Still, I wanted to see the looks on their faces when I presented, as an article of documentary consequence, as an anthropological artifact, as a postmodern relic of a species that had accomplished pyramids, the Taj Mahal, and Newgrange, the ethnographically denatured and, by the way, chemically inert, plastic golf-bag-shaped cremation urn. It's one of a kind. It came from a catalogue. There's also one that looks like a pair of cowboy boots—a "companion" urn for "pardners"—and one that looks like a duck decoy for hunters or possibly naturalists: variations on the theme of molded plastics. So I wanted to tell them about the paradigm shift that it signified.

I came up burying Presbyterians and Catholics, devout and lapsed, born-again and backslidden Baptists, Orthodox Christians, an occasional Zen Buddhist, and variously observant Jews. For each of these sets, there were infinite subsets. We had right old Calvinists who only drank single malts and were all good Masons and were mad for the bagpipes, just as we had former Methodists who worked their way up the Reformation ladder after they married into money or made a little killing in the market. We had Polish Catholics and Italian ones, Irish and Hispanic and Byzantine, and Jews who were Jews in the way some Lutherans are Lutheran—for births and deaths and first marriages.

My late father, himself a funeral director, schooled me in the local orthodoxies and their protocols as I have schooled my sons and daughter who work with me. There was a kind of comfort, I suppose, in knowing exactly what would be done with you, one's ethnic and religious identities having established long ago the fashions and the fundamentals for one's leave-taking. And while the fashions might change, the fundamental ingredients for a funeral were the same—someone who has quit breathing forever, some others to whom it apparently matters, and someone else who stands between the quick and dead and says something like, "Behold, I show you a mystery."

"An act of sacred community theatre," Dr. Thomas Long, writer, thinker, and theologian, calls this "transporting" of the dead from this life to the next. "We move them to a further shore. Everyone has a part in this drama." The dead get to the grave or fire or tomb whilst the living get to the edge of a life they must learn to live without them. Ours is a species that deals with death (the idea of the thing) by dealing with our dead (the thing itself).

Late in the twentieth century, there was some trending toward the more homegrown doxologies. Everyone was into the available "choices." We started doing more cremations—it made good sense. Folks seemed less "grounded" than their grandparents, more "portable," "divisible," more "scattered" somehow. We got into balloon releases and homing pigeons done up as doves to signify the flight of the dead fellow's soul toward heaven. "Bridge Over Troubled Water" replaced "How Great Thou Art." And if Paul's Letter to the Romans or the Book of Job was replaced by Omar Khayyam or Emily Dickinson, what harm? "After great pain, a formal feeling comes," rings as true as any sacred text. A death in the family is, as Miss Emily describes it: "First—Chill—then Stupor—then the letting go."

Amidst all the high fashions and fashion blunders, the ritual wheel that worked the space between the living and the dead still got us where we needed to go. It made room for the good laugh, the good cry, and the power of faith brought to bear on the mystery of mortality. The dead were "processed" to their final dispositions with a pause sufficient to say that their lives and their deaths truly mattered to us. The broken circle within the community of folks who shared blood or geography or belief with the dead was closed again through this "acting out our parts," as Reverend Long calls it. Someone brought the casseroles, someone brought the prayers, someone brought a shovel or lit the fire, everyone was consoled by everyone else. The wheel that worked the space between the living and the dead ran smoothly.

Lately I've been thinking that the wheel is broken or gone a long way off the track or must be reinvented every day. The paradigm is shifting. What with distanced communities of faith and family, the script has changed from the essentially sacred to the essentially silly. We mistake the ridiculous for the sublime.

Take Batesville Casket Company, for example. They make caskets and urns and wholesale them to funeral homes all over the globe. Their latest catalogue, called "Accessories," includes suggested "visitation vignettes"—the stage arranged not around Cross or Crescent or Star of David but around one of Batesville's "life-symbols" caskets featuring interchangeable corner hardware. One "life-symbol" looks like a rainbow trout jumping from the corners of the hardwood casket, and for dearly departed gardeners, there is one with little plastic potted mums. There is the "sports dad" vignette done up like a garage with beer logos, team pennants, hoops, and hockey skates and, of course, a casket that looks a little like a jock locker gone horizontal. There's one for motorcyclists and the much-publicized "Big Mama's Kitchen," with its faux stove, kitchen table, and apple pie for the mourners to share with those who call. Instead of Methodists or Muslims, we are golfers now; gardeners, bikers, and dead bowlers. The bereaved are not so much family and friends or coreligionists as fellow hobbyists and enthusiasts. And I have become less the funeral director and more the memorial caddy of sorts, getting the dead out of the way and the living assembled within a theatre that is neither sacred nor secular but increasingly absurd—a triumph of accessories over essentials, of stuff over substance, gimmicks over the genuine. The dead are downsized or disappeared or turned into knickknacks in a kind of funereal karaoke.

Consider the case of Peter Payne, dead at forty-four of brain cancer. His wife arranged for his body to be cremated without witness or rubric, his ashes placed in the golf-bag urn, the urn to be placed on a table in one of our parlors with his "real life"—which is to say, "life-size" golf bag standing beside it for their son and daughter and circle of friends to come by for a look. And if nobody said, "Doesn't he look natural?" several commented on how much he looked like, well, his golf bag. The following day, the ensemble was taken to the church, where the minister, apparently willing to play along, had some things to say about "life being like a par-three hole with plenty of sand traps and water hazards"—to wit, all too short and full of trouble. And heaven was something like a "19th Hole," where, after "finishing the course," those who "played by the rules" and "kept an honest score" were given their "trophies." Then those in attendance were invited to join the family at the clubhouse of Mystic Creek Golf Course for lunch and a little commemorative boozing. There is already talk of a Peter Payne Memorial Golf Tournament next year. A scholarship fund has been established to send young golfers to PGA training camp. Some of his ashes will be scattered in the sand trap of the par-five hole on the back nine with the kidney-shaped green and the dogleg right. The rest will remain, forever and ever, perpetual filler for the golf-bag urn.

Whether this is indeed a paradigm shift, the end of an era, or, as Robert Pogue Harrison suggests, an "all too human failure to meet the challenges of modernity," is anyone's guess. But we are nonetheless required, as he insists, to choose "an allegiance—either to the posthuman, the virtual, and the synthetic, or to the earth, the real and the dead in their humic densities."

"So, which will it be?" I posed rhetorically to the audience (which seemed oddly fixed upon the *objet de mort*). "The golf bag urn?" (read posthuman, virtual, and synthetic) "or some humus—the ground and graveyard, village, nation, place or faith—the nitty-gritty real earth in which human roots link the present to the past and future?"

They looked a little blankly at me, as if I'd held up five fingers and asked them what the square root of Thursday was. There was some shifting in seats, some clearing of throats. I thought I might have numbed them with the genius of it or damaged them in some nonspecific way.

I thought about wrapping up with a little joke about a widow who brings her cheapskate husband's ashes home, pours them out on the kitchen table, and begins to upbraid him for all those things she asked for but he never gave her—the mink coat, the convertible, etc.—but thought better of it and closed instead with an invitation to engage in a little Q & A on these and any other themes they might like to pursue. A man in the second row, whose eyes had widened when I produced the urn and who had not blinked or closed his mouth since the thing appeared, raised his hand to ask, "Is there anyone in there?"

"Why, no, no, of course not, no," I assured him.

There was a collective sigh, a sudden flash of not-quite-knowing smiles, and then the roar of uneasy silence, like a rush of air returned to the room.

The director of the Center for the Ethnography of Everyday Life hurriedly rose to thank me for "a thought-provoking presentation," led the assembled in polite applause, and announced that the buffet luncheon was ready and waiting in a room across the hall. Except for a man who wanted to discuss his yet-to-be-patented "water-reduction method" of body disposition, there was no further intercourse between the assembly and me.

It's only now, months later, the conference come and gone, the kindly stipend paid and spent, that it occurs to me what I should have said.

What I should have said is that ethnography seems so perilous just now, no less the everyday; that "life and letters and the field" seem littered more than ever with the wounded and the dead, the raging and the sad. That ethnicity, formerly a cause for celebration, now seems an occasion for increasing caution. That ethnic identity—

those ties by which we are bound to others of our kind by tribe and race, language and belief, geography and history, costume and custom and a hundred other measures—seems lately less a treasure, more a scourge.

WHEN I BEGAN this book, I had in mind something that would help my family reconnect to our little history as Irish Americans, something that would resonate with other hyphenated types who've come from every parish in the world. I wanted the names and the records kept—a text my grandchildren, not yet born, might dip into someday for their own reasons. Something like *Roots* for the freckled and redheaded set, the riverdancing and flash-tempered descendants of immigrants—the seven million "willing" Irish men and women who have crossed the Atlantic in the last four hundred years, seeking a future in this New World that had been denied to them in the Old. From the first Scots-Irish, tired of the tithes and rents in Ulster in the seventeenth century—Davy Crockett's people, westward pressing, sturdy and curious—to the hundreds of thousands of oppressed Catholics in the eighteenth century who would fight in our revolution and help to shape our nation, like the man with my name, from South Carolina, who signed the Declaration of Independence; to the million Famine Irish, sick with hunger, fever, and want in the nineteenth century, one of whom, my great-great-grandfather, came and returned, and another, my great-grandfather, came to stay; to the rising and falling tides of Irish who washed ashore here in the twentieth century, building our roads, working our Main Streets, filling our senates and legislatures, rectories, schools, and universities; to the sons and daughters of friends in Moveen who left home in the 1970s and 1980s and 1990s—Anne Murray and her sister Kay, a couple of the Carmodys, Downses and O'Sheas. They are still going out to America, although now they come and go as they please on 747s that every day fly over Moveen on their way to and from the airport at

Shannon. Ultimatum has become an option. American Wakes have become bon-voyage parties as the young in West Clare become, like the young in Michigan, working tourists in a smaller world full of portable opportunities and multiple possibilities.

By the time Alex Haley's *Roots* was published in 1976, I'd been back and forth to Ireland three times. Haley's hunger for knowing and reconstructing and reconnecting with the past was one I'd got a whiff of in my early travels. When the TV series the book inspired was aired in January 1977, I watched with a hundred thirty million other Americans who, thanks to Haley's gifts, saw, in the struggles of his family, something related to their own. For white Americans, it humanized blacks in a way that federal laws, however just and long overdue, had failed to do. For African Americans, it ennobled their struggle in a hostile world by connecting them to a formerly untold past.

When the African held his infant son, Kunta Kinte, up to the firmament and spoke his name into the dark face of creation, I understood the power of naming and keeping track of things, why all holy books begin with a litany of "begats," and how much each of our personal stories owes to the stories of our families and clans, our kind and kin. Second only to the forced migration of the African slave trade, the tide of Famine and post-Famine Irish marked the largest single wave of immigration in U.S. history.

SO, I WANTED a book that honored those who stayed and those who went, to bridge some of the distance that always swells between people who "choose" a different path, or find some footing in a life with few choices. I wanted to understand the man who left, the better to understand the man who returned to Moveen, to understand the ones who went between and who would follow after.

I wanted something chatty and jaunty like a good night's talk. Something that would find its market among even a fraction of the forty-some-million Americans alive today who trace their place back to the thirty-two thousand-square-mile island in the sea at the westernmost edge of Europe.

My agent and publishers oughtn't to be faulted for thinking of a kind of travel memoir, something with a little something for everyone, something that would earn back its advance and then some. Something that would offset the losses on poetry. Truth told, it's what I was hoping for, too.

The brother (about whom more anon), ever the raconteur, suggested at the outset a regimen of weekly audiences with himself and tendered *Wednesdays with Patrick* as a working title. "Or maybe *Paddy*—you know, for the folksy crowd—like that Paddy whiskey, easy sipping with a little bite. And maybe Thursdays, Tom. Yes, *Thursdays with Paddy.* That's just the t'ing." And the truth is I'd have no problem with that. He's a great man in all ways with a skeptic's temperament, a heart of gold, and a "fierce big brainbox," as Martin Roche once said about J. J. McMahon, our neighbor in West Clare.

I wanted it all to be a gift, in thanksgiving for the gift that had been given me, of Ireland and the Irish, the sense of connection, and the family I found there and the house they all came from that was left to me.

SEPTEMBER 11 CHANGED all of that. The book I first imagined was no longer possible. Just as our sense of safety here, protected by oceans and the globe's largest arsenal of weapons and resources, was forever shaken, irreparably damaged by the horrors of that day, so too was the sense that ethnicity is always and only quaint and benign.

Lost too was the luxury of isolation and purposeful ignorance of the larger world of woes, a taste for which I'd acquired in my protected suburban youth and overindulged throughout my adulthood—fattening, as Americans especially do, on our certainty that it will all be taken care of by whoever's in charge.

I remember telling prospective tourists, fearful of what they'd heard about the "Troubles" in Ireland—the last century's longest-running war in Western Europe—not to worry about a thing. Belfast and Derry were distant concerns, small towns in a tiny province—"little more," I'd assure them, "than a bar fight in Escanaba or Munising." I'd acquired the Irish gift for strategic understatement, too.

The day that terrorists bombed embassies in Africa, was it?—killing dozens or hundreds, I couldn't say—I was shopping in Kilrush for kitchen things at Brews and Gleeson's, certain that the troubles really didn't concern me and that out by Dunlicky the mackerel would be plentiful and the walk to the sea would do me good, and nothing could be better than fresh fish and tea.

So maybe what I should have said is that ethnography, which formerly seemed a parlor game, seems more a dangerous science now, especially "the ethnography of everyday life," because life, everyday life, here in the opening decade of the new millennium, constantly obscures, daily nullifies, and relentlessly confounds the needful work of such inquiry. The subgroup we were about to study is suddenly removed or written off by the first drafts of a history that our all-day-everyday news cycle proclaims.

"A Decade After Massacres, Rwanda Outlaws Ethnicity," proclaims the headline in the *New York Times* on April 8, 2004. Marc Lacey reports from the capital, Kigali:

> This country, where ethnic tensions were whipped up into a frenzy of killing, is now trying to make ethnicity a thing of the past. There are no Hutu in the new Rwanda. There are no Tutsi either. The government, dominated by the minority Tutsi, has wiped out the distinction by decree.
>
> Ethnicity has already been ripped out of schoolbooks and rubbed off government identity cards. Government documents no longer mention Hutu or Tutsi, and the country's newspapers and radio stations, tightly controlled by the government, steer clear of the labels as well.

It is not just considered bad form to discuss ethnicity in the new Rwanda. It can land one in jail. Added to the penal code is a crime of "divisionism," a nebulous offense that includes speaking too provocatively about ethnicity.

As elsewhere, there are the politically incorrect.

A Tutsi woman, who was raped in 1994 by so many Hutu militiamen in the village of Taba that she lost count, said she has difficulty interacting comfortably with Hutu.

"I don't trust them," said the woman, who, identified only as J. J., testified about her ordeal before the international tribunal in Rwanda.

Tutsi and *Hutu*—such neighborly words—equal in syllables and vowel sounds, trochees and pleasantly fricative "t's": who'd ever guess that they accounted for eight hundred thousand deaths in a hundred days a decade ago, most by machete, that the rest of the world largely ignored.

While marking another anniversary of the Rwandan genocide this year, we are avoiding naming what is happening in Sudan's Darfur region as "genocide." That particular noun requires verbs—by international convention, something remedial would have to be done—whereas *atrocity* or *ethnic cleansing* leaves us options. The systematic rape, pillage, and slaughter of tribal Africans by Arab Janjaweed militia, armed by the Sudanese government, are, like the atrocities of the twentieth century—Armenians in Turkey, Jews of the Holocaust, Cambodians, Kurds, Bosnians, Nigerians, Bengalis—all lamentable mostly after the fact.

Asked whether the recent run of genocides might finally get it to "stick in people's minds" that we've responsibilities, Samantha Power, author of *A Problem from Hell*, replies, "I think we tell ourselves, though, that that was the product of peculiar circumstances.

'Oh, that's Africa, you know, the tribes, they do that.' 'It's the Balkans, this stuff happens in the Balkans.' There's a way that we *otherize* [my italics] circumstances that challenge our universal premises." (Atlantic Unbound Interviews, March 14, 2003)

How do we *otherize* our fellow humans? How do we mistake them for something other than our kind? In what ways has our ethnicity poisoned the well of our humanity? Why must our religions so miscalculate our gods? If there is only one God, as all Muslims, Christians, and Jews believe, then isn't the One we believe in one and the same? If there is no God, aren't we only off by one? And if there are many, aren't there plenty to go around? In the wake of that godawful September, after bombing the bejaysus out of Afghanistan, after bombing, invading, and occupying Iraq, a book about the forty shades of green I'd encountered driving around the Ring of Kerry seemed a little like a golf-bag urn—plastic, silly, curious, but idiotic. All I saw was forty shades of gray, and in each of them still forty more.

FROM THE POST-FAMINE cottage of my great-great-grandfather, to the Moveen my great-grandfather left in 1890, to the West Clare that Dorothea Lang photographed in the mid-1950s, to the Ireland I found in 1970, the greatest change in a hundred years was light—electric light. So says my neighbor J. J. McMahon, a scholarly and insightful man. It illuminated the dark hours, lengthened the evenings, shortened the winter's terrible hold. Folks read later, talked later, went out in the night, certain their lamps would see them home. Still, life remained circumscribed by the limited range of transportation and communication. The immediate universe for most small farmers extended no farther than town, church, and marketplace, distances managed by ass and cart, or horse and trap, on Raleigh bike, or on foot—shank's mare, as it was locally called. Communication was by gossip and bush telegraph, from kitchen to kitchen, with the postman up the road, with the men to and from the creamery, with the priest or teacher on their daily rounds, with women returning from market stalls. Talk was almost entirely parochial. The "wireless"—electric light's chatty cousin—brought news of the larger world in thrice-daily doses whilst newspapers were read aloud, entirely. Still, these were one-sided communiqués. There was no escape, no geographical cures, no way to get out of the local into the world. Folks had to live with one another. This made them more likely to bear fellow feelings, to understand, to empathize. However much familiarity bred contempt—and it bred its share—the neighbors shared a common life experience, the same perils, the same hopes for their children, the same borders and limitations. They formed, if only by default, a community.

In the kitchens, shops, and snugs of those remote parishes, the visitor or stranger or traveler was, much like the bards of old, a bearer of tidings unheard before, like correspondence from a distant country, or a missionary or a circus come to town. The new voice at the fire relieved the tedium of the everyday, the usual suspects in the house, the same dull redundancy of the Tuesday that followed Monday, which in its turn followed Sunday, where the priest gave the same sermon he had last year at about the same time.

I was such a Playboy of the Western World, in the months of my first visit to West Clare. Deposed for hours on a variety of topics (music, money, presidential politics), and my opinion sought on all manner of things (the war in Vietnam, who shot Kennedy, the future of Ireland), I thought I must be a very interesting specimen indeed. It was years before I understood that, during those blustery winter evenings in Moveen, I provided only some little relief from habit and routine, what Samuel Beckett had identified years before as "the cancer of time." I was not so interesting as I was something, anything, other than the known thing.

But today, the easier communications become, the easier it becomes not to communicate. The more rapidly we travel to the ends of the earth, the more readily we avoid our nearest neighbors. The more communing we do, the more elusive a sense of community seems. We are each encouraged to make individual choices, to seek personal saviors, singular experiences, our own particular truth. We make enemies of strangers and strangers of friends and wonder why we feel alone in the world.

Americans seem terribly perplexed at all the hatred of us in the world. Where, we wonder, are all those happy Iraqis who were supposed to greet us with smiles and flowers after we had liberated them? Where have all the flowers gone? Anthology? Antigone?

In his unstintingly titled *How the Irish Saved Civilization*, historian Thomas Cahill comments on page 6 on the tendency of one "civilization" to miss the point of an "other":

> To an educated Englishman of the last century, for instance, the Irish were by their very nature incapable of civilization. "The Irish," proclaimed Benjamin Disraeli, Queen Victoria's beloved prime minister, "hate our order, our civilization, our enterprising industry, our pure religion [Disraeli's father had abandoned Judaism for the Church of England]. This wild, reckless, indolent, uncertain and superstitious race have no sympathy with the English character. Their ideal of human felicity is an alternation of clannish broils and coarse idolatry [i.e. Catholicism]. Their history describes an unbroken circle of bigotry [!] and blood." The venomous racism and knuckle-headed prejudice of this characterization may be evident to us, but in the days of "dear old Dizzy," as the queen called the man who had presented her with India, it simply passed for indisputable truth.

If this sounds a little like the conventional wisdom of the day, the policy and approved text on our "enemies in the war on terror," then perhaps we should be on the lookout for "venomous racism and knuckleheaded prejudice" of our own.

Cahill goes on to make his case of how Irish monks and scribes kept the candles burning and the texts illumined through the Dark Ages and recivilized and re-Christianized Europe from west to east in what he calls a "hinge" of history. Cahill's "hinges of history"—he has since done for the Jews and the Greeks what he did for the Irish—sound more than a little like what the German existentialist Karl Jaspers called the "Axial Age," from 800 to 200 BC, when most of religious thought was formed, an age marked by violence and upheaval.

Maybe it is time we looked to Ireland again for some clues to the nature of our ethnic imbroglios, our *jihads* and holy wars, and to how we might learn to live peaceably in the world with our "others." Surely the Shiite and Sunni of Iraq have something to learn from the Catholics and Protestants of Belfast and from the citizens of the Republic of Ireland. For here is a nation with a history of invasion, occupation, oppression, tribal warfare, religious fervor, ethnic cleansing, sectarian violence, and the tyrannies of churchmen, statesmen, thugs, and hoodlums. And yet it thrives on a shaky peace, religious convictions, rich cultural resources, and the hope of its citizens. It is a kind of miracle of civilization—where the better angels of the species have bested the bad. Such things could be contagious.

ON AUGUST 28, 1931, W. B. Yeats wrote "Remorse for Intemperate Speech," a line from which this book borrows for one of its chapters and organizing principles. "Out of Ireland have we come./Great hatred, little room,/Maimed us at the start." Yeats had witnessed and worked at the birth of a new Irish nation, had served as a Free State senator, and, after winning the Nobel Prize for literature, was at sixty-five the country's public man of letters. An Anglo-Irishman who had ditched his people's High Church Christianity in favor of swamis and Theosophists and his wife's dabbling in the occult, he was likewise deeply immersed in the fledgling nation's Celtic twilight, and torn between the right-wing politics of between-wars

Europe and the romantic, mystic past of Ireland. His poem confesses and laments that reason and breeding, imagination and good intention are trumped by what he called "a fanatic heart." The remorse is real. Surely the age in which we live requires such self-examination. In a world made smaller by its benign and malevolent technologies, out of whatever country we have come, great hatred, little room, maims us at the start. Regardless of our heritage, we carry from our mothers' wombs our own fanatic hearts.

IF THE BOOK I first had in mind was made more difficult by the ethnography of everyday life hereabouts, something Yeats wrote in a letter to Maud Gonne affords a kind of guidance. "Today I have one settled conviction 'Create, draw a firm strong line & hate nothing whatever not even (the devil) if he be your most cherished belief—Satan himself'. I hate many things but I do my best, & once some fifteen years ago, for I think one whole hour, I was free from hate. Like Faust I said 'stay moment' but in vain. I think it was the only happiness I have ever known."

The bookish habits of Michel de Montaigne ought likewise to be imitated. (Already I've become more tolerant!) The *essai*, as the sixteenth-century Frenchman named it, is less a certainty and more a search, an attempt at sense-making, a setting forth, as if in a boat of words, to see if language will keep the thought afloat; a testing of the air for what rings true, an effort at illuminating grays.

We are told he retired to his library at a certain age and made his way among its books, endeavoring to understand his species by examining himself. "Each man bears the whole of man's estate," he wrote, and figured humanity could be understood by the scrutiny of a single human. As it was easiest, he chose himself and began to look. He was among the first ethnographers of the everyday. Whereas Augustine gave us his *Confessions*, in Montaigne we get, as his present-day disciple Phillip Lopate says gorgeously, "more of the cat examining its fur." We get his table fare and toilet habits, his favorite poets and his favorite books, what he thought about the sexes, his take on the weather. From the tiniest of details, he essays the real, the human, and the true.

THIS BOOK WAS begun in my home in Moveen, in the easy early months of 2001. It was shaped between funerals and family duties over the next two years in Milford and was finished over the late winter and early spring of 2004 in northern Michigan, at a home we have on Mullett Lake, a half-hour south of the Straits of Mackinac. In each location, the "cancer of time," the duties and routine of the everyday follow something like Montaigne's regimen. I wake early, make the coffee, read the e-mail and the *New York Times* online, check the *Irish Times* and Clare FM, cook up some Odlums Pinhead Oatmeal. "Aptly named," my loved ones sometimes say. At 7:30, I listen to *The Writer's Almanac* with Garrison Keillor on the radio, a kind of writerly morning office or book of days during which he says what happened on the date, lists the birthdays, reads a poem.

Our calendars, once full of feasts of virgins, martyrs, and confessors, now are crowded with unholy days. The day they struck our shining cities; the day we leveled theirs; the day they killed our innocents; the day we did the same to theirs. So to have a poem and some better news, every day, is no bad thing.

Yesterday was the day they put Galileo on trial for claiming that the earth revolved around the sun. "You can think it," the pope told him, "just don't say so out loud." "*E pur si muove . . .*," the astronomer whispered, alas to no one in earshot.

And today is the birthday of Thomas Jefferson, born in 1743 in Virginia, we are told, and "though he had grown up with slaves, and later kept them himself, his first legislative act was a failed attempt to emancipate the slaves under his jurisdiction. He later said, 'The whole commerce between master and slave is a perpetual exercise . . .

in tyranny. . . . The man must be a prodigy who can retain his . . . morals undepraved by such circumstances.' "

And it's the birthday of Samuel Beckett, your "cancer of time" man, born on Good Friday in 1906 in a suburb of Dublin, who said of his childhood, "I had little talent for happiness." In 1928, he left for Paris to become James Joyce's acolyte. In 1937, he was stabbed in the chest by a pimp named Prudent. He visited his assailant in prison and when he asked the man why he had attacked him, Prudent replied, "*Je ne sais pas, monsieur.*" "I do not know, sir," became a prominent refrain in *Waiting for Godot*, his most famous play—in which, most famously, nothing happens.

We do not know. Such is the dilemma of the everyday. We rummage among books and newspapers, watch the fire go to ash, pace the room, walk out into the day that's in it, watch the snow give way to humus. The loons return. The first insuppressible flowers bloom. We find in our theatres and times, like Vladimir and Estragon, that life is waiting, killing time, holding to the momentary hope that whatever's supposed to happen next is scheduled to occur—wars end, the last thin shelf of ice melts, and the lake is clear and blue, like the ocean we are always dreaming of crossing, we get it right, we make it home—if not today, then possibly tomorrow.

TL

APRIL 13, 2004
MULLETT LAKE
MILFORD
MOVEEN WEST

THE BROTHER

Every so often the brother calls, ranting about having to get on a plane, fly over to Shannon, drive out to West Clare, and cut a finger off.

I blame myself for this.

"Not the finger again, Pat," is what I say.

He says he wants to leave it in Moyarta—the graveyard on the Shannon estuary where our people are buried in the ancient parish of Carrigaholt. He wants to leave his severed finger there—a part of himself—against the loneliness: the low-grade, ever-present ache he feels, like a phantom limb, whenever he's away from there too long. Will I come with him? He wants to know.

I blame myself for this. I know how it happens. I know it is only going to get worse. Lately he's been saying maybe better a thumb.

"Better yet two thumbs, Tom! That's it, both thumbs—one for the future and one for the past—there in Moyarta, that's just the thing. One for all that was and all that yet will be. . . ." He's waxing eloquent and breathing deeply.

"Never mind the thumbs, Pat," I tell him, but he knows it makes a kind of sense to me.

There's something about the impulse to prune and plant body parts on the westernmost peninsula of a distant county in a far country that goes a step beyond your standard tourist class. The brother is nothing if not a great man for the grim reaping and the grand gesture.

Maybe you're thinking the devil of drink, but neither of us has had a drop in years.

Big Pat swore off it decades ago, as a youth at university. He'd been given a football scholarship to the University of Dayton. He was a tight end and a good one. At six foot five and sixteen stone, he was fit and fast and difficult to tackle. Between games and his studies he would drink in the local bars, where invariably some lesser specimen would drink enough local lager to feel the equal of him. Pat found himself the target of too many drunken Napoleons—little men determined to have a go at the Big so as to make themselves feel, well, *enlarged.* He had bottles bashed over his head, sucker punches thrown, aspersions cast from every corner by wee strangers looking for a fight. After breaking a man's nose and spending a night in the lockup, Pat swore off the drink for the safety of all and everyone concerned. So he comes by his theory of thumbs quite soberly and knows that I know what he means to say.

IRELAND HAPPENED TO Big Pat in 1992 the way it happened to me in 1970, as a whole-body, blood-borne, core-experience; an echo thumping in the cardiovascular pulse of things, in every vessel of the being and the being's parts, all the way down to the extremities, to the thumbs. The case he got, like mine, is chronic, acute, and likely terminal. The symptoms are occasionally contagious. He became not only acquainted with but utterly submerged in his Irish heritage—a legacy of Lynches and O'Haras, Graces and McBradys, Ryans and Currys, and the mighty people he married into—shanty and lace-curtain tributaries of a bloodline that all return to Ireland for their source.

Of course, there are more orderly ways to do it.

You can dress up one day a year in the shamrock tie and green socks, haul out the beer-stained jacket, get a little tipsy cursing the Brits and the black luck of the draw into the wee hours from which you'll wake headachy and dry-mouthed the next morning and return to the ordinary American life—the annual mid-March Oiyrish.

Once, as luck would have it, I found myself in Manhattan for the St. Paddy's Day Parade. I stepped out from my hotel into 44th Street near Fifth Avenue thinking it was a day like any other. It was not. Maureen O'Hara was the Grand Marshal. There were cops and crazies everywhere. Cardinal O'Connor, may he R.I.P., said Mass in St. Patrick's, and I had to cancel a meeting with editors downtown. The sheer tidal force of Irishry, or of Irish impersonators—one hundred fifty thousand of them—all heading forty-some blocks uptown made perambulation against the grain of the parade impossible.

For most people, this Marchy excess is enough: the pipers and claddagh blather, the cartoon and caricature of what it means to be Irish and American. The next morning everyone returns to business as usual.

Or you might, after years of threatening to make the trip, get together with some other couples from the ushers' club and take the standard ten-day tour, bouncing in the bus from the Lakes of Killarney to the Blarney Stone with a stop at the Waterford factory, a sing-along in Temple Bar; you'll get some holy water and retail relics at the Knock Shrine and some oysters in Galway, where you'll buy one of those caps all the farmers are wearing this year, and spend a couple hours in the duty-free, buying up smoked salmon and turf figurines, Jameson whiskey and Belleek before you fly home with the usual stories of seeing Bill Clinton or Bono in a bar in Wicklow or the man with the big mitts and droopy earlobes you met in a chipper in Clogheen who was the image of your dearly departed mother's late uncle Seamus, or the festival you drove through in Miltown Malbay—fiddlers and pipers and tinwhistlers everywhere—the music, you will say, my God, the music!

Enough for most people is enough. Some photo-ops, some faith-and-begorras, maybe a stone from the home place, a sod of turf smuggled home in the suitcase, some perfect memories of broguey hospitalities and boozy light—something to say we are Irish in the way that others are Italian or Korean or former Yugoslavian: hyphenated, removed by generations or centuries, gone but not entirely forgotten, proud of your heritage—your Irish-Americanity.

Enough for most people is enough. But Pat was thrown into the deep end of the pool.

He landed in Shannon for the very first time on the Sunday morning of the 29th of March, 1992. A few hours later, instead of hoisting pints or singing along, or remarking on the forty shades of green, he was helping me lift the greeny, jaundiced, fairly withered body of Nora Lynch tenderly out of the bed she died in, out of the house she'd lived all her life in, out through the back door of her tiny cottage, into the coffin propped in the yard, on sawhorses assembled for this sad duty.

While most Americans spend their first fortnight tour rollicking through bars and countryside, searching none too intently for ruins or lost relations, Pat was driven straightaway to the home that our great-grandfather had come out of a century before, and taken into the room in which that ancient had been born. For Pat it was no banquet at Bunratty Castle, no bus ride to the Cliffs of Moher, no golf at the famous links at Lahinch, no saints or scholars or leprechauns. It was, rather, to the wake of Nora Lynch, late of Moveen West, Kilkee, County Clare—her tiny, tidy corpse laid out in a nunnish blue suit in a bed littered with Mass cards, candlesticks, and crucifix assembled on the bedside table, her bony hands wrapped in a rosary, her chin propped shut with a daily missal, folks from the townland making their visits; "sorry for your troubles," "the poor cratur, Godhelpus," "an honest woman the Lord've mercy on her," "faith, she was, she was, sure faith"; the rooms buzzing with hushed talk and the clatter of tableware, the hum of a rosary being said in the room, the Lenten Sunday light pouring through the deep windows. Big Pat stood between an inkling of the long dead and the body of the lately dead and felt the press of family history, like the sea thrown finally against the shore, tidal and undulant and immediate. He sighed. He inhaled the air, sweet with damp-mold and early putrefaction, tinged with tobacco and turf smoke, hot grease and tea, and knew that though he'd never been in this place before, among these stones and puddles and local brogues, he was, in ways he could neither articulate nor deny, *home*.

He and his Mary, and me and mine, had booked our tickets two mornings before when the sadly anticipated word had come of Nora Lynch's death at half-twelve in Moveen, half-past seven of that Friday morning in Michigan, March 27, 1992, four months into her ninetieth year, one month after she'd been taken to hospital in Ennis, six weeks after our father had died in the middle of the February of that awful year.

We had buried our father like the chieftain he was, then turned to the duties of the great man's estate when word came from across the ocean that Nora had taken a turn for the worse. Two days of diagnostics had returned the sad truth of pancreatic cancer. The doctors were anxious to have her moved. In dozens of visits to Moveen since 1970, I had become Nora's next of kin—a cousin twice removed, but still the first of her people ever to return to Ireland since her father's brother, my great-grandfather, had left at the end of the nineteenth century. Neither her sisters nor her sisters' children had ever returned. Her dead brothers had left no children. Nora Lynch was the last—the withered and spinsterly end of the line until, as she often said, I came. Two decades of letters and phone calls and transatlantic flights had tightened the ties that bind family connections between Michigan and Moveen. So when it looked like Nora was dying, they called me.

I LANDED IN Ireland on Ash Wednesday morning, March 4 that year, and drove from Shannon to the cathedral in Ennis, joining a handful of coreligionists for the tribal smudge and mumbled reminder that "you are dust and unto dust . . . ," et cetera, et cetera. Then out the road to the County Hospital, a yellow stucco building trimmed in white, behind a wall on the north end of town at a corner on the Galway road. I remember the eight-bed ward of sickly men and women and Nora in the far corner looking jaundiced and tiny and suddenly old under crisp white linens. Four months before, we'd all celebrated her eighty-ninth birthday in Mary Hickie's Bayview Hotel in Kilkee with cakes and tea and drinks all around. P. J. and Breda and Louise and Mary and me—there in Kilkee—all singing, "Happy Birthday," and Nora not knowing what to do. She'd never had a birthday party before.

And here she was now, a season later, the mightiness gone out of her, wasting away in the corner of a county ward, dying, according to the doctors, of cancer. And I remember wanting to have the necessary conversation with her—to say out loud what we both knew but did not want to speak, that she was not going to be getting any better.

"The doctors tell me they think you're dying."

"We're all dying, Tom. I just want to get home."

"Home is where we'll go then, Nora."

I asked the doctors for a day or two to organize some care for her in Moveen. I spoke to Dr. Cox, who promised palliative care. I spoke to Catherine O'Callaghan, the county nurse, who promised to come by in the mornings. I spoke to Breda and P. J. Roche, her renters and defenders, who promised to oversee the household details, and I spoke with Anne Murray, a young unmarried neighbor, herself a farmer and forever my hero, who said she would stay the nights with Nora.

I got a portable commode, a wheelchair, sheets and towels, fresh tea, bland foods, the *Clare Champion*. I called the priest to arrange a sacramental visit. I called home to see how the children were doing. I'd left my Mary with four teenagers in various stages of revolt. I promised to be home as soon as I could. "Do what you need to do," she said.

Once Nora was home from the hospital, the borders around her days became more defined by familiarity, gratitude, cancer, and contentment. She moved between bedroom and kitchen, sitting hours by the fire, half-sleeping in bed, whilst neighbors and professionals made their visits. Old friends came by to trade remembrances, old grudges were forgiven or set aside, old grievances forgotten or reconciled. After a sustainable pattern of care had been established in the house, I said my goodbyes to Nora on March 13, my dead father's birthday, and returned to my wife and children in Michigan to wait out the weeks or months it would be.

We deal with love by dealing with the ones we love, with sickness by dealing with the sick, and with death by dealing with the dead.

And after Nora died, it was the brother Pat who came to help me conduct her from one stone-walled incarnation to the next. We carried her out of her cottage to the coffin in the yard and processed down to the old church in Carrigaholt where Fr. Culligan, removed from his tea and paperwork, welcomed her with a decade of the rosary. The next morning Pat sang at Mass and followed us to Moyarta, where the Moveen lads had opened the old vault, built in 1889 by Nora's grandfather, our great-great-grandfather, Patrick Lynch. In the century since, it has housed the family dead, their accumulating bones commingled there in an orange plastic fertilizer bag at the side of the grave. And after the piper and tinwhistler played, and after Fr. Culligan had prayed, and after we lowered her coffin into the ground, we replaced the bag of our ancestors' bones, Nora Lynch's people and our own, three generations of kinsmen and women, and rolled the great flagstone back into place. Our Marys repaired to the Long Dock Bar, where food and drink had been prepared. And we stood and looked—the brother Pat and me—from that high place—the graveyard at Moyarta—out past the castle at the end of the pier, out over the great mouth of the Shannon whence our great-grandfather had embarked a century before, and landed in Michigan and never returned, out past the narrowing townlands of the peninsula, Cross and Kilbaha and Kilcloher, out past Loop Head and the lighthouse at the western end where, as the locals say, the next parish is America.

IT WAS THEN I saw Pat's thumbs begin to twitch, and the great mass of his shoulders begin to shake and wads of water commence to dropping from his eyeballs and the cheeks of him redden and a great heave of a sigh make forth from his gob and the hinge of his knees begin to buckle so that he dropped in a kind of damaged genuflection there at the foot of the family tomb into which poor Nora's corpse had just been lowered.

"Oh God," he half-sobbed through the shambles of his emotions, "to think of it, Tom, the truth and beauty of it."

And I thought it a queer thing to say, but admirable that he should be so overtaken with the grief at the death of a distant cousin whom he'd only met on a couple of occasions over the past twenty years when she'd made her visits to America. What is more, I remarked to myself, given that the brother and I were both occupationally inclined to get through these solemnities while maintaining an undertakerly reserve, I thought his emotings rather strange. Might it be the distance or the jet lag or maybe the sea air? It was his first time in Ireland, after all. It might all have overwhelmed him.

Truth told I was a little worried that my own bereavement didn't seem sufficiently keen compared to the way Pat had been leveled by his. All the same, I thought it my brotherly and accustomed duty to comfort the heart-sore with such condolence as I could bring to bear on such abject sadness.

"She'd a good life, a good death, and a great funeral, Pat. She's at peace now and there is comfort in that. It really was very good of you and Mary to come. My Mary and I are forever grateful."

He was still buckled, the thumbs twitching and the face of him fixed on the neighboring grave, and he was muttering something I made out to be about love and death because all he kept saying was, "In Love and in Death, together still." He was making an effort to point the finger of his left hand at the stone that marked the grave next to Nora's. I thought he might be quoting from the stone and examined the marker for "love" and "death." It was clean white marble, lettered plain, the name of *Callaghan* chiseled on it and not much else that was legible.

And then it came to me—his wife Mary's name is Callaghan.

"To think of it, Tom, here we are, four thousand miles from home, but *home* all the same at the grave of our great-great-grandparents; and the Lynches and Callaghans are buried together, right next to each other. In love and in death, they are together still. Who'd have ever imagined that?"

"Yes, yes, I see, of course. . . ."

"To think of it, Tom, all these years, all these miles. . . ."

"Yes, the years, the miles. . . ."

"Who'd have believed it, Tom?"

I helped him to his feet, brushed the mud from his trousers, and said nothing of substance for fear it might hobble the big man again. At the Long Dock he embraced his wife as a man does who has seen the ghosts.

PAT GOT SMITTEN at a funeral Mass one Saturday at Holy Name when Mary Callaghan, accompanied by her father on the organ, sang the "*In Paradisum*" as the sad entourage processed into church. First cross bearer and acolytes, then Fr. Harrington, then my father and Pat wheeling the casket in, the mourners rising to the entrance hymn. The brother stood at the foot of the altar holding the pall, transfixed by the voice of the angel come to earth in the comely figure of Mary Callaghan. When it came time to cover the casket with the pall as the priest read, "On the day of her baptism she put on Christ. In the day of Christ's coming may she be clothed in glory," Pat was elsewhere in his mind, imagining the paradise into which Miss Callaghan, what with her dark curls, blue eyes, and fetching attributes, might conduct him. My father thumped him ceremoniously on the shoulder to snap him back into the moment at hand. At the Offertory, she sang the "Ave Maria." Pat swooned at the back of church at the Latin for *Hail* and *Mary* and *the fruit of wombs.* At communion, "Panis Angelicus"; and for the recessional she sang an Englished version of the "Ode to Joy." It was all Pat could do to get the casket in the hearse, the family in the limousine, the cars flagged, and the procession on its way to Holy Sepulchre, so walloped was he by the music in her mouth and the beauty of her being.

When Fr. Harrington, riding shotgun in the hearse with Pat, wondered aloud, as he always did, had Pat met any fine young Catholic woman to settle down with yet—for a young man with a good job at the height of his sexual prowess untethered by the bonds of holy matrimony and indentured to nothing but his own pleasures is a peril second only to a young woman of similar station to any parish priest—Pat answered that he had indeed, and only within the hour. The priest looked puzzled.

When Pat explained further that he had only moments ago come to understand the trials of Job, the suffering of souls in purgatory, and meaning no blasphemy, the Passion itself—to behold such beauty and not to hold it, to have it, to take it home and wake to it, to be in earshot and eyeshot of such a rare specimen of womanly grace and gorgeousness and not be able to hold the hand of her, kiss the mouth of her, run a finger down the cheekbone of her—this was a suffering he had never had before. Fr. Harrington, blushing a little now, one supposes, had the brother exactly where he wanted him, on the brink of surrender to the will of God, ready to be delivered from the occasion of sin by the sacraments of the Church.

"Could you help me, Father?" Pat implored him.

"Leave it to me, boy. And say your prayers."

So it was a priest who made Pat's match with Mary Callaghan. Well, actually a bishop now. But back in that day it was Fr. Bernard Harrington, parish priest at Holy Name, who organized the courtship and consortium between the brother and the famous beauty.

Pat was twenty-three or twenty-four, recently finished with mortuary school, newly licensed and working funerals with our father and enjoying the life of the single man.

Mary was nineteen, an underclasswoman at Marygrove College studying theatre and voice under the tutelage of nuns. She was the fourteenth of the eighteen offspring of John F. Callaghan, a church organist, and Mary O'Brien Callaghan, whose once-promising operatic career was sacrificed to her marriage and motherhood duties. Of this prolific couple it was said that they had great music but never quite got rhythm.

It was the priest, later Bishop Harrington, who made discreet inquiries about the young woman's plans and prospects; the priest who put it in the organist's mind that a funeral director in the family would be no bad thing, the inevitabilities being, well, inevitable; and the priest who mentioned to the mother, "Queen" Mary, that a match between her namesake and heir to her vocal legacy and a tall and handsome Irish Catholic man, the son of famously honest people, would produce grandchildren of such moral, spiritual, intellectual, and physical pedigree as to ever be a credit to the tribe and race and species and, needless to say, to her own good self. It was the priest who advanced my brother's cause with the girl in question, letting it slip, more or less in passing, that he owned, albeit subject to a modest mortgage, his own three-bedroom bungalow in a good neighborhood, stood to take over the family business, was possessed, it was said, of a grand if untrained tenor voice, and sang "Danny Boy" with such aplomb that many's the young person and the old were set to weeping when he gave out with it.

It was the priest furthermore who blighted her other suitors, by novena or rosary or some other priestly medicine. One by one they all disappeared: the one in law school, the one with the family fortune, the one who later became a senator. Even Mary's twin brother Joe's best friend, a man of impeccable Irish-American stock who courted her with poems and roses and curried favor with the mother, even he was passed over. He went off to Ohio brokenhearted, married a Lithuanian woman, and was seldom heard from in these parts again. It was the priest who did it. And the priest who organized the first date, counseled them through the predictable quibbles, and after three years of courtship, pressed the brother to pop the question.

And standing before the dearly beloved and the church full of family assembled there—the Lynch and the Callaghan parents, like Celtic chieftains and their queens, the bride's seventeen siblings with their spouses and children and significant others, the groom's eight siblings with theirs as well, and the O'Brien and O'Hara cousins and uncles and aunts and host of friends all dressed to the nines for the nuptials—it was the priest who proclaimed it a great day for the Irish indeed.

INDEED, FOR THE IRISH and Irish Americans, the only spectacle more likely to bring out a crowd than a blushing couple at the brink of their marriage bed is a fresh corpse at the edge of its grave. Mighty at weddings, we are mightier still at wakes and funerals, to which we are drawn like moths to flame, where the full nature of our characters and character flaws are allowed to play out in a theatre that has deep and maybe pagan roots.

As Hely Dutton, an agriculturalist in the service of the Dublin

Society opined in 1808 in the final chapter of his *Statistical Survey of the County of Clare*:

> Wakes, quite different from what are so called in England, still continue to be the disgrace of the country. As it would be thought a great mark of disrespect not to attend at the house where the corpse lies, every person makes it a point, especially women, to shew themselves; and when they first enter the house, they set up the most hideous but dry-eyed yell, called the Irish cry; this, however, lasts but a short time. The night is usually spent in singing, not mournful dirges, but merry songs, and in amusing themselves with different small plays, dancing, drinking, and often fighting, &c.

When Pat's Mary's mother "Queen" Mary died, late last year at age eighty-five, we dispatched a hearse and driver to Pittsburgh to pick up a bespoke, carved-top mahogany casket for her. She'd have hated the expense but approved the bother. Mary O'Brien Callaghan was, like all the Irish dead, one of a kind. The much-doted-over only child of "Big Paul" O'Brien—a short man who made a respectable fortune as a lumber merchant—she passed her girlhood in Oswego, New York, with piano lessons, voice recitals, and the lace-curtain privilege of moneyed Irish. In high school she met her leading man, Jack Callaghan, when they played the love interests in *HMS Pinafore*. While attending Syracuse University on a voice scholarship, she married him and over the next twenty-two years gave birth to eight daughters and ten sons. He played the organ at daily Masses, directed choirs, and taught music at a women's college and a Christian Brothers school. They kept body and soul and household together. On the occasion of their fiftieth anniversary, an interviewer commented, "Mrs. Callaghan, you must really love children!" She replied, "Actually I just really love Mr. Callaghan." That same love—selfless, faithful, fierce, and true—still shines in the eyes of her sixty grandchildren, forty-some great-grandchildren, and one great-great-grandchild.

She had seen the generations grow up around her.

It was her grandson Paddy who helped his father wheel her casket into church, her granddaughter Caitlin whose soprano met the mourners at the door. It was her daughters who covered her with the pall and her sons who walked beside the hearse the few blocks to Greenwood Cemetery, then bore her body to the grave where another grandson piped the sad, slow air.

"Some say this is supposed to be a celebration of Mary's life," the priest said, "and we'll get to that, but not right now. Right now it hurts too much. We must first mourn her death." There was weeping and sighing, the breath of them whitening in the chill November air. Folks held hands and embraced one another.

The brother's thumbs were twitching.

THE THUMBS ARE safe for another season. Because we cannot go to Moveen this March, because Pat got himself elected president of the Funeral Directors' Association, because I'm finishing a book about the Irish and Irish Americans, because we are bound by duty and detail to the life in southeastern Lower Michigan, we head downtown to celebrate the high holy day in the standard fashion. A local radio station has a St. Patrick's Day party they broadcast from the lobby of the Fisher Theatre on West Grand Boulevard in Detroit. Then we make for Corktown and the annual Mass at Most Holy Trinity, where the blessed and elect, the great and small, will gather to give thanks for the day that's in it.

There's a crowd at the Fisher, and Paul W. Smith, the drive-time disc jockey, makes his way among the guests and celebrities and local business types who are keen for a little free air time to hawk their wares in their best put-on brogue.

Pat does "Danny Boy" and I recite a poem about a dream of going home, because here we are in a city of immigrants and their descendants from every parish on the globe and all of them wearing the green today, and hoisting Guinness and humming sweet ditties about the Irish. I see my mother's cousin, Eddie Coyle, and Mayor Kwame Kilpatrick, the self-described "first six-foot, six-inch Irish African American." We laugh and glad-hand and then get on our way for Corktown on the southwest side of the city.

Corktown is the oldest neighborhood in Detroit. It was settled in the 1830s by Irish who came west on the Erie Canal from the eastern slums and the West of Ireland. Most Holy Trinity was the first English-speaking parish in the city that was, in the middle of the nineteenth century, still mostly French. The factory and railway and civil-service jobs that grew with the city attracted plenty of the Famine Irish and after the Irish, the Maltese came, and after the Maltese, mostly Mexicans. In a city that has been blighted by white flight, segregation, and racism, Corktown remains a little broken jewel of stable integration and diversity. There are blacks and whites and Hispanics sharing the row houses, family businesses, churches, schools, and community halls. New townhouses, vetted by the historical society for architectural correctness, fill in the old lots cleared for parking when the Detroit Tigers played at the stadium at the corner of Michigan Avenue and Trumbell until 1999.

This morning it's a mix of city people and suburbanites who fill Most Holy Trinity to celebrate the 170th anniversary of the church's founding. Sister Marietta always saves a place for Big Pat down front with the politicos, heavy donors, and dignitaries. We are seated near the plaster statue of the saint Himself whose life and times in the fifth century still seems relevant for the new millennium. He was kidnapped in his teens by Irish marauders, taken to Antrim and kept as a slave, escaped to Gaul where he became a priest and returned to the country of his captors to convert them to Christianity. The snakes and shamrocks might have been added in by overly enthusiastic biographers.

The cardinal is here and his concelebrants, the governor and her smiling aides, the county executives and secretary of state, the president of the Ancient Order of Hibernians and the president of the "Ladies" AOH and a detail of knights from the Knights of Columbus. And the "Maid of Erin" and her pretty attendant court sponsored by the United Irish Societies, and all of them piped in by a corps of pipers and drummers in full regalia.

Everyone is wearing some paper shamrocks or a green carnation or a bright green scarf or tie or a badge that says something like, "Kiss Me I'm Irish" or "Erin Go Bragh." And as the pipes and drums begin, we rise, all smiles, because it's a great day for the Irish and Irish eyes are smiling and Oh Danny Boy things are good in Glocca Morra and God is in heaven and here, now, if only for a moment, all's right with the world.

But of course it's not. The litany of the world's woes expands exponentially from the local to the regional to the global.

There's famine in Africa, plagues in Asia; quiet little homicides and suicides and genocides go on around the globe while wars and rumors of war are everywhere, everywhere. The pitiful species remains its own worst enemy.

Fr. Russ Kohler, the pastor of Holy Trinity since 1991, steps to the lectern to welcome everyone. After the requisite niceties, he makes mention of the two young police officers from the neighborhood shot to death in the line of duty last month.

> I personally knew 21-year-old Officer Matthew Bowens and instead of a marriage I officiated at his funeral. And I personally knew 26-year-old Officer Jennifer Fettig and officiated not at her wedding, but her funeral. Illegal drug distribution throughout Michigan renders our cities into virtual free fall. Inept political maneuvering demoralizes police departments. Using sworn officers for after-hours escorts to rave parties renders the whole city one big market for drug distribution and consumption.

The cardinal speaks about the War on Terror and the violence of euthanasia, abortion, the need for repentance, the hunger for justice, forgiveness, and peace in the world.

The governor is concerned about the loss of manufacturing jobs from Michigan to Mexico, where workers are paid much less. There's an influx of illegal immigrants taking low-wage jobs around the state. She has brought a proclamation to honor the parish for one hundred seventy years of service to the immigrant and homeless, the helpless and those in need, many of whom are from, well, Mexico. The parish runs a free legal clinic, a free medical clinic, an outreach to sailors through the Port of Detroit.

The third-graders from the school sing, "I believe that children are our future." Their faces are black and brown and white and every shade in between. They are from everywhere. Watching their performance, the Maid of Erin weeps, the governor is beaming and singing along, the cardinal is enraptured or possibly dozing in a post-communion reverie.

The Taoiseach (prime minister of Ireland) is in Washington, D.C., to give the president a bowl of shamrocks.

In Chicago they dye the river green.

There's music and marching in Melbourne and Moscow and Montreal.

AND OUT ACROSS the world the roseate Irish everywhere are proclaiming what a good thing it is to be them, possessed as they are of this full register of free-range humanity: the warp-spasms and shape-changing of their ancient heroes, their feats and paroxysms and flights of fancy, their treacheries and deceits, sure faith and abiding doubts—chumps and champions, egomanias and inferiority complexes, given to fits of pride and fits of guilt, able to wound with a word or mend with one, to bless or curse in impeccable verse, prone to ornamental speech, long silences, fierce tirades, and tender talk.

Maybe this is why the couple hundred million Americans who do not claim an Irish connection identify with the forty-five million who do—for the license it gives them, just for today, for a good laugh, a good cry, a dirge or a dance, to say the things most in need of saying, to ignore the world's heartbreaks, the Lenten disciplines, their own grievous mediocrities, the winter's last gasping hold on the soul, and to summon up visions of a home-place where the home fires are kept burning, where the light at the window is familiar, the face at the door a neighbor's or friend's, the sea not far beyond the next field over, the ghosts that populate our dreams all dear and welcome, their voices sweet with assurances, the soft day's rain but temperate, the household safe for the time being from the murderous world's worst perils; home among people at one with all immigrants, all pilgrims, all of the hungry and vanquished and evicted strangers in a strange place, at odds with the culture of triumphalists and blue bloods.

Who's to know?

As for the brother, as for me, after making the rounds at the union hall in which all had assembled for corned beef and cabbage, we made for the road home before rush hour hit, singing the verses of "The Hills of Moveen," counting our blessings as we had come to see them: that here we were, the sons of an undertaker who was the son of a parcel-post inspector who was the son of a janitor and prison guard who was the son of an ass and cart farmer from a small cottage on the edge of West Clare to which our own sons and daughters do often repair, for the sense that it gives them of who they are and where they've come from and where they might be going still.

Along the way were the cute fools puking out their excesses of spuds and green beer or leaning out of their car doors pissing their revelries into ditches, or being taken into custody by the police. We drove past them all, out beyond the old cityscape of slums and ruins and urban renewal, out past the western suburbs, with their strip malls and parking lots, bearing the day's contentment like viaticum, singing the old songs, that "Wild Mountain Thyme" what with its purple heather, Pat tapping the time with his thumbs on the dashboard, out toward Milford where the sun was declining, where the traffic was sure to be thinning, and the last light of the day would be reddening and the false spring oozing from the earth might hold a whiff of turf smoke, a scent of the sea, and our Marys would have a plate of chicken and peas, a sup of tea, our place by the fire ready and warm for us to nod off in the wingback chairs, the brother and me, dreaming of the ancients and our beloveds and those yet to be—Nora and Tommy and Mrs. Callaghan and all the generations that shared our names; the priests and the old lads in the stories, our dear parents, gone with years, and our wives and daughters and sons, God bless them, and the ones coming after us we'll never see, bound to the bunch of them by love and death.

THE SAME BUT DIFFERENT

It is mid-June, nearly solstice, and I am adding a room onto the house in West Clare. A small room only—12 by 12—enough for a bed and a bureau and a chair. P. J. Roche has put up the block walls and Des O'Shea is roofing it, after which the work inside might proceed apace—flagstones and plaster and decor. There'll be a window to the east looking out on the haggard and a glass door to the south looking down the land, over the Shannon to Kerry rising, hilly on the other side.

It is an old house and changing it is never easy.

Near as I can figure it's the fifth addition and will make the house nearly seven hundred square feet, adding this wee room to what is here now: an entrance hall, the kitchen, a bathroom and bedroom—my cottage in Moveen West—my inheritance.

I'm returning in a month's time with my wife and her sister and her sister's friend, Kitty, for a fortnight's stay; and while the company of women is a thing to be wished for, sleeping on the sofa whilst they occupy the house's one existing bedroom—my ancestral bedroom—is not a thing I am prepared to do.

Back in the century when this house was first built, we'd have all bedded down together maybe, for the sake of the collective body heat, along with the dog and the pig and the milch cow if we could manage it. But this is the twenty-first century and privacy is in its ascendancy.

So P. J. and I hatched this plan last year of adding a room at the east side of the house. He understands the business of stone and mortar, plaster and space, time and materials, people, place. He has reconfigured this interior before, nine years ago after Nora Lynch died.

We have settled on particulars. Gerry Lynch will help with the slates and Matty Ryan will wire things. Damien Carmody from across the road will paint. And Breda, P. J.'s wife, is the construction manager. She sorts the bills and keeps them at it. "There's no fear, Tom," she assures me. "It'll all be there when you're home in August." There are boards and blocks and bundles of slates in the shed from Williams's in Kilkee. We've been to Kilrush to order curtains and bedding from O'Halloran's and buckets of paint from Brew's. The place is a permanent work in progress.

MY GRANDFATHER'S GRANDFATHER, Patrick Lynch, was given this house as a wedding gift when he married Honora Curry in 1853. They were both twenty-six years old and were not among the more than a million who starved or the more than a million who left Ireland in the middle of the nineteenth century in what today would be called a Holocaust or Diaspora but in their times was called the Famine.

On the westernmost peninsula of this poor county, in the bleakest decade of the worst of Irish centuries, Pat and Honora pledged their troth and set up house here against all odds. Starvation, eviction, and emigration—the three-headed scourge of English racism by which English landlords sought to consolidate smaller holdings into larger ones—had cut Ireland's population by a quarter between 1841 and 1851. Tiny parcels of land and a subsistence diet of potatoes allowed eight Lynch households to survive in Moveen, according to the Tithe books of 1825. Of these eight, three were headed by Patricks, two by Daniels, and there was one each by Michael and Anthony and John. One of these men was my great-great-great-grandfather. One of the Patricks or maybe a Dan—there's no way of knowing now for certain. Their holdings ranged from three acres to nearly thirty. Of the eleven hundred acres that make up Moveen West, they were tenants on about a tenth. They owned nothing and were "tenants at will"—which is to say, at the will of a gentrified landlord class who likely never got closer to Moveen than the seafront lodges of Kilkee three miles away, always a favorite of Limerick Protestants. Their labor—tillage and pasturage—was owned by the landlord. The Westropps owned most of these parts then—James and John and later Ralph. The peasants were allowed their potatoes and their cabins. Until, of course, the potato failed. Of the 164 persons made homeless by the bailiffs of John Westropp, Esq., in May of 1849, in Moveen, thirty were Lynches. All of Daniel Lynch's family and all of his son John's family were evicted. The widow Margaret Lynch was put out of her cabin and John Lynch the son of Martin was put off of his nine acres. Another John Lynch could not afford the seven pounds, ten shillings rent on his small plot. The roofs were torn from their houses, the walls knocked down, their few possessions put out in the road. The potato crop had been blighted for four out of the last five years. Some of the families were paid a pittance to assist with the demolition of their homes, which made their evictions, according to the landlord's agents, "voluntary." Along with the Lynches evicted that day were Gormans and McMahons, Mullanys and Downses—the poor cousins and sisters and brothers of those marginally better situated economically or geographically who were allowed to stay but were not allowed to take them in. It was, for the class of landlords who owned the land, a culling of the herd of laboring stock, to make the ones who were left more fit, more efficient laborers. For those evicted, it was akin to a death sentence. For those who stayed, it was an often-toxic mix of survivors' pride, survivors' guilt, survivors' shame. Like all atrocities, it damns those who did and those who didn't. Like every evil, its roots and reach are deep.

In proportion to its population, County Clare had the highest number of evictions in all of Ireland for the years 1849 through 1854. The dispossessed were sent into the overcrowded workhouse in Kilrush, or shipped out for Australia or America or died in a ditch of cholera or exposure. As John Killen writes in the introduction to *The Famine Decade*, "That a fertile country, the sister nation to the richest and most powerful country in the world, bound to that country by an Act of Union some forty-five years old, should suffer distress, starvation and death seems incomprehensible today. That foodstuffs were exported from Ireland to feed British colonies in India and the sub-continent, while great numbers of people in Ireland starved, beggars belief."

But the words George Bernard Shaw puts into the mouths of his characters in *Man and Superman* get at the truth of it:

> MALONE: My father died of starvation in Ireland in the Black '47. Maybe you heard of it?
> VIOLET: The famine?
> MALONE (with smoldering passion): No, the starvation. When a country is full of food, and exporting it, there can be no famine.

The words of Captain Arthur Kennedy, the Poor Law inspector for the Kilrush Union who meticulously documented the particulars of the horror in West Clare, are compelling still:

> The wretchedness, ignorance, and helplessness of the poor on the western coast of this Union prevent them seeking a shelter elsewhere; and to use their own phrase, they "don't know where to face"; they

linger about the localities for weeks or months, burrowing behind the ditches, under a few broken rafters of their former dwelling, refusing to enter the workhouse till the parents are broken down and the children half starved, when they come into the workhouse to swell the mortality, one by one. Those who obtain a temporary shelter in adjoining cabins are not more fortunate. Fever and dysentery shortly make their appearance when those affected are put out by the roadside, as carelessly and ruthlessly as if they were animals; when frequently, after days and nights of exposure, they are sent in by relieving officers when in a hopeless state. These inhuman acts are induced by the popular terror of fever. I have frequently reported cases of this sort. The misery attendant upon these wholesale and simultaneous evictions is frequently aggravated by hunting these ignorant, helpless creatures off the property, from which they may perhaps have never wandered five miles. It is not an unusual occurrence to see 40 or 50 houses leveled in one day, and orders given that no remaining tenant or occupier should give them even a night's shelter.

The evicted crowd into the back lanes and wretched hovels of the towns and villages, scattering disease and dismay in all directions. The character of some of these hovels defies description. I, not long since, found a widow whose three children were in fever, occupying the piggery of their former cabin, which lay beside them in ruins; however incredible it may appear, this place where they had lived for weeks, measured 5 feet by 4 feet, and of corresponding height. There are considerable numbers in this Union at present houseless, or still worse, living in places unfit for human habitation where disease will be constantly generated.

The mid-nineteenth-century voice of Captain Kennedy, like mid-twentieth-century voices of military men proximate to atrocity, seems caught between the manifest evil he witnesses and the duty to follow orders he has been given.

> I would not presume to meddle with the rights of property, nor yet to argue the expediency or necessity of these "monster" clearances, both one and the other no doubt frequently exist; this, however, renders the efficient and systematic administration of the Poor Law no less difficult and embarrassing. I think it incumbent on me to state these facts for the Commissioners' information, that they may be aware of some of the difficulties I have to deal with. —*Reports and Returns Relating to Evictions in the Kilrush Union: Captain Kennedy to the Commissioners*, July 5, 1848

IT WAS A starvation, a failure of politics more than crops that cleared the land of the poor, killed off thousands in the westernmost parishes, and dispersed the young to wander the world in search of settlements that could support them.

Moveen, of course, was never the same.

By August of 1855, when Griffith's Valuation was done, only three households of Lynches remained in Moveen—Daniel Lynch, the widowed Mary Lynch, and the lately married Patrick Lynch. It was Mary who gave Patrick and Honora their start, putting in a word for her son with the landlord and making what remained of the deserted cabin habitable.

My guess is Honora came from an adjacent townland, nearer the Shannon—Kilfearagh maybe, or Lisheen where her famous granduncle Eugene O'Curry, the Irish language scholar, came from; or north of here, toward Doonbeg, where the Currys were plentiful in those days. Maybe her people and Pat's people were both from the ancient parish of Moyarta and it is likely they met at church in Carrigaholt or in one of the hedge schools.

Pat came out of the house above, on the hill where the land backs up to the sea, where James and Maureen Carmody live now with their daughter Rachel and their son, Niall. James would be descended from Pat's brother, Tom; and, of course, from Mary, the widowed mother. We'd all be cousins many times removed.

The newlyweds leased twenty-six acres from Ralph Westropp, the English landlord. The house had, according to the records, "stone walls, a thatched roof, one room, one window and one door to the front." In the famous illustration of "Moveen after the Evictions," which appeared in the *Illustrated London News* on December 22, 1849, there are sixteen cottages of this kind, most of them roofless, their gables angled into the treeless hillocks of Moveen, their fires quenched, their people scattered to Liverpool and the Antipodes and the Americas. In 1855, the Griffith Valuation assigned the place a tax rate of ten shillings. The more windows and doors a house had, the more the tax. No doubt to accommodate their ten children, Pat added a bedroom to the south.

On October 3, 1889, Honora died. She was buried in the great vault at Moyarta, overlooking the Shannon and the estuarial village of Carrigaholt. Hers was a slow death from stomach cancer, giving time for her husband and his brother Tom to build the tomb, there near the road, with its cobblestone floor, tall gabled end, and huge flagstone cover that was inscribed with her particulars by Mick Troy, the stonecutter from Killballyowen, famous for his serifs and flourishes. The brother Tom lost an eye to the tomb's construction when a chunk of stone flew off of Pat's sad hammering. The work must have taken most of a month—to bring the round gray rocks up from the Shannon beach by the cartload for the floor, ledge rocks from the cliff's edge to line the deep interior and build the gable he would plaster over, and finally the massive ledger stone that would serve as tomb roof and permanent record. Grave work, in anticipation of his grief—the larger muscles' indenture to the heart—it was all he could do for the dying woman.

For months after his mother's death, my great-grandfather, looking out the west window of this house at the mouth of the River Shannon and the sea beyond, must have considered the prospects for his future. As ever in rural Ireland there were no guarantees. The labor and poverty were crushing. Parnell and land reform were distant realities. Their lease on the land would support just one family. A sister Ellen had gone off to Australia. A brother Michael married in a hurry when he impregnated a neighbor girl and moved far away from the local gossip, first to Galway and then to a place in America named Jackson, Michigan. Another brother, Pat, passed the exam to become a teacher but the Kilkee School already had a teacher, so he was given an offer in The North. His mother, Honora, had forbidden his going there, fearful for his soul among Protestants, so Pat sailed off to Australia to find his sister Ellen in Sydney. He was said to be a wonderful singer. "But for Lynch, we'd all do," is what was said about him after he'd regaled his fellow passengers on the long journey. He was, it turned out, good at seafaring too, keeping logs and reading the stars and charts. The captain of the ship offered him work as a first mate and it is rumored that after a fortnight's visit with his sister in Sydney, he returned to the ship and spent the rest of his days at sea. No one in Moveen ever heard from him again. He famously never sent money home. Dan and John, two other brothers, had died young, which left Tom and Sinon and their sister Mary who was sickly and their widowed father still at home.

Tom Lynch booked passage for America. He was twenty-four. I'm guessing he sailed from Cappa Pier in Kilrush and went through Canada, working his way from Quebec to Montreal to Detroit and then by train out to Jackson. He settled in a boardinghouse near his brother Michael and the wife, Kate, there in Jackson—a place their father, Pat, had been to briefly years before—where a huge state prison and the fledgling auto shops promised work. Maybe it was in memory of his dead mother, or maybe because there was a space on the forms, or maybe just because it was the American style, he identified himself in his new life in the new world as Thomas Curry Lynch. Or else it was to distinguish himself from the better-known and long-established Thomas B. Lynch, proprietor, with Cornelius Mahoney, of Jackson Steam Granite Works, "Manufacturers of Foreign and Domestic Monuments," situated on Greenwood Avenue, opposite the cemetery. Maybe to better his job prospects or his romantic ones, he shaved four years off his age in the same way.

Among his new liberties was to identify himself as he saw fit. The stone in Jackson in St. John's Cemetery maintains his version of it. *Thomas C. Lynch*, it reads, *1870–1930*. Back at the Parish House in Carrigaholt, his baptism is recorded in 1866.

Before he was buried in Jackson, in consort with Ellen Ryan, the Canadian daughter of Irish parents, to whom he was married in 1897, Thomas Curry Lynch fathered a daughter, Gertrude, who became a teacher, and two sons: Thomas Patrick who would become the priest I'd be named for, and Edward Joseph who would become my grandfather.

According to the *Jackson City Directory*, Thomas Curry Lynch worked as a "fireman," a "helper," a "laborer," a "painter," a "foundry man," and as a "janitor" at I. M. Dach Underwear Company. In September 1922, he was hired as a guard for the Michigan State Prison in Jackson. The picture on his employee pass shows a bald man with a long, square face in a three-piece double-breasted suit and white shirt, collar pin and tie. He is looking straight into the camera's eye, neither smiling nor frowning; his closed mouth is a narrow level line between a good nose and a square chin—a sound man, as they say in Clare, able and airy and dressed to the nines. He bought a small frame house at 600 Cooper Street, a block south of St. John's Church, outlived his wife by nine years, and died in September of 1930. He never lived to see his son receive his Holy Orders in 1934 or die of influenza in 1936. He is buried there in Jackson among the Morrisseys and Higginses and others from the western parishes of Clare, between Ellen and his youngest son. He rests in death, as in life, as Irish men have often done, between the comforts and vexations of priest and the missus, far from the homes they left as youths.

SINON, THE BROTHER Tom had left at home, stayed on and kept his widowed father. In 1895 he married Mary Cunningham from Killimer, east of Kilrush, and they raised sons and daughters, the youngest of whom, Tommy and Nora, born in 1901 and 1902, waited in the land and tended to their aging parents and kept this house.

The census of a hundred years ago records a house with stone walls, a thatched roof, two rooms, two windows, and a door to the front. Early in the twentieth century, another room was added to the north and divided by partition into two small rooms. So there was a room for the parents, a room for the girls, a room for the boys, and a room for them all where the table and the fire were. The farm, at long last, was a freehold, the first in the townland, bought from the landlord in 1903 under the provisions of the Land Purchase Act. Cow cabins and out-offices appeared, and a row of whitethorns that Pat Lynch had planted years before to shelter the east side of the house were now full grown. He bought them as saplings in Kilrush when he'd gone there for a cattle fair. He paid "two and six": two shillings and sixpence, about thirty cents, and brought them home as a gift for Honora who had them set beside some native elder bushes. They still provide shelter and berries for birds.

This is how I found it when I first came here—sheltered by whitethorns and elders on the eastern side, stone walls, stone floors, thatched roof, an open hearth with the fire on the floor, a cast-iron crane and hooks and pots and pans and utensils. There were three windows and one door to the front, three windows and a door to the back, four lightbulbs, strung by wires, one in every room, the kitchen at the center, the bedroom to the south, and two smaller rooms, divided by a partition, to the north. There was a socket for the radio perched in the deep eastern window, a socket for the kettle and the hotplate, and a flickering votive light to the Sacred Heart. There were pictures of Kennedy and the pope, Jesus crowned with thorns, the Infant of Prague, St. Teresa, St. Martin de Porres, and a 1970 calendar from Nolan's Victuallers. There was a holy-water font at the western door. The mantel was a collection of oddments—a wind-up clock, a bottle of Dispirin, some antiseptic soap, boxes of stick matches from Maguire & Patterson, plastic Madonnas and a bag of sugar, a box of chimney-soot remover called Chimmo, and cards and letters, including mine. There was a flashlight, and a tall bottle of salt and a bag of flour. Otherwise the house remained unencumbered by appliance or modernity—unplumbed, unphoned, dampish and underheated, unbothered by convenience, connection, or technology. It resembled, in its dimensions, the shape of a medieval coffin or an upturned boat, afloat in a townland on a strip of land between the mouth of the Shannon and the North Atlantic. It seemed to have as much in common with the sixteenth century as the twentieth. Perpendicular to the house on the south side was a cow cabin divided into three stalls, each of which could house half a dozen cows. On the north side of the house, also perpendicular, was a shed divided into two cabins. Hens laid eggs in the eastern one. In the western one was turf.

Last week for the first time in more than thirty years, I could see it all—as the Aer Lingus jet made its descent from the northwest, over the Arans to the Shannon Estuary, the cloud banks opened over the ocean, clear and blue from maybe 5,000 feet, and I could see the whole coastline of the peninsula, from the great horseshoe strand at Kilkee out the west to Loop Head. The DC-9 angled over Bishop's Island, Murray's Island, and Dunlicky, the cliffs and castle ruins, and the twin masts atop Knocknagaroon that the pilots aim for in the fog. I could see the quarry at Goleen and the Holy Well and James and Maureen Carmody's house on the hill and Patrick and Nora Carmody's, Jerry Keane's and J. J. McMahon's, and Sonny and Maura Carmody's and the Walshes' and Murrays' and there, my own, this house and the haggard and the garden and outbuildings and the land and the National School and Carrigaholt Castle and banking eastward Scattery Island and the old workhouse in Kilrush and the ferry docks at Tarbert and then, in a matter of minutes, we landed.

I never saw it so clearly before. The first time I came here, it was just a patchwork of green emerging from the mist, the tall cliffs, ocean, river, houses, lands.

Nothing had prepared me for such beauty.

I was the first of my people to return.

My great-grandfather, Thomas Curry Lynch, never returned to this house he was born in nor ever saw his family here again. My grandfather, Edward, proud to be Irish, nonetheless inherited the tribal scars of hunger and want, hardship and shame, and was prouder still to be American. He never made the trip. He worked in parcel post at the Main Post Office in Detroit, wore a green tie on St. Patrick's Day, frequented the bars on Fenkell Avenue until he swore off drink when my father went to war and spoke of Ireland as a poor old place that couldn't feed its own. And though he never had the brogue his parents brought with them, and never knew this place except by name, he included in his prayers over Sunday dinners a blessing on his cousins who lived here then, "Tommy and Nora," whom he had never met, "on the banks of the River Shannon," which he had never seen, and always added, "Don't forget."

Bless us, O Lord
And these thy gifts
Which we are about to receive
From thy bounty
Through Christ Our Lord.
Amen.

And don't forget your cousins
Tommy and Nora Lynch
On the banks of the River Shannon.
Don't forget.

The powerful medicine of words remains, as Cavafy wrote in his poem "Voices":

Ideal and beloved voices
of those dead, or of those
who are lost to us like the dead.
Sometimes they speak to us in our dreams;
sometimes in thought the mind hears them.

And with their sound for a moment return
other sounds from the first poetry of our life—
like distant music that dies off in the night.

And this is how my grandfather's voice returns to me now—here in my fifties, and him dead now "with" forty years (in Moveen life and time go "with" each other)—"like distant music that dies off in the night," like "the first poetry of our life."

Bless us, O Lord.
Tommy and Nora.
Banks of the Shannon.
Don't forget. Don't forget.

He is standing at the head of the dining-room table in the brown brick bungalow with the green canvas awning on the porch overlooking Montavista Street two blocks north of St. Francis de Sales on the corner of Fenkell Avenue in Detroit. It is any Sunday in the 1950s and my father and mother and brothers, Dan and Pat and Tim, are there and our baby sister, Mary Ellen, and Pop and Gramma Lynch and Aunt Marilyn and Uncle Mike and we've been to Mass that morning at St. Columban, where Fr. Kenny, a native of Galway, held forth in his flush-faced brogue, and we've had breakfast after Mass with the O'Haras—our mother's people—Nana, and Uncle Pat and Aunt Pat and Aunt Sally Jean and Uncle Lou, and then we all piled in the car to drive from the suburbs into town to my father's parents' house for dinner. And my grandfather, Pop Lynch, is there at the head of the dining-room table, near enough the age that I am now, the windows behind him, the crystal chandelier, all of us posing as in a Rockwell print—with the table and turkey and family gathered round—and he is blessing us and the food and giving thanks and telling us finally, "Don't forget" these people none of us has ever met, "Tommy and Nora Lynch on the banks of the River Shannon. Don't forget."

This was part of the first poetry of my life—the raised speech of blessing and remembrance, names of people and places far away about whom and which we knew nothing but the sounds of the names, the syllables. It was the repetition, the ritual almost liturgical tone of my grandfather's prayer that made the utterance memorable. Was it something he learned at his father's table—to pray for the family back in Ireland? It was his father, Thomas Lynch, who had left wherever the banks of the Shannon were and come to Jackson, Michigan, and painted new cellblocks in the prison there and striped Studebakers in an auto shop there. Was it that old bald man in the pictures with the grim missus in the high-necked blouse who first included in the grace before meals a remembrance of the people and the place he'd left behind and would never see again?

Bless us O Lord, Tommy and Nora. Banks of the Shannon.
Don't forget.

When I arrived in 1970, I found the place as he had left it, eighty years earlier, and the cousins we'd been praying for all my life. Tommy was holding back the barking dog in the yard. Nora was making her way to the gate, smiling and waving, all focus and calculation. They seemed to me like figures out of a Brueghel print: weathered, plain-clothed, bright-eyed, beckoning. Words made flesh—the childhood grace incarnate: *Tommy and Nora. Don't forget.* It was wintry and windy and gray, the first Tuesday morning of the first February of the 1970s. I was twenty-one.

"Go on, boy, that's your people now," the taxi man who'd brought me from Shannon said. I paid him and thanked him and grabbed my bag.

I'VE BEEN COMING and going here ever since.

The oval welcome in my first passport—that first purple stamp of permission—remains, in a drawer in a desk with later and likewise-expired versions. *3 February 1970. Permitted to land for 3 months.*

The man at the customs desk considered me, overdressed in my black suit, a jet-lagged dandy with his grandfather's pocket watch, red-eyed, wide-eyed, utterly agape. "Gobsmacked," I would later learn to call this state.

"Anything to declare?" he asked, eyeing the suitcase and the satchel.

"Declare? Nothing."

"Passport." I handed it over.

"The name's good," he said, and made an "X" on my luggage with a piece of chalk. "You're welcome home."

I walked through customs into the Arrivals Hall of Shannon Airport. At the Bank of Ireland window I traded my bankroll of one hundred dollars for forty-one Irish punts and change—huge banknotes, like multicolored hankies folded into my pocket. I walked out into the air sufficiently uncertain of my whereabouts that when a taxi man asked me did I need a lift, I told him yes and showed him the address.

"Kilkee—no bother—all aboard."

That first ride out to the west was a blur. I was a passenger on the wrong side of a car that was going way too fast on the wrong side of roads that were way too small through towns and countryside that were altogether foreign. Cattle and parts of ruined castles and vast tracts of green and towns with names I'd seen on maps: Sixmilebridge, Newmarket on Fergus, Clarecastle, then Ennis where the signpost said, KILKEE 35 MILES, then Kilrush, where another said, KILKEE 8.

"How long are you home for?" the driver asked. I'd never been so far from home before.

"I don't know," I told him. I didn't know. I didn't know what "home" meant to the Irish then, or what it would come to mean to me. I'd paid two hundred and nineteen dollars for a one-way ticket from Detroit to New York to Shannon. I had my future, my passport, my three months, no plans.

The ride from Shannon took about an hour.

What a disappointment I must have been—deposited there in the road outside the gate, the Yank, three generations late, dressed as if for a family photo, fumbling with a strange currency for the five-pound note I owed for the ride, bringing not the riches of the New World to the Old, but thirty-six pounds now and a little change, some duty-free tobacco and spirits, and the letter that Nora Lynch had sent that said it was all right for me to come. Blue ink on light blue lined paper, folded in a square, posted with a yellow stamp that bore a likeness of "Mahatma Gandhi 1869–1948" and a circular postmark: *CILL CHADIOHE CO AN CHLAIR*, which I later learned to English as "Kilkee, Co. Clare." The handwriting was sturdy, angular, and stayed between the lines.

Moveen West

Kilkee

Jan 8. '70

Dear Thomas

We received your letter before Xmas. Glad to know you are coming to Ireland. At the moment the weather is very cold. January is always bad. I hope it clears up before you land. Write and say when you expect to come so we'd get ready for you. I hope all your family are well.

With Best Regards to All the Lynch's

Nora & Tom

Of course she hadn't a clue about us—"All the Lynch's," as she called us. Whatever illusions Americans have about the Irish—that they are permanently good-natured, all saints and scholars, tidy and essentially well-intentioned drunks, cheerful brawlers—all that faith-and-begorra blindness behind *The Quiet Man* and the Irish Spring commercials, what the Irish knew about Americans was no less illusory.

The taxi man told me a joke en route, about the "Paddy" he called him, from Kilmihil, who'd gone off to the States to seek his fortune, having heard that the money there grows on trees and the streets are "literally paved with it," et cetera, and "he's after stepping off the boat in Boston of a Sunday and making his way up the road when what does he see but a ten-dollar bill in the street, plain as day. And your man, you know, is gobsmacked by the sight of it, and saying to himself, 'The boyos back home were right after all, this place is nothing but money, easy as you please,' and he bends to pick up the tenner when the thought comes to him. He straightens up, kicks it aside, and says to himself, 'Ah hell, it's Sunday. I'll start tomorrow.' "

Still Nora Lynch would have known I was one of her people. She would have sorted out that her grandfather was my grandfather's grandfather. Old Pat Lynch, whose heart failed at eighty on the twelfth of June in 1907, would be our common man. His body buried with his wife's, long dead, and Nora's twin who had died in infancy of encephalitis, and Nora's father who had died in 1924—all of them returning to dust in the gabled tomb by the road in Moyarta. We'd be cousins, so, twice removed. She could twist the relations back the eighty years, back to the decade before she was born when her father's brother Tom left for America. Old Pat had gone to America himself years before, stayed for several months, and returned to Honora and the children. Maybe he was the one who discovered Jackson, Michigan, and the huge prison, opened in 1838, the largest in the world back then, and all the work it provided for guards and cooks and the building trades. And Nora's brother Michael had gone to Jackson as a young man, following others from the west of Clare to "Mitch-e-gan." The records at Ellis Island show him landing there in 1920, off the *Adriatic* from Southampton. He'd married there and when his wife died, he returned to Moveen, where he died of a broken heart one warm August day in 1951 while saving hay. Nora would have had word from him about the Jackson crowd—about their uncle, Thomas Curry Lynch, and his wife, "a Ryan woman, wasn't she?" and about his boys, Eddie and Tommy, and their sister Gertrude, raised at 600 Cooper Street. Hadn't he brought a picture of his first cousin the priest, Fr. Thomas Patrick Lynch, for whom I'd be named a dozen years after the young priest had died—my father's uncle—there in the wide-angled photo of them all gathered out front of St. John's Church on Cooper Street in Jackson, Michigan, in June of 1934 shortly after his ordination. My father, ten years old, wearing knickers and knee socks, is seated between his father and mother. And Nora's brother Mikey, somewhere in that crowd, posed for the camera with his young wife who would be dead before long, the way they are all dead now. Nora and Tommy four thousand miles away, in the prime of their lives, will get word from one of them, about the new priest in the family.

And years later she will sort it all out: her Uncle Thomas married Ellen Ryan, "a great stiff of a woman," she had heard, and their son, Edward, married Geraldine, "some shape of a Protestant, but she converted," and their son Edward married Rosemary, and then this Yank, twentyish, out of his element, in the black suit standing in the rain at the gate, the dog barking, the cab disappearing down the road, all family, "all the Lynch's," all long since gone, and now returned.

"So, Tom that went," she said, connecting eight decades of dates and details, "and Tom that would come back. You are welcome to this part of the country."

After the dog, Sambo, was subdued, we went indoors. There was a fire on the floor at the end of the room, a wide streak of soot working up the wall where the chimney opened out to the sky. And the rich signature aroma of turf smoke I'd smelled since landing in Shannon. I was given a cigarette, whiskey, a chair by the fire, the household luxuries.

"Sit in there now, Tom. You'll be perished with the journey," Tommy said, adding black lumps to the fire. "Sure faith, it's a long old road from America." There were odd indecipherable syllables between and among the words I could make out.

Nora was busy frying an egg and sausage and what she called "black pudding" on the fire. She boiled water in a kettle, cut bread in wedges from a great round loaf, pulled the table away from the wall into the middle of the room, settled a teapot on some coals in front of the fire. She set out cups and plates and tableware. Tommy kept the fire and interrogated me. How long was the trip, how large the plane, were there many on it, did they feed us well? And my people would be "lonesome after" me. I nodded and smiled and tried to understand him. And there was this talk between them, constant, undulant, perfectly pitched, rising and falling as the current of words worked its way through the room, punctuated by bits of old tunes, old axioms, bromides, prayers, poems, incantations. "Please Gods" and "The Lord've mercies" and "The devil ye know's better than the one ye don't"—all given out in a brogue much thicker and idiomatically richer than I'd ever heard. They spoke in tongues entirely enamored of voice and acoustic and turn of phrase, enriched by metaphor and rhetoricals and cadence, as if every utterance might be memorable. "The same for some, said Jimmy Walsh long 'go, and the more with others." "Have nothing to do with a well of water in the night." "A great life if you do not weaken." There was no effort to edit, or clip, or hasten or cut short the pleasure of the sound words made in their mouths and ears. There were "Sure faith's" and "Dead losses" and "More's the pities." And a trope that made perfect sense to Nora, to wit: "The same but different"—which could be applied to a variety of contingencies.

"The same but different," she said when she showed me the wallpaper she'd lately pasted to the freshly plastered walls of the room she had prepared for me. "The same as America, but different." There was a narrow bed, a chair on which to put my suitcase, a crucifix, and the picture of the dead priest I'd been named for. The deep window ledge gave me room for my briefcase. There was a chamber pot on the floor and a lightbulb hung from the ceiling. The room was five feet wide and ten feet long, like a sleeper on a night train or a berth in steerage class, snug and monkish, the same but different.

After tea she took me down in the land. Out past the cow cabins and the tall hay barn, we stepped carefully along a path of stones through the muddy fields. Nora wore tall rubber boots she called Wellingtons and moved with a deliberate pace along the tall ditch banks that separated their land from the neighbors'. She carried a plastic bucket. She seemed immediately and especially curious about my interest in farming. I told her I didn't know a thing about it. "There's nothing to it," she told me. "You'll have it learned like a shot. A great block of a boy like you, it'll be no bother for ye. You'd get a tractor, and a wife, and there'd be a good living in it."

"What do you grow?" I asked her.

"Mostly cows."

We made our slow way down the soggy land, dodging pools of standing water and thickening mud.

"Mind the fort, Tom," Nora said, pointing to a tall, circular mound that occupied the corner of the next field over. "Never tamper with a fort."

Then she knelt to an open well in the middle of the land, skimmed the surface with the bucket, then sank it deep and brought it up again with clear water spilling over the edges.

"Have a sup, Tom, it's lovely water and cold and clean."

We walked the half a mile uphill back to the house. I carried the bucket and was highly praised for doing so.

Back at the fire, Nora told me how she and Tommy had been the youngest of their family. How her father died young and all their siblings had left for America except for Nora's twin brother who died in infancy. Two sisters had gone to Buffalo, New York, married well, and never returned. Mikey had gone to Jackson, "Mitch-e-gan," and worked there in the factory and married but his wife died young and he came home to Moveen and died saving hay in the big meadow in 1951. He was fifty-three. So it fell to Tommy and Nora to keep the place going and care for their widowed mother who was always sickly and feeble. Neither married, though they had many chances, "you can be sure of that, Tom." Both had stayed. Now, nearing seventy, they had their health, their home, and their routine. "Thanks be to God," they wanted for nothing. God had been good to them. "All passing through life." Sambo dozed in the corner. A cat curled on the window ledge. Another nursed her litter in the clothes press near the fire. There was a goose in the storage room waiting on an egg. There was rain at the windows, wind under the doors. The clock on the mantel was ticking. The day's brief light was fading rapidly. The coals reddened in the fire on the floor.

Now I was nodding, with the long journey and the good feed and the warmth of the fire at my shins, and the chanting of cattle in the adjacent cabin and the story Nora was telling me of lives lived out on both sides of the ocean—an ocean I'd seen for the first time that day. I might've drifted off to sleep entirely, awash in bucolia, talk, and well-being, if all of a sudden Tommy didn't rise, tilt his head to some distant noise, haul on his tall boots, and disappear out the door. Nora quickly filled a large pot with water and hung it from the crane over the fire. She brought lumps of coal from a bag in the storage room and added them to the turf. She rolled a piece of newspaper and fanned the coals to flames in the turf. She brought a bucket of meal from a tall bag in the same room. I wondered what all of the bustle was about.

Within moments, Tommy was back in the door holding in a slippery embrace a calf still drenched with its own birthing. It was the size of a large dog, and shaking and squirming in Tommy's arms.

Nora mixed meal in a large plastic bowl and filled it with boiling water—a loose oatmeal that she took out to the cow cabin. Tommy dried the new calf with straw and kept it close to the warm fire and tried to get it to suckle from a bucket of milk and meal. "Fine calf, a fine bullock God bless 'oo," he kept repeating, "that's it now, drink away for yourself." Nora reappeared and disappeared again with another bucket of hot meal. All of this went on for most of an hour. The calf was standing now on its own spindly legs. Tommy took it out to suck from its mother. It was dark outside; the night was clear and cold. The cow cabin, though it stank of dung, was warm with the breath of large bodies. Tommy squirted the new calf from its mother's teat and said, "Go on now, go on now, sup away for yourself, best to get the beastings right away, there's great medicine in the first milk." He got hay from the hay barn and spread it about and traded one of his Woodbines for my Old Gold. We stood and smoked and watched the new bullock suckle, its mother licking it with great swipes of her tongue.

"Haven't they great intelligence after all?" said Tommy. "That's it then, Tom, we'll go inside."

I was chilled and tired, tired to the bone. But Nora made fresh tea and put out soda bread and cookies and praised the good fortune of a healthy calf, God bless him, and Tommy who was a "pure St. Francis" with the animals. "None better. Ah, no boy. Of that you can be sure." Then she filled an empty brown bottle with boiling water and put it in my bed to warm the sheets. She brought out blankets and aired them by the fire then returned them to the room I was given to sleep in. I crawled in and despite the cold and damp could feel my body's heat beneath the heavy bed linens and was soon asleep.

Sometime in the middle of that first night I woke, went out the back door to piss the tea and water and whiskey in the dark, and looking up I saw a firmament more abundant than anything I'd ever seen in Michigan. It was, of course, the same sky the whole world sees—the same but different—as indeed I felt myself to be, after that first night on the edge of Ireland, in the townland of Moveen with the North Atlantic roaring behind the fields above, and the house full of its nativities, and the old bachelor and his spinster sister sleeping foot-to-foot in their twin beds and common room and myself out pissing under the stars asking the heavens how did I ever come to be here, in this place, at all?

IN THE LATE 1960s, my life was, like the lives of most American men my age, up for grabs. The war in Vietnam and the Selective Service draft made us eligible to be called up when between the ages of nineteen and twenty-six. For able-bodied suburban men, that meant going to college for the deferment. As the war grew increasingly unpopular, the draft was rightly seen as a class war being waged against the disadvantaged—mostly black or Hispanic or poor who were disproportionately sent into battle. In December 1969, Richard Nixon held the first draft lottery since World War II. The pressing need for more young men as fodder, the gathering storms of protest and public outrage, the inequities of the draft all coalesced into this theatre of the absurd. Three hundred sixty-six blue capsules with the dates of the year were drawn out of a fishbowl in Washington, D.C., on Monday evening, December 1. I was playing gin rummy in the student union of Oakland University. The first date drawn was September 14. Men born on that day were going to war. October 16, my birthday, wasn't pulled until 254. The first hundred drawn were reckoned to be goners. They'd be suited up and enroute for Southeast Asia before spring of the coming year. The next hundred or so were figured to be relatively safe. The last third drawn were the jackpot winners. They would not be called up for Vietnam. They would not be given guns and sent off to an unwinnable war and told to shoot at strangers who were shooting at them. It was like a sentence commuted. I was free to go.

Up until then, I'd been going nowhere. I was twenty-one, a lackluster student in a state university studying nothing so much as the theory and practice of pursuing women, a variety of card games, the pleasures of poetry and fiction and drink. I had been biding time, doing little of substance, waiting to see what would become of my life. I was living in a sprawling rental house in the country not far from the university with seven other men and the women they could occasionally coax to stay with them. We each paid fifty dollars a month rent and a few bucks for light and heat. The place had five fireplaces, a stream out front, half a mile of woodlands to the main road, acres of scrub grass and ponds out back. We had our privacy. We'd play cards around the clock, listen to the music of the day, drink and drug and arrange great feasts. I was working part-time at my father's funeral home to pay for the rent and the car and my habits but had steadfastly avoided making career choices yet. It was a life of quiet dissipation from which the number 10-16, the date of my birth, in concert with the number 254, delivered me. It seemed arbitrary, random, surreal. I could do the math—that 1016 was divisible by 254—but couldn't make out the deeper meaning. As with many of life's blessings, it was mixed. The certainty that I would not be going to war was attended by the certainty that I would have to do something else. As long as the draft loomed, I could do nothing. But I had escaped it. This was the good news and the bad news.

I considered the options. I had met a woman but was uncommitted. I had a job but no career. I was taking classes but had no focused course of study. I had a future but hadn't a clue as to what to do with the moment before me.

My closest friend, then as now, was the poet Michael Heffernan, with whom I drank, read poems, and discussed the fierce beauties of women and the manifest genius of the Irish. He had regaled me with talk of his own travels in Ireland and read me what he'd written about the people and the places. At his instruction, I read Joyce and Yeats and Kavanaugh. I switched from vodka to whiskey—it seemed more Irish. I asked my widowed grandmother for an address. She still dutifully sent Christmas and Easter greetings to her dead husband's distant old-country cousins.

Moveen West Kilkee County Clare Ireland

The syllables—eleven, prime, irregular—then as now belong to this place only: townland, town, county, country, place—a dot on an island in an ocean in a world afloat in the universe of creation to which I was writing a letter. No numbers, no street names, no postal box or code. Just names—people, places, postage—sent. Postmarked all those years ago now: December 10, 1969.

Tommy and Nora Lynch
Moveen West
Kilkee
Co. Clare
Ireland

Like a telescope opening or a lens focusing, each line of this addressing reduces the vastness of space by turns until we get to this place, this house, these people, who are by degrees subtracted from the vastness of humanity by the place they live in and the times they occupy and the names they have.

Since 1970, everything here has changed. Ireland has gone from being the priest-ridden poor cousin of Western Europe to the roaring, secularized Celtic Tiger of the European Union. For the first time in modern history, people are trying to get *into* rather than *out of* Ireland, and a country of emigrants has become a nation of commuters. Once isolated as an island nation at the edge of the Old World, the Irish are wired and connected and engaged with the world in ways they never would have imagined even a decade ago. There are more cars, more drugs, more TVs and muggings, more computers and murders, more of everything and less time in the day. Ireland has come, all swagger and braggadocio, into its own as a modern nation. Its poets and rock stars and fiddlers and dancers travel the wide world as citizens of the globe and unmistakably Irish.

Still, looking out the window my ancestors looked out of, west by southwest, over the ditch bank, past Sean Maloney's derelict farm, upland to Newtown and Knocknagaroon, tracing the slope of the hill to the sea at Goleen and out to the river mouth beyond Rehy Hill, I think nothing in the world has changed at all. The same fields, the same families, the same weather and worries, the same cliffs and ditches define Moveen as defined Moveen a hundred years ago, and a hundred years before a hundred years ago. Haymaking has given way to silage, ass and cart to tractor and backhoe, bush telegraph to telecom and cell phones. But the darkness is as dense at night, the wind as fierce, the firmament as bright, the bright day every bit as welcome.

Everything is the same, but different.

Everything including me. In my fifties, I imagine the man in his twenties who never could have imagined me. I consider the changes in this house and its inhabitants—my people, me.

IS IT POSSIBLE to map one's life and times like a country or topography or geography? To chart one's age or place or moment? To say: I was young then, or happy, or certain, or alone? In love, afraid, or gone astray? To measure the distances between tributaries, wellsprings, roads and borders? Or draw the lines between connected lives? Can the bigger picture be seen in the small? Can we see the Western World in a western parish? Can we know the species by the specimen? Can we know the many by the few? Can we understand the way we are by looking closely at the way we've been? And will the language, if we set ourselves adrift in it, keep us afloat, support the search, the pilgrimage among facts and reveries and remembrances?

Is it possible to understand race and tribe, sect and religion, faith and family, sex and death, love and hate, nation and state, time and space and humankind by examining a townland of the species, a parish of people, a handful of humanity?

It was in Moveen I first got glimpses of recognition, moments of clarity when it all made sense—my mother's certain faith, my father's dark humor, the look he'd sometimes get that was so distant, preoccupied, unknowable. And my grandmothers' love of contentious talk, the two grandfathers' trouble with drink, the family inheritance of all of that. And the hunger and begrudgments and fierce family love that generation after generation of my people makes manifest. And I got the flickering of insights into our sense of "the other" and ourselves that has informed human relations down through time. Can it be figured out, found out, like pointing to a spot on a peninsula between now-familiar points and saying: It came from there, all of it—who we are, how we came to be this way, why we are the way we are—the same but different as the ones that came before us, and will come after us, and who came from other townlands, peninsulas, islands, nations, times—all of us, the same but different.

Those moments of clarity, flickering wisdoms, were gifts I got from folks who took me in because I had their name and address and could twist relations back to names they knew. When I stood at their gate that gray February morning, going thirty-five years ago, they could have had me in to tea, then sent me on my way. They could have kept me for the night, or weekend, or the week and then kindly suggested I tour the rest of the country. Instead they opened their home and lives to me, for keeps. It changed my life in ways I'm still trying to understand.

Tommy Lynch died in 1971. He was laid out in the room I sleep in now. After his funeral I rented a TV for Nora from Donnelan's in Kilrush, thinking it would shorten the nights. Because she was an elderly woman living on her own, Nora got the first phone in Moveen in 1982. She added a roomlet out front to house the new fridge and the cooker. She closed in the open hearth for a small and more efficient firebox. In 1982, my friend Dualco De Dona and I ran a water line in from the road, through the thick wall, into a sink that sat on an old clothes press and gave her cold water on demand. "A miracle," is what she called it, and praised our "composition" of it all. In 1986, she built a room on the back in which went a toilet and a shower and a sink.

Nora died here in 1992 in the bed I sleep in now. She left her home to me.

P. J. Roche pulled up the old flagstones and damp-coursed underneath them, then knocked out an inside wall to enlarge the kitchen, put in storage heaters, a back-boiler, radiators, and new windows. The place is dry and snug and full of appliances. The civilizers of the twentieth century—toilets and tap water, TV and a kind of central heat, the telephone and tractor and motor car—all came to this place in the past thirty years. Still, little in the landscape out of doors has changed. The fields green, the cattle graze on the topography that rises to the sea out one window and leans into the river out another. The peninsula narrows to its western end at Loop Head, where gulls rise in the wind drafts and scream into the sea that every night the sun falls into and on either side of which I keep a home. Folks love and grieve and breed and disappear. Life goes on. We are all blow-ins. We all have our roots. Tides come and go in the estuary where the river's mouth yawns wide into the ocean—indifferent to the past and to whatever futures this old house might hold.

The plans for the new room include a sliding glass door out to the rear yard where the whitethorn trees my great-great-grandmother. Honora planted a century and a half ago still stand. According to their various seasons, they still berry and flower and rattle their prickly branches in the wind. It was her new husband Patrick who brought them home—mere saplings then—from a cattle mart in Kilrush where the old woman who sold them told him it was whitethorn that Christ's crown was fashioned from.

There's shelter in them and some privacy for those nights when, here in my fifties after too much tea, rather than the comforts of modern plumbing, I choose the liberties of the yard, the vast and impenetrable blackness of the sky, the pounding of the ocean that surround the dark and put me in mind of my first time here.

Those rare and excellent moments in my half-life since, when the clear eyes of ancients or lovers or babies have made me momentarily certain that this life is a gift, whether randomly given or by design; those times when I was filled with thanksgiving for the day that was in it, the minute only, for every tiny incarnate thing in creation—I've measured such moments against that first night in Moveen where staring into the firmament, pissing among the whitethorn trees, I had the first inkling that I was at once one and only and one of a kind, apart from my people yet among them still, the same as every other human being, but different; my own history afloat on all history, my name and the names of my kinsmen repeating themselves down generations, time bearing us all effortlessly, like the sea with its moon-driven, undulant possibilities: we Irish, we Americans, the faithfully departed, the stargazers at the sea's edge of every island of every hemisphere of every planet, all of us the same but different.

THE SISTERS GODHELPUS

My sister Brigid's yellow Lab bitch Baxter was put to death last Monday. What can be said of such proceedings? That every dog has its day? The following from my sister's partner, Kathy, tells the tale.

> It is with a heavy heart that I write this e-mail to notify family of the death of Baxter Bailey (11 1/2 years old) on Monday, July 14th. Kidney failure. She was buried in a deserved spot, at Mullett Lake. She is survived by her sister, Bogey Bear (who is a little lost as to what has transpired) and her mother/best friend/companion—Brigid. A brief ceremony will be held the weekend of the 25th on Mullett Lake.
>
> Whether you loved her, feared her or were entertained by her, she will never be forgotten. Long live her memory.
>
> *Kathy*

In receipt of which I replied:

Dear Kathy and B,

Thanks for the sad and tidy news. I will not pretend to have admired the deceased. She was, however, a walking (more lately hobbled) example of the power of love. She was not bright, not lovely, less communicative than most mum plants, and drugged into a stupor for most of her life. But here is the mystery—the glorious mystery—that a woman as bright and lovely, articulate and sober as our B loved her, loved her unambiguously. For a man of my own limitations (and they are legion) the love B showed to Baxter was a reminder of the lovability of all God's creatures—even me. In that sense she was a constant beacon of faith and hope and love. If this is what they call the Dog's Life, I say more of it is the thing we need.

You and B will be in my prayers for a brief if deserved bereavement.

Love & Blessings,

T

PS: Pat and I will get the stone and willn't stint.

It was a hasty but heartfelt sentiment, managed between the usual mélange of mortuary, literary, and family duties. I meant only comfort by it. And though we get the headstones at wholesale, the gesture was genuine.

Part of the comeuppance for calling our small chain of funeral homes Lynch & Sons is that the daughters—our sisters—control the purse. Three of my father's six sons, I among them, went off to mortuary school and got licensed, years ago, to embalm the dead and guide the living through the funerary maze. Before our father died, we bought the enterprise from him. His three daughters—ever his favorites—went to university and business schools and were installed in various key positions. Mary is the bookkeeper and paymistress.

Julie Ann is her factotum. Brigid handles trusts and insurance and pre-need finance and is the de facto comptroller at my brother Pat's funeral home. We call them "The Three Furies," and they travel between my establishment and Pat's, bringing light and joy and accountability.

When I see them together—Mary, Julie, and Brigid—I often think of the headlands on the Dingle Peninsula called "The Three Sisters," which rise in a triad of sweeping, greeny peaks to protect the Irish countryside from the ravages of the North Atlantic. Like those features in the West Kerry topography, they are strikingly beautiful, immovable, and possessed of powers we know nothing of. They are, it is well known, Irish in origin—the powers, the sisters. The source of all that is holy and hazardous about them is a matrilineage that finds its way back to a kitchen and cauldron in a boggy parish in the old country where only marginally post-Celtic mystics bedded with poor farmers who never knew what they were getting into. It is a lineage of women who emigrated on their own, in numbers equal to or greater than men, enduring steerage and indignity, years of indenture, to better themselves and their American children.

The sisters come by their powers honestly. They are their late mother's daughters and have inherited that sainted woman's charms and spells, blue eyes and Parian complexion, intellect and idolatries. They are, as she was, devotees of the votive and vigil, rosary and novena, perpetual adorations, lives of the saints, imitations of Christ, statues of the Blessed Virgin Mary and Sacred Heart, Stations of the Cross, relics, waters, ribbons and badges, prayerbooks and scapulars—all of which make them morally superior and spiritually dangerous. The arsenal of their godly wraths and blessed tempers would, in the best of circumstances, be turned on their spouses, to their betterments. But as each has partnered and consorted with the most amiable soulmate, they've only to train their tantrums upon their older brothers, whose puny potvaliances, collective and individual, are no match for The Furies. It makes them, I suppose, easier women to come home to.

Wednesdays Mary and Julie come to my funeral home in Milford for payroll and accounts—receivable and payable. Brigid remains at my brother's office but calls to consult with her sisters three or four times on the day.

Last Wednesday, when Mary and Julie read my sympathy note, they rolled their eyes and smote me with their disapproval. "How could you say such an awful thing about Baxter to your grieving sister?"

"What awful thing?" I asked, "a beacon of faith and hope and love?"

"This bit about the mum plant and stupor. . . . Couldn't you have just said something nice? Something about her loyalty?"

They did not see that stating the obvious about Baxter's life and times was central to the art of condolence and, a fortiori, the construction of the note's kindlier sentiment.

Truth told, the dog was a disaster, which had worn out her welcome by eleven years with everyone except, of course, my sister Brigid. A female assigned a fashionably suburban, chicly Anglo-Irish, but still oddly mannish name, "Baxter Bailey" never seemed to know whether she was coming or going, whether to hump or be humped, whether she ought to lift a leg or squat. When she had just achieved adult size and indoor continence, she bit my sister—quite literally the hand that was feeding her—thereby missing the only requisite point of Dog 101, to wit: Don't bite the humans. B had her neutered. Later she growled and snapped at B's infant and toddling nieces and nephews as they approached to pet her. On the strength of these misdemeanors and distempers, I once had B talked into putting her down, citing the liability presented by a dog that might attack neighbors or their pets or children, houseguests or passersby. I reminded her of the One-Bite Rule, with roots in the Book of Exodus, near where the ordinances on the seduction of virgins are recorded (alas, the emergent patriarchy!), which held that an owner would be called to account for the second infraction of a domestic animal. I'd gone so far as to set an appointment with the vet for the euthanasia and had Baxter leashed and loaded in the backseat and B agreeably disposed to the good sense of it all. But when she got there, she waffled in her resolve. She asked the vet, instead, for medication, something, she pleaded, "to calm her down"—Baxter, not Brigid. The cocktail of pharmaceuticals thus prescribed amounted to the nonsurgical equivalent of lobotomy. She was given phenobarbital to control her seizures, Lasix as a diuretic, something for her stomach disorders and insomnia, and a giant daily dose of canine Thorazine—enough I daresay to dull an orangutan—to quiet her demons, real and imagined. Baxter remained more or less on the edge of a coma for the rest of her life. Like some of those old lads you'd see in the pubs, the tooth gone out of them, supping up their daily sedation. She never snapped at anyone or anything again. She roamed about, bumping into the landscape and geography and furniture, like an outsize, spongy orb in a game of pinball or bumper-pool. At the lake, Mullett Lake—where we've recreated *en famille* for years and ruined the property values—she would sometimes walk into the water, as if some distant memory of her breed still flickered in her. Brigid would have to wade in and lead her ashore. People would toss Frisbees and tennis balls in her direction, hoping to engage her in the usual play. They would bounce off her snout and hindquarters, causing not so much as a flicker in Baxter's glassy eyes. The customary commands—"Sit," "Fetch," "Heel," "Come"—meant no more to Baxter than a recitation from the *Tain* or the *Annals of the Four Masters.* To the voice of her mistress or any human directive, Baxter was uniformly nonresponsive. The only trick she ever performed was, "Breathe, Baxter! Breathe."

"Where there's life there's hope," Brigid would say, ever the loyal human, as if the dog's damage were reversible. It was a sad thing to witness, this zombified miscreant working her way through a decade and then some of meaningless days. Her end was a mercy to all and sundry.

But what my sisters Mary and Julie seemed to be saying was that no empathy or fellow feeling could be tendered that did not include the ruse that Baxter was Rin Tin Tin done up in drag, or Lassie or Old Yeller—a great dog to be greatly grieved and greatly missed—a loyal, loving, exceptional specimen of Man's (read Woman's too) Best Friend. When I protested that Baxter would not want to be placed on a pedestal, or to be loved for other than the amalgam of distress and misfortune that she was, that authentic feeling could not be based upon a vast denial of reality, they both rolled their eyes in counterclockwise turns and said, one to the other, "He just doesn't get it."

That I just don't "get it" is the conventional wisdom and the conversation's end with the several women in my life. Though I am the son of a good woman, now deceased and lamented, and sibling of three of them; though I am the father, friend, and spouse of females, like most of the men of my generation, and almost all of the men of my extraction, I just don't get it and maybe never will. A library of literature currently exists on the whys and whatnots about Irish men—with the notable exceptions of Bono and Liam Neeson—which render them denser than other specimens when it comes to "getting it" so far as women are concerned. The Irish-American male is similarly disposed, unless there is a remedial dose of Italian, Mexican, or Russian in his genealogy, in which case not getting it gives way to not giving a rap.

FIVE MORNINGS OUT of every seven, the woman across the street in the gingerbready Queen Anne with the Martha Stewart garden emerges with her two snow-white toy poodles to attend to what Victorians called "the duties of their [the dogs'] toilet." Each is the size of a bowling ball and their tiny feces like wee, green, cat-eyed marbles—about which more, alas, anon. These daft and dainty little sexless things are named for their mistress's favorite libations, "Chardonnay" and "Champagne," which are shortened in the diminutive to "Chardy" and "Champy," as she is heard to call out when they go bouncing about the neighborhood in search of somewhere to take their tiny designer shits. Most mornings the entourage looks a little dazed, as if they all might've gotten into the vodka-and-tonic late. But who am I to say?

She doesn't like me—the woman across the street. The list and variety of our quarrels and quibbles on civic, cultural, and neighborhood issues is a long and exhaustive one. I'm sure she thinks I just don't get it. Truth told, I'm not that gone on her. Except for the occasional wave or sidelong glance and nod, we make no effort at neighborliness. We knew from the get-go we would not be friends. And though I admire her refusal to maintain any pretense or decorum, it is better to do so from afar. Maybe we remind each other of each other's former spouses.

Still, I uphold her right to her ways as she upholds my right to mine. This is America, after all. Though we hold forth from opposite sides of the street, the name of the street is Liberty. So the insipid little dogs, the fellow she's married to (who must on the weekends attend to Chardy and Champy's morning office), the overgrowth of garden—these are situations I accept like variations on the theme of weather. It could be worse, is what I tell myself. In the same way, she tolerates me and mine: the overflow parking from the funeral home, the mysterious vans arriving at all hours, the bright *Impatiens* we plant every year among the uninspired juniper and yews and, the Dear knows, my manifest personal foibles. Like me, she has much to tolerate.

It's only when she brings Chardy and Champy over to the funeral home to sniff about in search of a proper shitting ground that I take especial umbrage. To give her and her poodles their due, she always comes armed with a plastic bag and a rubber glove—the latter effecting the transfer of the turdlettes from my greensward into the former. She is, in keeping with local and regional custom, fastidious about the fecal matters. I think she uses them with her prized delphinium. But for some reason I cannot shake the sense that I and my real estate have been shat upon, and that there is a kind of message hidden in the act, that there is some intelligence she intends for me to "get" by the witness of it. Nor can I shake the temptation, so far resisted, to mosey on over and shit on hers. There's liberty in it, and a kind of truth.

AFTER MY FIRST wife and I divorced, I was the custodial parent of a daughter and three sons from the time they were ten, nine, six, and four—until I was married again, some seven years later, to the Woman of My Dreams. It's when I most wanted to be a feminist. The divisions of labor and money, power and parental duties—those good-for-the-goose-and-gander concerns of the third-wave feminism of the day—were themes I found the most intriguing. I read de Beauvoir and Friedan, Brownmiller and Millett, Germaine Greer and Gloria Steinem. I read Robin Morgan's man-hating rhetoricals on "cock privilege" and castration and Doris Lessing's *Golden Notebook* and Andrea Dworkin's sad and incomprehensible screed and wondered if there were miseries out of which such people could really never be put. I was a card-carrying, contributing member of NOW. I vetted my personal lexicon for sexist terms. *Postman* became *mail carrier*; *chairman* became *chairperson*, *ladies* became *women*. I never said "girl." I made my sons wash dishes and my daughter take out the trash and filed for child support from my former spouse, in keeping with the equal-rights amends I was trying to make. I was encouraged by the caseworker from the Friend of the Court's office—a fetching woman with green eyes and a by-the-bookish style—who said the children should get fifty percent of their noncustodial parent's income. This, she assured, was a gender-indifferent directive. The state-prescribed formula called for twenty percent for the first child and ten percent for every one after that. "It's what you'd be paying," she said matter-of-factly, "if the shoe were on the other foot." I figured I could save it for their higher educations.

The judge, however, overruled the caseworker's recommendation. Her honor conceded that while in theory our sons and daughter deserved the benefits of both of their parents' gainful labors, she could not bring herself to order a mother to pay child support, even one who saw her children but every other weekend. It was enough that the erstwhile missus was making her own way in a difficult world. Supplemental payments for the support of her children were more of an indenture than the judge was prepared to order. During the brief hearing, I was advised by her pinstriped counsel to leave well enough alone. I just didn't get it after all.

In Ireland at the time, they had no ex-wives and more than once I thought, "How very civilized." There was no shortage of domestic misery, of course, no shortage of abuse, just no divorce. It wasn't allowed. So people moved apart and lived their lives as, more or less, ex-spousal equivalents. There was a Divorce Referendum in 1986, but the priests all preached against it in the country places. It failed by a convincing margin. Still men and women wanted civil disunions and lobbied for them until the measure passed just as convincingly in 1992. Now gay men and lesbians want to get married, and who could blame them, what with the bliss, for lobbying for the blessings and paperwork?

Back in those days, I kept a lovely cur, free of any registered pedigree or jittery habits. She had a small head, a large body, and an agreeable temperament. We called her Heidi. When she was a puppy, I walked her 'round our little city lot at the corner of Liberty and East Streets and the half-block next door occupied by the funeral home and its parking lot and told her that she could come and go as she pleased but that if she showed up at home, more nights than not, she'd be fed and petted and sheltered well; she'd be loved and cuddled, bathed and brushed. In short, if she would do her part, we'd do ours. Such was the nature of our covenant.

And though Heidi traveled widely, she never strayed. She would follow the mail carriers on their rounds, forfending them from more vicious dogs. She'd find her way to the corner butcher shop and beg for bones and to the bakery on Main Street to beg for day-old donuts. She was particularly fond of custard-filleds. She would stare balefully into the doorway of the delicatessen for hours until someone proffered some Polish ham or Havarti cheese or some other succulent or delicacy. Later in the day, she would make her way to the schoolyard to accompany my younger sons home from their day's studies. Evenings she'd position her repose in the driveway of the funeral-home parking lot, acting the speed bump and sentinel whilst the children practiced their skateboarding or Frisbee or whiffle-ball. On weekends she'd be in Central Park, fishing with my oldest son or accompanying my daughter and her friends on their rounds through town, field-testing their ever-changing figures and fashions. She died old and fat and happy and was buried under the mock-orange bush where she used to shade herself against the summer heat. Near two decades since, she is still remembered with reverence; her exploits and loyalties are legendary.

Which is all I ever wanted out of love and husbanding, family and parenting—to be fondly regarded by the ones I loved; to be known for how I came home at night, minded the borders, kept an eye out for impending dangers, paid the piper, did my job, loved them all fiercely to the end. It was the dream I inherited from my mother and father for whom a division of labor did not mean a disproportion of power.

I WAS, IN those times, a casualty of the gender wars waged by the men and women of my generation over duties and identities. It was, I suppose, a necessary battle, which we did not choose and were powerless to avoid—damned if we did and if we didn't fight. We all took too seriously the carping and dyspepsia of a generation for whom sexism was a sin only men could commit, and only and always against women. Power and money were zero-sum games. Sex and love were often trophies. Women of the day kept their litany of injustices—the glass ceilings, the hostile work environments, the sixty-three-cents-on-the-dollar deal, the who-does-the-most-work-in-the-house debate. The little tally of inconsistencies I maintained kept driving me crazier and crazier. That the courts gave reproductive options to women but not to men was a bother. There was no clinic to which men could repair to terminate their impending paternity. If "choice" were such a fine thing, it occurred to me, oughtn't one and all, not one and half of the population have it? That my daughter might "choose" a career in the military but only my sons had to register for the draft struck me as odd. No less the victim-chic status of the feminist intelligentsia who were always ranting about "women and other minorities" while quietly ignoring the fact that women had been the majority for years. The planet was fifty-two percent female. That women not only out-numbered men, they outlived them—by years, not months, in every culture—seemed a thing that ought to be, at least, looked into. Never mind the incessant sloganeering, or the militia of women who blamed Ted Hughes for Sylvia Plath's suicide or who blamed their husbands for the history of the world or who turned men into the tackling dummies for their chronic discontents. Maybe it was all that "every intercourse is an act of rape" hysteria, or "a woman needs a man like a fish needs a bicycle," or the way they joked about the man who had his penis cut off by his angry wife. I used to wonder what late-night talk-show host would survive any less-than-reverential comment about a woman's genitalia if the damage had been reversed.

Violence against women was quite rightly abhorred whilst violence against men was generally ignored. Nothing in the literature rang more true to me than something I had overheard in a conversation between pathologists who were autopsying a fatal domestic case: "A man will kill his wife, then kill himself," one said grimly; "a woman kills her husband, then does her nails." Whatever else I did not "get," I got that one loud and clear: the higher ground of entitlement that victims, self-proclaimed, could occupy. I'm certain there were additional grievances, like so much else, I've forgotten now.

In ways that were not so for my parents' generation and, please God, will not be so for my sons' and daughter's, the men and women of my generation suffered a kind of disconnect that left them each wary of the other's intentions, each ignorant of the other's changing, each speaking a dialect the other could not cipher, each wondering why the other just didn't get it. Such are the accidents of history and hers—that we make aliens of our intimates, enemies of friends, strange bedfellows entirely that crave the common ground but rarely really find it.

So it is with nations and neighbors, parents and children, brothers and sisters, family and friends—the list we keep of grievances keeps us perpetually at odds with each other, alone in a world that is growing smaller, more distant from each other, more estranged.

The sisters, Godhelpus, are praying for peace and reconciliation and forgiveness. They are praying to be vessels of God's love and mercy. They say it will take a miracle and that the world changes one heart at a time. They have unleashed the hounds of their Hibernian faith—the rubrics of which involve candles, moonlight, chrisms, icons, incense and every manner of mystic unguents, passions, immersions, aromatics, and possibly herbs, the recipes for which were no doubt published in the Gnostic Gospels, found in those jars.

I STILL DON'T get it. And I've quit trying to. Years of living with and among women have convinced me I'm as well off with no dog in that fight. My daughter, my sisters, my beloved wife (in the associative, not possessive sense), and no few women that I count as lifelong friends, the memory of my mother, aunts, and grandmothers—they've all been and remain powerful and courageous and selfless humans, gifted with a dignity and calm that has made me wish I knew them better and all the more wary of their mysterious medicines. Most days I recite a litany of gratitudes for the pleasures of their company, the beauty and beatitudes of their intellections. I'm resolved to say nice things about their dogs. It keeps me, so far, safe from the hounds.

Young neighbor couples and their designer dogs go walking with leashes now on weekend mornings. Their puppies and their babies are all pedigreed. Everyone is better trained and behaved. At every corner there are dangers and warnings; at every intersection, flashing lights and signs. The lesson, of course, is to mind the traffic. They learn to speak and heel and fetch and to return. The men, as is their custom, bark out wisdoms. They pose and sniff, they howl and growl and whine. Their wives and pets grow weary of listening. Some things only the dogs hear, some the women.

I ORDERED A mum plant for Baxter's obsequies scheduled for later this month at Mullett Lake. I asked the florist to write, "Sorry," on the card.

I hope they get it.

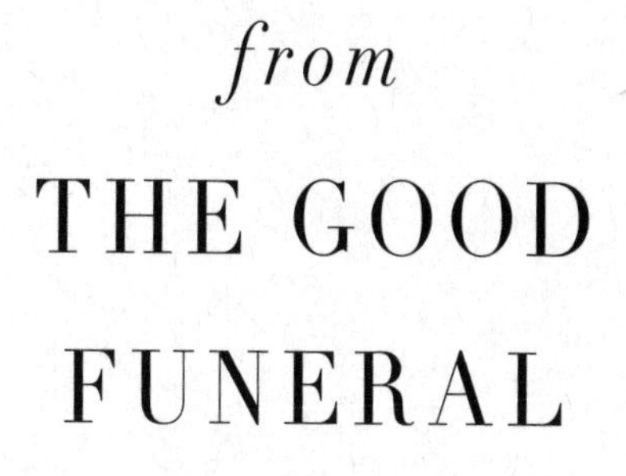

from

THE GOOD FUNERAL

Death, Grief, and the Community of Care

HOW WE COME TO BE THE ONES WE ARE

In the summer of 2012, Gus Nichols, one of Dublin's great undertakers and the President of FIAT-IFTA, the International Federation of Thanatologists Associations, invited me to Ireland to speak on a subject of my choosing. FIAT-IFTA is a congress of funeral directors from around the world and at this, their twelfth international convention, there would be representatives from thirty nations, two hundred and fifty registrants in all, from places as far-flung as Malaysia and Sierra Leone, Argentina and Australia, Canada and China and Columbia. My brother Patrick was the immediate past president of our National Funeral Directors Association and traveled with me as a delegate from the United States to thank Gus, Finbarr O'Connor and, indeed, several members of the Irish Association of Funeral Directors for having traveled to Chicago the year before to participate in Pat's convention. There would be a gala banquet and golf outing, tours of Glasnevin Cemetery and the Titanic Exhibition in Belfast, and plenty of good shopping in Grafton Street. The conference was held in Dublin Castle, a huge, walled compound in the center of that ancient city, with turrets and towers, dungeons and courtyards, dating to early in the thirteenth century—eight hundred years of history oozing from its stones. And I found myself constructing a line for the obituary I am always editing in my head that would someday in the long-distant future read, "He had presented to funeral directors from around the world." Travel and castles will do that to you. I was grateful for the invitation.

I had been to the castle once before. Indeed, I'd been to Ireland dozens of times in the forty-some years since my first visit there in the winter of 1970, in search of my roots and my future, as twenty-somethings are wont to do. But my first visit to Dublin Castle was in the late 1980s, to the offices of Poetry Ireland, which were housed there in Bermingham Tower, to arrange for a reading tour of the country after my first book of poems was published.

And now, twenty-five years and several books later, rising to speak about our common calling to a room full of mortuary sorts from Asia and Africa and the Americas, from Europe and the Antipodes and just down the road, it seemed as if my life's works and preoccupations—poetry and funerals, the literary and the mortuary arts—were finally melding into one. They were, in many ways, the same but different: equal tributaries of the one enterprise. So much so, in fact, that I had titled my presentation after a poem I intended to read them called "Local Heroes." How many funeral directors from small-town, middle America, I asked myself, get to hold forth their ideas and recite their poems to colleagues from around the world in Dublin Castle in the middle of June? It felt like a gift and I felt lucky and exceptionally fortunate and it made me wonder, as Gus Nichols was giving me a generous introduction and I was gathering my papers and thoughts together and readying to rise to the august occasion, and praying, as we do, not to make the huge fool of myself that I have in me to do, I wondered *what exactly am I doing here?*

How do we come to be the ones we are?

I was raised by Irish Catholics. Even as I write that it sounds a little like "wolves" or some especially feral class of creature. Not in the apish, nativist sense of immigrant hordes, rather in the fierce faith and family loyalties, the pack dynamics of their clannishness, their vigilance and pride. My parents were grandchildren of immigrants who had mostly married within their tribe. They'd sailed from nineteenth-century poverty into the prospects of North America, from West Clare and Tipperary, Sligo and Kilkenny, to Montreal and Ontario, upper and lower Michigan. Graces and O'Haras, Ryans and Lynchs—they brought their version of the "one true faith," druidic and priest-ridden, punctilious and full of superstitions, from the boggy parishes of their ancients to the fertile expanse of middle America. These were people who saw statues move, truths about the weather in the way a cat warmed to the fire, omens about coming contentions in a pair of shoes left up on a table, bad luck in some numbers, good fortune in others. Odd lights in the nightscape foreshadowed death; dogs' eyes attracted lightning; the curse of an old woman could lay one low. The clergy were to be "given what's going to them," but otherwise, "not to be tampered with." Priests were feared and their favor curried—their curses and blessings opposing poles of the powerful medicine they were known to possess. Everything had meaning beyond the obvious. The dead were everywhere and their ghosts inhabited the air and memory and their old haunts, real as ever, if in an only slightly former tense, in constant need of care and appeasement. They were, like the saints they'd been named for, prayed over, prayed to, invoked as protection against all enemies, their names recycled through generations, reassigned to new incarnations.

My mother thought I might become a priest. Not because I was especially holy; rather, as a devout and Catholic mother of six sons and three daughters, she would've known the expected ecclesiastical surtax on so many healthy babies would be a curate or two and maybe a nun to boot. "Be stingy with the Lord and the Lord will be stingy with you," was the favorite wisdom of her parish priest and confessor, Father Thomas Kenny, of the Galway Kennys in Threadneedle Road.

I WAS NAMED for a dead priest, my father's uncle. Some few years after surviving the Spanish flu epidemic of 1918, he got "the call." "Vocations follow famine," an old bromide holds. No less the flu? He went to seminary in Detroit and Denver and was ordained in the middle of the Great Depression. We have a photo of his First Solemn High Mass on June 10, 1934, at St. John's Church in Jackson, Michigan, a block from the clapboard house he'd grown up in.

His father, my great-grandfather, another Thomas Lynch, did not live to get into this photo of women in print dresses and men in straw boaters on a sunny June Sunday between world wars. My great-grandfather had come from the poor townland of Moveen on the West Clare peninsula that forms the upper lip of the gaping mouth of the river Shannon—a treeless sloping plain between the ocean and the estuary, its plots of pasturage divided by hedgerows and intermarriages. He'd come to Michigan for the work available at the huge penitentiary there in Jackson where he painted cellblocks, worked in the laundry, and finished his career as a uniformed guard. He married Ellen Ryan, herself an immigrant. Together they raised a daughter who taught, a son who got good work with the post office, and another who would become a priest—like hitting the trifecta for poor Irish "Yanks," all cushy jobs with reliable pensions. He never saw Ireland again.

In the middle of the retinue of family and parishioners posed for the photo at the doors to the church around their freshly minted, homegrown priest, is my father, Edward, aged ten years, seated next to his father and mother, bored but obedient in his new knee breeches. Because the young priest—he has just gone thirty—is sickly but willing, the bishop in Detroit will send him back out West to the bishop in Santa Fe, who will assign him to the parish of Our Lady of Guadalupe, in Taos, in hopes that the high, dry air of the Sangre de Cristo Mountains might ease his upper respiratory ailments and lengthen his days.

The young curate is going to die of pneumonia just two years later at the end of July, 1936. The Apache women whose babies he baptized, whose sons he taught to play baseball, whose husbands he preached to, will process his rough-sawn coffin down the mountains from Taos, along the upper reaches of the Rio Grande, through landscapes Georgia O'Keeffe will make famous, to the Cathedral in Santa Fe where Archbishop Rudolph Gerken will preside over his requiems, then send his body back to his people, C.O.D., on a train bound for Michigan and other points east.

A moment that will shape our family destiny for generations occurs a few days later in the Desnoyer Funeral Home in Jackson. The dead priest's brother, my grandfather, is meeting with the undertaker to sort details for the hometown funeral at St. John's. He brings along my father, now twelve years old, for reasons we can never know. While the two elder men are discussing plots and boxes, pallbearers and honoraria, the boy wanders through the old mortuary until he comes to the doorway of a room where he espies two men in shirtsleeves dressing a corpse in liturgical vestments. He stands and watches quietly. Then they carefully lift the freshly vested body of his dead uncle from the white porcelain table into a coffin. They turn to see the boy at the door. Ever after my father will describe this moment—this elevation, this slow, almost ritual hefting of the body—as the one to which he will always trace his intention to become a funeral director. Perhaps it aligned in his imagination with that moment during the masses he attended at St. Francis De Sales when the priest would elevate the host and chalice, the putative body and blood of Christ, when bells were rung, heads bowed, breasts beaten in awe? Might he have conflated the corruptible and the incorruptible? The mortal and immortality? The sacred and the profane? We have no way to know.

"Why," we would often ask him, "why didn't you decide to become a priest?"

"Well," he would tell us, matter-of-factly, "the priest was dead."

It was also true that he'd met Rosemary O'Hara that year, a redheaded fifth-grader who would become the girl of his dreams and who would write him daily when he went off to war with the Marines in the South Pacific; who would marry him when he came home and mother their nine children and beside whom he'd be buried half a century later.

"God works in strange ways," my mother would remind us, smiling, passing the spuds, all of us marveling at the ways of things.

And so these "callings," such as they were, these summons to her life as a wife and mother and his to a life as a father and undertaker—a life's work he would always describe as "serving the living by caring for the dead," or "a corporal work of mercy," or "not just a living, but a way of life." And his sons and daughters and their sons and daughters, who now operate half a dozen funeral homes in towns all over lower Michigan, were all called to a life of undertaking. And all are tied to that first week of August, 1936 when a boy watched two men lift the body of a dead priest into a box.

How we come to be the ones we are seems a useful study and lifelong query. Knowing how we got to where we are provides some clues to the perpetual wonder over what it is we are doing here—a question that comes to most of us on a regular basis. Indeed, a curiosity about one's place and purpose keeps one, speaking now from my own experience, from going too far astray.

"Listen to your life," the writer and minister Frederick Buechner tells us. "See it for the fathomless mystery that it is."[1]

Thus a book that endeavors to say what I've learned from forty years as a funeral director might well be improved by some notes on how I came to be one.

"In the boredom and pain of it," Buechner continues, "no less than in the excitement and gladness: touch, taste, smell your way to the holy and hidden heart of it because in the last analysis all moments are key moments, and life itself is grace."[2]

---

1 Frederick Buechner, *Now and Then: A Memoir of Vocation* (New York: HarperOne, 1991), 87.

2 Buechner, *Now and Then*, 87.

All these years later it feels like grace—life itself—chancy as any happenstance, and yet we get these glimpses of a plan and purpose behind how we come to be the ones we are.

POSSIBLY MY FATHER was trying to replicate that moment from his boyhood for me in mine when he took me to work with him one Saturday morning when I was eight or ten.

The old funeral home in Highland Park was a storefront chapel on Woodward Avenue that served mostly a Romanian clientele because the owner, William Vasu, was part of that immigrant community. There was an apartment upstairs, offices that flanked the parlors, caskets in the basement, and, at the rear of the building, the embalming room. I've written elsewhere of this occasion—my first sighting of a dead human—how what I saw raised curiosities about the dead man in particular, adverbial sense, and how my father's presence and steady answers, his willingness to share his own bewilderments around mortality were sufficient to me on the day. I have written that the presence of the dead human body, first encountered that Saturday morning in my boyhood, changed the gravity in the room, and still changes it today, well into my anecdotage; when one shares a room with a corpse, whether outstretched on a table, laid out on a bed or in a box, the ontological stakes are always raised, the existential ante upped, and the press of our impermanence, our mortality, flexes its terrible gravity in every aspect of our being. Possibly this is why a funeral, the ritual by which we get the dead buried or burned or cast into some particular abyss, seems a weightier enterprise than the ubiquitous celebration of life from which something essential always seems to be missing.

That was another received truth of my father's nunnish upbringing and my own—that life and time were not random accretions of happenstance. On the contrary, there was a plan for each and every one of us, and ours was only to discern our vocation, our calling, our purpose here. No doubt this is how the life of faith, the search for meaning, the wonder about the way of things first sidles up to the unremarkably curious mind.

When I was seven, my mother sent me off to see the priest to learn enough of the magic Latin—the language of ritual and mystery—to become an altar boy. Father Kenny, our parish priest, had been at seminary with my father's uncle and had hatched a plan with my sainted mother to guide me toward the holy orders. This, the two of them no doubt reckoned, was in keeping with the will of God—that I should fulfill the vocation and finish the work of the croupy and tubercular young man I'd been named for. I looked passably hallowed in cassock and surplice, had a knack for the vowel rich acoustics of Latin, and had already intuited the accountancy of sin and guilt and shame and punishment so central to the religious life. This tuition I owed to *Father Maguire's Baltimore Catechism* and the Sister Servants of the Immaculate Heart of Mary, who had prepared me for the grade school sacraments of Confession and First Holy Communion. I had learned to fast before communion, to confess and do penance in preparation for the feast, to keep track of my sins by sort and number, to purge them by prayer and mortification, supplication and petition. To repair the damage done by impure thoughts or cursing at a sibling, a penance of Our Fathers and Hail Marys would be assigned. *Mea culpa, mea culpa, mea maxima culpa* became for me the breast thumping idioms of forgiveness and purification, atonement, reconciliation and recompense that are so central to the holy sacrifice of the Mass we Catholic school kids daily attended. Thus were the connections early on established between holiness, blight and blessedness, contrition and redemption; and these powerful religious metaphors gathered themselves around the common table. It was all a way to be ever ready for the unpredictable death that might suddenly claim us. This theater replayed itself each night at our family meals where our father and our blessed mother would enact a home version of the sacrifice and feast, the brothers and sisters and I returning prodigals for whom the fatted calf, incarnate as stew or goulash, meatloaves or casseroles had been prepared. On Fridays my father brought home bags of fish and chips. Whatever our sins were, they seemed forgiven.

Likewise were we made aware of the assistance we might lend the dead in their pilgrimage between this life and the next. Purgatory was the way station between the joys of heaven and this "vale of tears"—a place where sinners were purged of the guilt of their trespasses by the cleansing of temporary flames. Our prayers, it was well known, could shorten this purging for "the suffering souls," and on certain days, notably the Feast of All Souls, we could pray them immediately into their eternal reward by coming and going into church with the proper combination of Our Fathers, Hail Marys and Glory Bes. There was a meter and mathematical aspect to our rituals and observances, and the dead, though gone, were not forgotten in our talk or daily rounds.

We were not alone in this. A version of my ethnically flavored religious training played out in the homes of my Lutheran friends and Methodists, Jews and Buddhists, Muslims and Humanists—each had a narrative about life and death, right and wrong, sickness and health, goodness and evil, life's endless litany of gains and losses, joyful and sorrowful mysteries.

FOR ALL OF my mother's and the priest's well-intentioned connivances, and though I kept my ears peeled for it, I never ever heard the voice of God. I remember seeing the dead priest's cassock hanging from a rafter in my grandparents' basement, a box with his biretta and other priestly things on a shelf beside it. I tried them on but nothing seemed to fit, and over time my life of faith came to include an ambivalence about the church that ranged from passion to indifference—a kind of swithering brought on, no doubt, by mighty nature. A certain sense awakened in me when I was twelve or thereabouts that among the Good Lord's greatest gifts to humankind were the gifts he gave us of each other. Possibly it was meditating on the changes I could see in bodies all around me and sense in my own body, late in my grade school years, that there were aspects of the priestly life that would be, thanks be to God, impossible for me.

If pubescence foreclosed any notion I might have had of the celibate priesthood, it was the early sense of mortality and of my father's association with it that shaped my adolescence.

I remember the neighborhood celebrity my brothers and sisters and I enjoyed because our father was an undertaker. And though it would be years before I understood that word, I knew it meant that he had a lot to do with dead bodies, which would eventually find their way "under" the ground.

As my brothers and I got older we were given jobs at the funeral home. Cutting lawns and painting parking blocks at first, then washing cars. When the first of our sisters was a teenager, she was put in the office to learn bookkeeping. And while she went on to become bookkeeper and comptroller of my father's business, my brothers and I matriculated to removals from homes and hospitals, dressing and casketing bodies, swinging the door during visitations, and working funerals.

We were dressed up in black suits, white shirts, and grey ties, shod in wingtips and barbered like men of another generation rather than the pimply boys we actually were, and we were paid by the hour to do whatever came up: cover the phones, work visitations, carry flowers, set up chairs, valet cars. It was a job. And it paid for our own cars, gas and maintenance, and left us enough money to go out on dates and other adventures. The summer days were long ones and we'd pile up a lot of overtime and lived like moguls. During the school year we would work shorter hours—evening visitations and Saturday funerals.

I think it was swinging the door where I first learned the powers of language and of presence. It was standing in the lobby of my father's funeral home that I first heard bereaved humans shaping the narratives that would carry them through their particular sorrow.

There were abridged versions:

> "We couldn't wish him back, the way he was suffering."
>
> "He sat in the chair and smiled at me and was gone."
>
> "She never would have wanted to trouble any of us."
>
> "She just slept away and never felt a thing."
>
> "At least he died doing what he loved to do."

And longer renditions, which touch on existential themes:

> She woke in the middle of the night complaining of a pain in her back. And it was hard to know what to do or what she needed. I got her the heat pad and plugged it in. She asked me would I bring her a glass of water and one of her pills. But by the time I got back to the bed, she wasn't breathing. She'd rolled on her shoulder and her face was blue. It's as if the switch was thrown and the power was off. I still can't believe she's gone. I just always assumed I'd be the first and she'd outlive me by years.

Or the father of a dead soldier:

> God must just have looked down and said that Ben had learned everything life on the earth is supposed to teach you, even though he was only twenty-two years old, and we'll always treasure every day we had with him, so God must have said, "Come on home to heaven, Ben," and that was that. My son was a hero, and everyone enjoying freedom tonight has boys like Ben to thank for it all.

Or the daughter of a woman dead of cancer:

> She fought the good fight against it—surgery, chemo, radiation, even holistic cures—but in the end it just overcame her. But her courage, her stamina, her relentless passion for life has been an example to all of us.

Beyond the colloquies of the bereaved and the sympathies of family and friends, beyond the obituaries and eulogies and testimonials, were the raised speech and sacred texts of ritual and rubric: the Orthodox *saracustas* (prayers for the dead), the Blue Lodge services of the Masonic orders, the Catholics with their rosaries and wake services, and the inevitable obsequies and committals—ceremonies laden with Scripture and poetry, hymns and plainchants, psalms and litanies of praise. Both as helpless humans and as people of faith it was evident that language, with all its powers and nuances, became the life raft that kept the bereaved afloat in the unfamiliar seas of immediate grief.

It is nearly impossible to overestimate the balm that language can be. The familiar prayer, even to the lapsed and apostate, evokes a nearly protective order in an otherwise unspeakable circumstance. It became clear to me, early on, that a death in the family presented both the most faith shaking and religiously charged among life's many changes. And it is certain that many souls have been irreversibly won and irretrievably lost because of something said or read or sung over the dead in earshot of the living.

My fascination with language and its powers began very early. Sundays were, in particular, a feast of nothing so much as the various and best deployments of the lexicon. We'd go to church at St. Columban's in the morning, where the Latin liturgy was full of mystery and intrigue and the sense that we were communing in a supernatural and magical tongue. Father Kenny's homiletics—often red-faced and passionate disquisitions on the obligations of stewardship—were tirades in which the priest played every part of the conversation and always won the arguments he'd set up for himself, albeit ten or fifteen minutes after most of his parishioners had ceased to listen. The liturgy, laden with religious and spiritual metaphors that could be cyphered by the interlinear translations in the missal, gave even the most indifferent witness a sense of how the word did, indeed, become flesh. Sunday afternoons were spent at home with our large extended family. Often the aunts and uncles and cousins came, but always my two widowed grandmothers were there. My father's habit was to get them both a little liquored up and sit them in the living room and set them to arguing about something the priest failed to cover in his sermon, invariably involving religion or sex or politics—subjects that were studiously avoided in more refined families were just as studiously pursued in ours. When I would question my father on his motives, he would simply advise that I listen closely to "those old women," and I would learn more from their contretemps than I'd ever learn in school.

Of course, the sharpness of their discourse proceeded from the fact that they were opposites. My mother's mother, Marvel Grace O'Hara, it might be safely assumed, never suffered any low self-esteem. She was punctilious, grandiloquent, a rabid Democrat and union organizer. She became, eventually, superintendent of music in the Detroit Public Schools, raised three daughters and a son, outlived her harried husband by nearly thirty years, never discussed her age, and voiced her opinion on each and every one of her grandchildren whether she was asked to or not. She did everything in the faintly idolatrous style of the Irish-American Catholic for whom *The Bells of St. Mary's* and *The Quiet Man* were the principal studies.

My father's mother, on the other hand, was a quiet, formerly Methodist woman, a fine cook, quilter, gardener, and Eisenhower Republican who, I am sure, voted for him well into the 1980s; she wore print dresses, sensible shoes, her hair in a bun, and kept her own counsel, never giving any offense or scandal until early in the 1920s when she fell in love with an Irish-American Catholic. This did not please her Methodist kin, nor did her decision, in keeping with the custom of the times and to appease his parish priest, to "convert" to what she would ever after call "the one true faith?" (appending a lilt of uncertainty to the end of that phrase, as if the doubting saint whose name I also share, his finger aquiver over the wounded palm of Christ, was none too certain when he was heard to ask, "My Lord, my God?").

My grandmother would describe her conversion experience to us saying, "Ah the priest splashed a little water on me and said, 'Geraldine, you were born a Methodist, raised a Methodist, thanks be to God, now you're Catholic.' "

Some weeks after the eventual nuptials she was out in the backyard of their bungalow in Northwest Detroit, grilling beefsteaks for my grandfather on the first Friday in Lent, when a brother-knight from the local Knights of Columbus leapt over the back fence to upbraid her for the smell of beef rising over a Catholic household during the holy season. And she listened to the man, nodding and smiling in her quiet, formerly Methodist way, and when he had finished with his sermonette, she went over to the garden hose, splashed water on the grill and pronounced, "You were born cows, raised cows, thanks be to God, now you are fish." Then she sent the nosy neighbor on his way.

"Ah surely we are all God's children," she concluded her narrative, "the same but different, but all God's children, either way."

This notion that we are all "the same but different," struck me, on the one hand, as quite impossible—like being short but tall, thin but fat, old but young, this but that—and on the other it rang entirely true. It remains among the most serviceable wisdoms of my life. As does the bromide advanced by my other grandmother, to wit: "The ridiculous and the sublime belly up to the one bar." I did not, as a boy, know the meaning of this, but it had nonetheless the ring of truth about it, and in the lifetime since has proven to be among the most useful of the verities.

This, of course, was my first brush with author(ity)—the power of language to name and proclaim and pronounce and transform. Words could change cows into fish, Methodists into Catholics, things that were different into things that were the same. They held the power to redeem and reclaim and remake the everyday objects and people and concepts I was surrounded by. The voices of those dearly departed old women, quibbling over whatever came to mind, occupy one section of the chorus of voices that call us to become the ones we are.

Ideal and beloved voices
of those who are dead, or of those
who are lost to us like the dead.

Sometimes they speak to us in our dreams;
sometimes in thought the mind hears them.

And with their sound for a moment return
other sounds from the first poetry of our life —
like distant music that dies off in the night.[3]

So wrote the great Alexandrian, Constantine P. Cavafy in his poem, "Voices." And this is how I still hear now *the first poetry* of my life, not in the voice of God speaking to me out of a whirlwind or out of the sky or burning bush, but in the voice of my parents and peo-

[3] Constantine P. Cavafy, "Voices," http://users.hol.gr/~barbanis/cavafy/voices.html.

ple, my elders and ancients and imagined ones—"ideal and beloved voices, of those dead or lost to us like the dead"—speaking to me, as if in dreams, like distant music that dies off in the night.

Sundays ended as all other days did, with our mother or father tucking us into bed with the prayer we all were required to say:

Angel of God, my guardian dear
to whom God's love commits me here,
ever this night be at my side
to light, to guard, to rule and guide.

This prayer, said at bedside—a grim little plea for protection against darkness and death—was the first poetry of my life. Long before I ever understood its deeper meanings, I heard the memorable, and not incidentally, memorizable rhymes between "dear" and "here," "side" and "guide." And the thumping heart-beating iambic code of the last line—to *light*, to *guard*, to *rule* and *guide.*

Its acoustic pleasures were immediate. Before it made sense, it made "sound" to me. It rang true in my ear. There were others:

God is great.
God is good.
Let us thank him for our food.

That is how they prayed before meals at Jimmy Shryock's house. I loved the off-rhyming between "good" and "food." Or when I spent the night at Mark Henderson's I was taught:

Now I lay me down to sleep
and pray the Lord my soul to keep.
If I die before I wake
I pray the Lord my soul to take.

It was a Protestant version of my Angel of God—involving the same grim contingencies, the same hopes, the same sense, and slightly different sounds that were metrical cousins to the secular poetics the world seemed full of:

> Twinkle twinkle little star.
> How I wonder what you are.
> Up above the world so high,
> like a diamond in the sky.

Or

> ABCDEFG
> HIJKLMNOP

Or

> Tyger! Tyger! Burning bright
> In the forests of the night
> What immortal hand or eye
> Could frame thy fearful symmetry?[4]

Or

> Irish poets learn your trade
> Sing whatever is well made
> Scorn the sort now growing up
> All out of shape from toe to top[5]

---

[4] William Blake, "The Tyger," in *The Complete Poetry & Prose of William Blake*, ed. David V. Erdman, et al. (New York: Anchor, 1984), 24.

[5] William Butler Yeats, "Under Ben Bulben," *The Collected Poems of W. B. Yeats*, 2nd ed., ed. Richard Finneran (New York: Simon & Schuster, 1996), 325.

That quatrain about the Irish poets is part of a longer poem, "Under Ben Bulben," written by the Irish master, William Butler Yeats, some months before he died in late January of 1939.

When the English master, W. H. Auden, got word of the great man's death, he wrote his elegy, "In Memory of W. B. Yeats," which includes this homage quatrain:

Earth receive an honored guest
William Yeats is laid to rest
Let the Irish vessel lie
Emptied of its poetry.[6]

And all of these sounded the same but different to me—nursery rhymes, prayers, alphabets, and poems—little seven-syllable meters, seasoned with rhymes to make them memorizable formulas:

Twinkle, twinkle little star
Now I lay me down to sleep
ABCDEFG
God is great and God is good,
let us thank him for this food.
Irish poets learn your trade
Earth receive an honored guest
William Yeats is laid to rest.

It was William Yeats who wrote in a letter to a woman he was trying to impress that the only subjects of interest to a studious mind were sex and death. How nice for me, I remember thinking in my early twenties, because I was predictably fond of sex, and the dead, as it turned out, were everywhere.

Thus were the hours spent working wakes and visitations at my

---

[6] W. H. Auden, "In Memory of W. B. Yeats," *Collected Poems: W. H. Auden*, ed. Edward Mendelson (New York: Vintage, 1991), 247.

father's funeral home, listening to the colloquies of mourners we met at the door, a daily instruction in the way of things—life and death and the shape of relations that gave them meaning and the rituals that tried to make some sense of the existential mysteries of coming to be and being and ceasing to be.

"If God speaks to us at all . . . then I think that he speaks to us largely through what happens to us."[7] That's Frederick Buechner again, in *Now and Then: A Memoir of Vocation.*

WHAT HAPPENED TO me while working at my father's funeral home was that folks began to treat me like a hero. They were so grateful when we would show up at the hospital or nursing home or family home in the middle of the night, so grateful for the way we handled their dead carefully and with respect. Or leaving after a long day's visitation at the funeral home, when a widow would hold me by the shoulders and tell me how very comforting it was to have us parking the cars and holding the doors and taking the coats and casseroles, directing folks to the proper parlor and bringing the flowers and for "just being there." Or turning from the graveside once everything that could be done had been done, how they would shake my hand or hug me and thank me profusely because "we couldn't have done this without you . . . thank you. . . . God bless you . . ." or heartfelt words to that effect. Such effusions made me feel useful and capable and helpful, as if I'd accomplished the job well done and all I really did was show up, pitch in, do my part. Before long I began to understand that showing up, being there, helping in an otherwise helpless situation was made heroic by the same gravity I had sensed when I first stood in that embalming room as a boy—the presence of the dead made the presence of the living more meaningful somehow, as if it involved a basic and intuitively human duty to witness.

By now I was beginning to think about sex and death almost exclusively—the former because I was in my twenties, the latter because,

7 Buechner, *Now and Then*, 3.

as the son of a funeral director, death and the dead were part of our daily lives. I was twenty-two and casting about for my calling. A high number in the Nixon Draft Lotto had kept me out of Vietnam, my college career had been spent reading poetry and playing cards and traveling back and forth to Ireland and the Continent in search of diversion and direction, I suppose. My younger brother Pat was starting mortuary school that fall and, possibly sensing my dilemma, my father asked if I'd like to go with him to the NFDA convention in Kansas City that year. They convened—nearly five thousand of them from across the country—on Halloween in the Hotel Muehlebach where all the meetings would be held in the Imperial Ballroom. There was to be a dinner on Sunday night with music "by Woody Herman, in concert" for dancing; a "Special Ladies' Program"; another dinner "with radio and T.V. personality, Art Linkletter!"; the usual sessions to elect officers, conduct association business, and take reports from various committees; and a list of morning educational seminars. There was what they called an "educational display of funeral merchandise and supplies in the Municipal Auditorium" across the street. This display involved more than a hundred manufacturers and suppliers of caskets and hearses and other accessories to the trade: vaults and embalming fluids, printers of holy cards and thank you notes, suits and shrouds and gowns for burial, canned music, candles and plastic flowers, grave markers, flags and insignia—all the stuff that can be bought at wholesale, sold at retail just like books and burgers and pharmaceuticals. There was a deep shine to the limousines and hearses and I remember the odd names of things, "Frigid Fluid" and "Progress Caskets," "Con-O-Lite" and "Phoenix Embalming." It was a bit bizarre to be spending Halloween filling our bags with freebees and samples from suppliers to the mortuary trade—yard sticks and tie clips shaped to look like shovels and models of headstones and horse-drawn coaches—something for everybody, trick or treat.

But the stars of the exhibits were the casket companies: Batesville and National, the biggest and best, and Marsellus, which made the mahogany cabinet President Kennedy had been buried in. Springfield, Aurora, Boyertown, Belmont, and Merit were there along with local and regional jobbers like Artco, Chicago, Missouri, Boyd, Delta, Quincy, Royal, and Flint. Each came with an entourage of salesmen, always smiling and glad-handing, eager to add to their accounts. And each of the caskets had its own name too, "The President" or "Permaseal" or "Praying Hands," which became a kind of litany of mostly metal caskets in those days, and polished woods, with plush velvet and crepe and satin insides that gave the impression in their collective display that funerals were mostly about the boxes.

Of course this was precisely the argument that Jessica Mitford had made less than a decade before with the publication of her muckraking classic, *The American Way of Death.* Because I was his bookish son, my father gave it to me to read when I was fifteen years old and told me to tell him what was in it. I told him I thought the style would earn her a lot of readers and that she would change the way people thought about funerals and that much of what she wrote was true and much of what she wrote missed the point entirely.

It was on the Feast of All Souls—that Tuesday in convention week—that the stuff began to give way to substance and the ridiculous began to make room for the sublime. That morning, NFDA's educational consultant, Robert C. Slater, who taught at the mortuary school at the University of Minnesota, arranged for what was called a "Think Tank" of scholars and teachers and clergy, each of whom had served as a consultant to NFDA. Robert Fulton, a sociologist; Dr. Vanderline Pine, a funeral director and sociologist; Dr. William Lamers, a psychiatrist and hospice pioneer; Robert Habenstein, author of *Funeral Customs the World Over* and *The History of American Funeral Service*; and Roger Blackwell, the marketing and consumer guru who taught at Ohio State University's School of Business, were joined by clergy-authors Rabbi Earl Grollman, Pastor Paul Irion, and Reverend Edgar Jackson, along with NFDA's Howard C. Raether and Robert Slater, to carry on an open discussion about the place of the funeral and the funeral director in American culture. Much of the discussion was shaped by questions from the more than 1,200 funeral directors in the ballroom. It was the best-attended session of the convention. These were writers and thinkers and professors and preachers and, in ways that casket salesmen were not, these were men of studious minds whose version of my father's work was much more serious than the cartoon that Jessica Mitford and the display of mortuary goods across the street would give one to believe. If psychologists, sociologists, consumer gurus, statisticians, the reverend clergy, and historians all found the funeral worthy of study, possibly the literary and mortuary arts could be commingled. And their topic was the funeral, as an event unique to humankind, as old as the species. Whereas the exhibits across the street proclaimed that the chief product of the mortuary were the cars and caskets and vaults and urns, piped in music and embalming, this think tank viewed such things as accessories only to the fundamental obligation to assist with the funeral. A death in the family was not a sales op, rather it was an opportunity to serve, in concert with the community of civic and religious, neighborhood and family circles that endeavored to respond to the facts of death.

"Take care of the service," I can still hear my father's good counsel: "and the sales will take care of themselves."

That night I told my father I'd be going to mortuary school. Some months later I was enrolled at Wayne State University's Department of Mortuary Science. After which I graduated, got my license, and the following year moved to Milford to take up residence in and management of the funeral home that our family purchased to accommodate the growing number of our funeral directors.

MY FRIEND AND fellow in this book's endeavor, Thomas G. Long, writes with insight and candor about the changing religious landscape of America and the place of the clergy in a nation that is increasingly secular. The remarkable changes in religious practice over the past half century are coincident with, correlated to, and in many instances, trafficked in cause-and-effect with changes in our mortuary customs. Unlike the clergy who have fallen from great heights of approval, funeral directors have never been generally popular. It is the same with poets. While many people might approve the idea of poetry and are passably glad that there are poets at work, only a fraction of a fraction of the population can tolerate actually having to read a poem. Thus, a funeral director who writes poems is the occupational equivalent of a proctologist with a sideline in root canals. No less a preacher with a specialty in final things. Folks are glad to see us coming when there is pain or trouble, and gladder still to see us gone with their good riddance in tow. It was ever thus.

Thus, for two such unpopular sorts as my coconspirator and me to take on the toxic and oxymoronic topics of good death, good grief, and good funerals presumes there are others like ourselves for whom such things might be of interest.

As it often is among writers, I read Thomas G. Long before I met him. He published an article titled "The American Funeral Today—Trends and Issues" in the *Director*, published by the National Funeral Directors Association (NFDA). It was thoroughly original, full of original notions and insights and real scholarship and written in a way that even I could get. Some months later, Mark Higgins, a friend and fellow funeral director from North Carolina, secured for me an e-mail introduction. Reverend Long and I met in New York on the twenty-fifth of June in 1998. I was between stops on a book tour and he was teaching at Princeton then. He picked me up at LaGuardia, took me to lunch in the city, and told me about the project, just underway, which would eventually become *Accompany Them with Singing—The Christian Funeral*, the most important book on the Christian response since Paul Irion's *The Funeral: Vestige or Value* was published in 1977. Our views, shared over salads, arrived at so many of the same conclusions—some provisional, some hard-earned, some in search of replication—from our different vantage points and professional experiences. It is safe to say that the years Dr. Long has spent in ministry and teaching, coincident with the years I have spent in funeral service, have seen more changes in the nation's religious and mortuary customs and practices than in any generation before.

We first began working together doing daylong multidisciplinary conferences sponsored by the Michigan Funeral Directors Association for hospice, clergy, and funeral directors. The public relations firm hired by the association to work up some advance publicity advised that we could never get an audience for a conference called "The Good Death, Good Grief, Good Funerals." They saw it as a triple dose of the dire and dismal. "Think, 'good war, good plague, good famine,'" I distinctly remembered one of them saying. They proffered other more welcoming, heartwarming titles involving health and healing, celebration and memories. But we insisted that people who played on the front line of final things, the ones you would find out in the middle of the night en route to a home where a death had occurred, were among those rare and indispensable local heroes—hospice volunteers, pastors, good neighbors, and funeral directors—who drove towards such trouble rather than away from it. They would understand quite readily, we told the PR firm, what could, in fact, be "good" about death and grief and funerals. And they knew what could be bad. It is just such an audience this book hopes to find, those local heroes who ante up the power of their presence, their words that ring true, the quiet they can keep through the difficult vigils, and all they have learned of compassion, in service to their fellow pilgrims among the dying, the dead, and the bereaved.

One more thing: named, as I am, for a sickly priest and a famous doubter, the life of faith for me is constantly in flux. Some days it seems like stating the obvious to say that God is good, whoever she is. Still on others it seems we are entirely alone. Years ago I quit going to church on Sunday. I found myself second-guessing the sermons and the society of it all. It is a character flaw of mine, I readily confess. But compared to what I had seen and heard at funerals, when faith and hope and love are really up for grabs, the Sunday routine seemed, well, routine. When there's a body in the box at the front of the room or the foot of the altar and a family gathered round with a fist about to be shaken in the face of their maker and the reasonable questions about why such sadness and grief always seems to attend this life, that's when ministers really earn their keep. Baptisms, weddings, Sundays with the full choir and fashions on parade are nothing compared to the courage it takes to stand between the living and the dead and broker a peace between them and God. And inasmuch as I was going to funerals six days a week and hearing the clergy bring their A-games to them, on Sundays I began going to one of those places where they do twelve steps and smarmy bromides like "one day at a time" and "fake it till you make it," "let go, let God"—things like that. In the way things happen as they are supposed to happen, I arrived by the grace of Whomever Is in Charge Here at a provisional article of faith, to wit: if there's a God, it is not me. In the years I've been working and writing with Reverend Long, my faith has been emboldened by his own fierce faith. I think it is what we are all called to do: to embolden, encourage, behold, ennoble, instruct, and inspire our fellow humans in troubling times. It's what Tom Long's faith does for mine. It is what I hope this book will do.

FORTY YEARS SINCE deciding, at a conference in Kansas City, to follow my father into funeral service, and two months after addressing in Dublin an international confab of fellow funeral directors, I find myself presenting to several hundred attendees of the Greenbelt Festival in Cheltenham, in the Cotswalds in greeny England. These are mostly Anglicans and Methodists and seekers after some truth who come for a long bank holiday weekend to listen to Christian rock music and talks by poets and priests, the lapsed and beleaguered and devout. After my remarks, a woman in the audience stands to ask how might we "redeem" the funeral—that is her word—how we might redeem it from its failed and fallen ways.

Her question is at the heart of this book. And my answer is the same as it was to the funeral directors in Dublin: that we are all called to become local heroes; that the dead and the bereaved are the same but different everywhere, in need of someone who answers the call to show up, pitch in and do their part, to serve the living by caring for the dead; to be what Tom Long calls "undertakers." Because just as a good death does not belong exclusively to doctors or nurses or hospice workers, nor good grief to therapists, psychologists, or social workers, a good funeral belongs to the species, all of us, not just the clergy and funeral directors. Each of us must reclaim these last things for our own and for each other. Then I thought I'd finish with a poem, so I gave them the one that I was asked to write for undertakers in my country who answered the call to care for the victims and families of the 9-11 attacks. It has come to be for me an homage to the men and women who serve on the front lines of dying, death, and bereavement: the first responders, police and firefighters, doctors and nurses, hospice volunteers and clergy, funeral directors, no less the family, friends, and neighbors. These are the folks who can be counted on in times of trouble; they go out in the middle of the night, in the middle of dinner, in the middle of the weekday and weekend, holiday and holy day. Theirs are kindnesses that can't be outsourced or off-shored or done online. They are hand-delivered, homemade, deeply human, do-it-yourself. These are the ones whose voices make up the chorus that calls each of us in our own way to serve the living by caring for the dead and they are the ones for whom this book is written.

LOCAL HEROES

Some days the worst that can happen happens.
The sky falls or evil overwhelms or
the world as we have come to know it turns
towards the eventual apocalypse
long prefigured in all the holy books—

the end-times of old grudge and grievances
that bring us each to our oblivions.
Still, maybe this is not the end at all,
nor even the beginning of the end.
Rather, one more in a long list of sorrows
to be added to the ones thus far endured
through what we have come to call our history—
another in that bitter litany
that we will, if we survive it, have survived.
God help us who must live through this, alive
to the terror and open wounds: the heart
torn, shaken faith, the violent, vengeful soul,
the nerve exposed, the broken body so
mingled with its breaking that it's lost forever.
Lord send us, in our peril, local heroes.
Someone to listen, someone to watch, someone
to search and wait and keep the careful count
of the dead and missing, the dead and gone
but not forgotten. Some days all that can be done
is to salvage one sadness from the mass
of sadnesses, to bear one body home,
to lay the dead out among their people,
organize the flowers and the casseroles,
write the obits, meet the mourners at the door,
drive the dark procession down through town,
toll the bell, dig the hole, tend the pyre.
It's what we do. The daylong news is dire—
full of true believers and politicos,
bold talk of holy war and photo ops.
But here, brave men and women pick the pieces up.
They serve the living, caring for the dead.
Here the distant battle is waged in homes.
Like politics, all funerals are local.

THE THEORY AND PRACTICE OF CREMATION

"When I'm gone just cremate me," Hughey MacSwiggan told his third and final wife as she stood at his bedside while the hospice nurse fiddled with the morphine drip that hadn't kept his pain at bay. The operative word in his directive was "just." He wasn't especially fond of fire. He hadn't picked out a favorite urn. He saw burning not so much as an alternative to burial as an alternative to bother. He hadn't the strength to force the moment to its crisis. He didn't know if he was coming or going. He just wanted it all to be over—the cancer, the second guessing, the wondering whether he'd done irreparable harm, what with the years of drinking, the divorces, all of that carrying on.

It's not that he lacked faith. On the contrary, after long years of sobriety in the fellowship of Alcoholics Anonymous, he had sought through prayer and meditation to improve his conscious contact with God as he understood Him, praying only for knowledge of His will for him and the power to carry that out. He was, in extremis, ready and willing, grateful and gracious. He'd had enough. He just wanted whatever was going to happen to happen.

Loosened from his own ethnic and religious traditions, which were lost in the shuffle of postmodernity, he hadn't any particular sense of "the done thing" when it came to funerals. He just didn't want to be a burden to anyone, least of all the ones he loved. So when pressed by his family for some direction, "just cremate me" is what he told them all. And so they did.

They dispensed with the presbyters and processions, with casket, graveside, and monument. "Never mind the marines," they said, when I told them that his service during World War II, from Cape Gloucester to Peleliu to Okinawa, entitled him to military honors. "Daddy wouldn't want any of that." Neither flag nor flowers, hymns or limousines, obits or an open bar. His son-in-law put the charges on a credit card, which earned him frequent flier miles.

And Hughey was just cremated, which is to say his body was placed on a plywood pallet, covered with a cardboard carapace and, after the paperwork and permits were secured, loaded into the hearse and driven to a site toward the back of an industrial park where a company that makes burial vaults operates a crematory on the side. The line of boxes along the wall—a couple dozen of them—contained the bodies of other pilgrims, dropped off by discount cremation services and other mortuaries. They were waiting, like planes on the tarmac, for a clear runway, an open retort.

Because our funeral home's protocols require us to see the dead all the way into the fire, just as we see the dead who are buried all the way into the ground, the crematory operator lets us jump the line. We arrange this by appointment, same as for burials. It seems the last if not least that we can do.

When I invited—as is also our policy—any and all of his family to come with us to the crematory, or to designate one among them to come along, "just to see that everything is done properly," they winced and shook their heads as if I'd invited them to a root canal or public stoning: a necessary but noxious procedure, the less talked about the better, thank you.

So it was one of the crematory staff who helped me roll Hughey out of the hearse and onto the hydraulic lift and stood by wordlessly while I recited the Lord's Prayer, which Hughey would have heard at AA meetings, and set the little numbered metal disk atop the cardboard box and helped me push it into the retort, closed the door and pushed the red button that started the fire that turned Hughey MacSwiggan's corpse into his ashes. Three hours later, after everything had cooled, the remnants of his larger bone structures were "processed" into a finer substance and all of it placed in a plastic bag inside a plastic box with a label that bore his name, the date, and the logo of the crematory. This greatly reduced version of Hughey was given to me to take back to the funeral home to await a decision from his family about what would be done with what remained.

"In a funeral we are carrying the body of a saint to the place of farewell," writes Thomas G. Long in his study of American funeral practice, *Accompany Them with Singing—The Christian Funeral.*[1] In short, we are carrying a loved one to the edge of mystery, and people should be encouraged to stick around to the end, to book passage all the way. If the body is to be buried, go to the grave and stay there until the body is in the ground. If the body is to be burned, go to the crematorium and witness the burning.

Ask any gathering of your fellow Americans—students at university, clergy or hospice workers, medical or mortuary sorts—how many have ever been to a graveside or watched a burial, and 95 out of every 100 raise a hand. The hillside and headstones, the opened grave and black-clad mourners are fixtures in our commemorative consciousness. If not in real life, then on TV, we've seen enough burials to know the drill. Next ask how many have been to a retort or crematory or witnessed a cremation and roughly the reverse is true: less than 5 percent have been there, done that.

Forty or fifty years ago, when the cremation rate in the U.S. was

---

[1] Thomas G. Long, *Accompany Them with Singing: The Christian Funeral* (Louisville, KY: Westminster John Knox Press, 2009), 177.

still in the low single digits, this would have made perfect sense. But today, when the national rate is over 40 percent and is predicted to be over 50 percent before another decade turns, it represents a kind of disconnect. How is it that so many people claim a preference for cremation but so few have any interest in knowing more about it? As a people we have thoroughly embraced the notion of cremation as an exercise in simplicity and cost-efficiency. But we remain thoroughly distanced from the fire itself and all its metaphors and meaning, its religious and ritual significance as a station in our pilgrimage of faith. For Christians, in particular—who, along with secular humanists, account for most of the nation's increase in cremations—this disconnect is even more telling.

In *Accompany Them with Singing*, Long documents a troublesome shift in religious practice. In the place of funerals—the full-bodied, full gospel, faith-fit-for-the-long-haul and heavy lifting of grief events our elders were accustomed to—what has evolved, especially among white suburban Protestants, is a downsized, "personalized," user-friendly, Hallmarky soiree: the customized, emotively neutral and religiously ambiguous memorial service to which everyone is invited but the one who has died. The dead have been made more or less to disappear, cremated as a matter of pure function and notably outside the context of faith. The living gather at their convenience to "celebrate the life" in a kind of obsequy-lite at which therapy is dispensed, closure proclaimed, biography enshrined, and spirits are, it is supposed, uplifted. If not made to disappear entirely, the presence of the dead at such services is minimized, inurned, denatured, virtualized, made manageable and unrecognizable by cremation. The "idea" of the deceased is feted for possessing a great golf swing or good humor, a beautiful garden or well-hosted parties, while the thing itself—the corpse—has been dispensed with in private, dispatched without witness or rubric.

Even when the cremation follows a wake or visitation and a public service in the church or elsewhere, we rarely process to the crematory, not least because the retort is often housed in an industrial park, not a memorial park. This disinclination to deal with the dead we burn has something to do with our conflicted notions about fire, which Western sensibilities and Western religious traditions still often associate with punishment and wastefulness.

"IF THERE IS a problem with cremation in regard to a funeral," says Long, "it is that the cremated remains are required to stand in for the whole body of the deceased, which at its worst could be like asking Ralph Fiennes's hat to play Hamlet."[2]

This minimization of what Long calls a "worshipful drama" suggests more than a shift in religious fashion. The issue is not cremation or burial but rather the gospel, the sacred text of death and resurrection, suffering and salvation, redemption and grace—the mystery that a Christian funeral ought to call us to behold the mystery of life's difficult journey and the faithful pilgrim's triumphant homegoing. The memorial service, by avoiding the embodied dead, the shovel and shoulder work, the divisions of labor and difficult journey to the grave or pyre, too often replaces theology with therapy, conviction with convenience, the full-throated assurances of faith with a sort of memorial karaoke where "everyone gets to share a memory."

Thence to the fellowship hall for "tea and cakes and ices," having dodged once again those facts of death that, as T. S. Eliot famously says, "force the moment to its crisis."[3]

"The fact is," writes Long, "that many educated Christians in the late nineteenth century, the forebears of today's white Protestants, lost their eschatological nerve and their vibrant faith in the afterlife, and we are their theological and liturgical heirs."[4] Long is citing not a change of fashions but a lapse of faith in the promise of eternal life: a core principle of Christianity.

---

[2] Long, *Accompany Them with Singing*, 174.

[3] T. S. Eliot, "The Love Song of J. Alfred Prufrock," in *Collected Poems: 1909–1962* (New York: Harcourt, Brace, Jovanovich, 2001), 5–6.

[4] Long, *Accompany Them with Singing*, 73.

The crisis presented by a death in the family has not changed since the first human mourners looked into the pit or cave or flames they'd just consigned their dead to and posed the signature questions of our species: Is that all there is? Why did it happen? Will it happen to me? Are we alone? What comes next? The corpse, the grave, the tomb, and the fire became fixtures in the life of faith's most teachable moment. We learned to deal with death by dealing with our dead; to process mortality by processing mortals from one station to the next in the journey of grief. The bodiless obsequies that have become the standard practice in many mainstream Protestant churches represent not only a shift of mortuary fashions from custom and tradition toward convenience, but also a fundamental uncertainty about eternal life. They lack an essential task and manifest—to assist all pilgrims, living and dead, in making their way back home to God.

Abject grief, spiritual despair, anger at God, and serious doubt are common responses to suffering and loss. And while doubt is unexceptional in the life of faith, and most certainly attends a death in the family, the role of pastor, priest, minister, and congregation, indeed the raison d'être of the Christian community, is to uphold and embolden believers, shaken in their bereavement, with the promise of the gospel. This is how the faithful bear both death in the abstract and the dead in the flesh. It is by bearing our dead from one station to the other—deathbed to parlor, parlor to altar, altar to the edge of eternal life—that we learn to bear death itself. By going the distance with them we learn to walk upright in the faith that God will take care of God's own, living and dead.

But how, Long asks, should the living take seriously a church from which the dead have been gradually banished, as if not seeing were believing? If dead Christians are redeemed saints bound for heaven, oughtn't we accompany them with singing? Oughtn't we bring them to church and go the distance with them, proclaiming the gospel on the way to the grave or tomb or fire, and there commend our dead to God?

To the extent that cremation has become an accomplice in the out-of-sight and out-of-mind nature of memorial services, it is at cross-purposes with the life of faith and the mission of the church. Of course, the problem is not with cremation, which is an ancient and honorable, efficient and effective means of disposing of our dead. Nor is the fire to burn our dead any less an elemental gift of God than is the ground to bury them in. The problem is not that we cremate our dead, but how ritually denatured, spiritually vacant, religiously timid, and impoverished we have allowed the practice to become. It is not *that* we do it, but *how* we do it that must be reconsidered.

It was back in the Gilded Age that the first modern cremation in America took place. In Washington, Pennsylvania, in 1876, the corpse of Baron De Palm was burned in a retort built by a local doctor. A hundred years later, cremation remained very much the exception to the general rule—still less than 7.5 percent.[5] But the past thirty years has seen a steadily growing acceptance of cremation. Across the nation, more than a third of all deaths are now followed by cremation. Among Protestant Christians the numbers are even higher if we consider that Jews, Muslims, and Orthodox Christians almost never cremate their dead and that Catholics still bury the large majority of theirs.

The reasons for this change are manifold. For our ancestors in the nineteenth and early twentieth centuries, the land remained foundational. Borders, boundaries, beliefs were all fixed and settled. But modern American culture seems in constant transit and flux. We are more mobile, more modular, less grounded than our grandparents. Our ethnic, religious, and family ties do not bind so tightly as in former times. We multitask and travel light through lives that seem to be in constant states of revision. Careers are a series of five-year plans. Communities have become virtual entities—social networks—as home pages replace home places as a key to identity. Marriages and families have been reconfigured. Cremation seems to suit many of us better—making us more portable, divisible, and easier to scatter.

---

5 See Stephen Prothero, *Purified by Fire: A History of Cremation in America* (Berkeley: University of California Press, 2002), especially 15–45.

But while technology has made the process odorless, smokeless, and highly efficient, the culture remains ritually adrift when it comes to fire, consigning it most often to private, industrial venues rather than public, ceremonial ones.

In cultures where cremation is practiced in public, among Hindus and Buddhists in India and Japan, its powerful metaphorical values—purification, release, elemental beauty, and unity—add to the religious narratives the bereaved embrace. The public pyres of Bali and Calcutta, where the firstborn brings fire from the home fire to kindle the fire that will consume a parent's body, are surrounded by liturgical and civic traditions. Elsewhere, however, cremation is practiced in private, the fire kept purposefully behind closed doors. Whereas the traditional funeral transports the corpse and mourners from parlor to altar, then to place of disposition, cremation, as it is practiced in the U.S., often routes around, not through, such stations in the pilgrimage. We miss most if not all of the journey, the drama, and the metaphor.

Of course, some of this has to do with consumer dissatisfaction with a mortuary marketplace interested more in sales than in service, inclined more toward the stuff than the substance, and geared more toward Hallmark sentiments than real meaning. Still, a death in the family is not a retail event; rather it is an existential one. It involves core values rather than commodities; a marketplace that spends more time and energy cataloging the possible purchases and their price points instead of the ways to engage and participate in this first among the human rubrics is of little lasting value.

For persons of faith, the essential elements of a good funeral remain few and familiar: the dead pilgrim, the living to whom the death matters, and someone to broker the mystery between them and enunciate the new status of the soul. Last but not least among the essentials is the task at hand: to get the dead and the living where they need to be. For the former that means the tomb or fire or grave or sea. For the latter it means to the edge of the life they will be living without the deceased, whose blessed body is consigned to the elements and whose soul is commended to God. Everything else is accessory. Coffins and flowers, obits and eulogies, bagpipers and dove releases, organ music and stained-glass windows, funeral homes and funeral directors—all accessories; though helpful certainly, comforting sometimes, maybe even edifying, whether costly or bargain priced, they are but accessories. Corpse and mourners, gospel and transport: these are the requisites. Everything else is incidental. To Christianize cremation requires only that Christians—clergy and laypeople—treat it as an alternative to burial, rather than an alternative to bothering. The fireside, like the graveside, is made holy by the death of saints, the witness of faithful pilgrims, and the religious context in which the living take leave of their dead.

Long writes:

> Resistance to going the full distance with the dead will occasionally be encountered from some crematoriums, which are not accustomed to people who want to stay for the firing up of the retort, and some cemeteries, which view trudging to the grave as an inefficient use of employee time or don't like the idea of families being present for the dirt being placed on the coffin in the grave. These cemeteries much prefer for funeral processions to end not at graveside but in some plastic pseudo chapel where the ceremonies can be peremptorily put to an end and the worshipers dispatched without delay, thus freeing up the burial crew to get on with their business unimpeded. These so-called chapels—why mince words?—are Chapels of Convenience and Cathedrals of Funeralia Interruptus. Tell the cemetery owner or crematorium manager, kindly of course, to step out of the way, that they are impeding the flow of traffic. You have been walking with this saint since the day of baptism; the least you can do is go all the way to the grave, to the end, with this child of God. They may refuse, but if enough clergy demand to be able to go the last few yards with the dead, change will happen.[6]

[6] Long, *Accompany Them with Singing*, 177.

So much of what I know of final things I have learned from the reverend clergy. These men and women of God drop what they're doing and come on the run when there is trouble. These are the local heroes who show up, armed only with faith, who respond to calls in the middle of the night, the middle of dinner, the middle of already busy days to bedsides and roadsides, intensive care and emergency rooms, nursing homes and hospice wards and family homes, to try and make some sense of senseless things. They are on the front lines, holy corpsmen in the flesh-and-blood combat between hope and fear. Their faith is contagious and emboldening. Their presence is balm and anointing. The Lutheran pastor who always sang the common doxology at graveside: "Praise God from Whom All Blessings Flow," his hymn sung into the open maw of unspeakable sadness, startling in its comfort and assurance. The priest who would intone the Gregorian chant and tribal Latin of the "In Paradisum" while leading the pallbearers to the grave, counting on the raised voice and ancient language to invoke the heavenly and earthly hosts. The young Baptist preacher who, at a loss for words, pulled out his harmonica and played the mournful and familiar notes of "Just as I Am" over the coffin of one of our town's most famous sinners. "Between the stirrup and the ground," he quietly promised the heartsore family and upbraided the too eagerly righteous, "mercy sought and mercy found."

MY FRIEND JAKE ANDREWS, an Episcopal priest, now dead for years but still remembered, apart from serving his little local parish, was chaplain to the fire and police departments and became the default minister, the go-to guy for the churchless and lapsed among our local citizenry. Father Andrews always rode in the hearse with me, whether the graveyard was minutes or hours away, in clement and inclement weather, and whether there were hundreds or dozens or only the two of us to hear, he would stand and read the holy script such as it had been given him to do. When cremation became, as it did elsewhere, the norm among his townspeople and congregants, he would leave the living to the tea and cakes and ices in the parish hall and ride with me and the dead to the crematory. There he would perform his priestly offices with the sure faith and deep humanity that seems to me an imitation of Christ.

It was Jake Andrews's belief that pastoral care included care of the saints he was called on to bury and cremate. Baptisms and weddings were, he said, "easy duties," whereas funerals are "the deep end of the pool." I think he had, as we all do, his dark nights of the soul, his wrestling with angels, his reasonable doubts. His favorite studies were on the book of Job. But still, he believed the dead to be alive in Christ. He met the mourners at the door and pressed the heavens with their lamentations. It was Jake who taught me the power of presence, the work of mercy in the showing up, pitching in, bearing our share of whatever burden, and going the distance with the living and the dead. He taught me that a living faith founded on a risen corpse and empty tomb ought not be estranged from death's rudiments and duties.

IN THE END Hughey MacSwiggan was scattered in Scotland. "He never made the trip but always wanted to go" is what his family told me. They knew my writerly duties often took me to the British Isles. "Take him with you the next time you go," his third wife said. And so I did. I'd been invited to launch a book at the Edinburgh Festival.

When the X-ray at the airport showed "some dense packaging" in my carry-on, I told the security guard it was Hughey MacSwiggan's cremated remains and asked if she'd like to inspect them further. She shook her head and let me pass. I did not declare Hughey at customs in Heathrow and kept my own counsel on the train ride north and checking in at the Channings Hotel. I considered the gardens off Princess Street or maybe some corner of the castle grounds, but the mid-August crowds made those sites impossible. I toyed with the notion of leaving him in a pub near Waverley Station on the theory that heaven for Hughey might mean that he could drink again.

But it was the view from Dean Bridge, the deep valley, the "dene" that names the place, the river working its way below under the generous overhang of trees—the valley of the shadow of death, I thought—that beckoned me further in my search. I worked my way down into Belgrave Crescent where I found an open, unlocked gate to the private gardens there. But it was a little too perfect, a little too rose-gardenish and manicured, and I was drawn by the sound of falling water. So I went out and around past the Dean Parish Church and the graveyard there.

I made my way down to the water by the footpath, and working back in the direction of the bridge I found a wee waterfall, apparently the site of an old mill. Kneeling to my duties, I poured Hughey's ashes out—some into the curling top waters and the rest into the circling pool below. I remember the quick pearlescent cloud, the puff of white it made in the rush of current, almost like what you'd see when salmon spawn. And watching what remained of him disappear downstream, what I thought of was the thing they said whenever the masked man rode off at the end of the cowboy show I watched as a boy: "A fiery horse with the speed of light, a cloud of dust, and a hearty 'Hi-yo, Silver!' . . . The Lone Ranger!"

There goes Hughey now, I thought—hi-yo, Silver, away. The little bone fragments, bits and pieces of him, glistened in the gravel bed of the Waters of Leith while his cloud of dust quickly worked its way in the current downstream to the eventual river mouth and out, I supposed, into the Firth of Forth and the North Sea and the diasporic waters of the world. One with all the elements now—the earth and wind and fire and water—Hughey was like the Holy Spirit of God: everywhere or nowhere, in everything that lives or in nothing at all, endlessly with us or always alone; blessed and blissful nonetheless I prayed, at his first glimpse of whatever is or isn't.

NEW ESSAYS

INTROIT

Argyle, the sin-eater, came into being in the hard winter of 1984. My sons were watching a swashbuckler on television—*The Master of Ballantrae*—based on Robert Louis Stevenson's novel about two Scots brothers and their imbroglios. I was dozing in the wingback after a long day at the funeral home, waking at intervals too spaced to follow the narrative arc.

But one scene I half wakened to—the gauzy edges of memory still give way—involved a corpse laid out on a board in front of a stone tower house, kinsmen and neighbors gathered round in the gray, sodden moment. Whereupon a figure of plain force, part pirate, part panhandler, dressed in tatters, unshaven and wild-eyed, assumed what seemed a liturgical stance over the body, swilled beer from a wooden bowl and tore at a heel of bread with his teeth. Wiping his face on one arm, with the other he thrust his open palm at the woman nearest him. She pressed a coin into it spitefully and he took his leave. Everything was gray: the rain and fog, the stone tower, the mourners, the corpse, the countervailing ambivalences between the widow and the horrid man. *Swithering* is the Scots word for it—to be of two minds, in two realities at once: grudging and grateful, faithful and doubtful, broken and beatified—caught between a mirage and an apocalypse. The theater of it was breathtaking, the bolt of drama. I was fully awake. It was over in ten, maybe fifteen seconds.

I knew him at once.

The scene triggered a memory of a paragraph I'd read twelve years before in mortuary school, from *The History of American Funeral Directing*, by Robert Habenstein and William Lamers. I have that first edition, by Bulfin Printers of Milwaukee circa 1955.

The paragraph in Chapter III, page 128, at the bottom reads:

> A nod should be given to customs that disappeared. Puckle tells of a curious functionary, a sort of male scapegoat called the "sin-eater." It was believed in some places that by eating a loaf of bread and drinking a bowl of beer over a corpse, and by accepting a six-pence, a man was able to take unto himself the sins of the deceased, whose ghost thereafter would no longer wander.

The "Puckle" referenced was Bertram S. Puckle, a British scholar, whose *Funeral Customs, Their Origin and Development* would take me another forty years to find and read. But the bit of cinema and the bit of a book had aligned like tumblers of a combination lock clicking into place and opening a vault of language and imagination.

By broaching the notion of substitutionary atonement—that Jesus came to die for our sins, in particular the residual stain of Original Sin that closed the gates of Paradise to us—upon which much of western religiosity rests, the film image of the sin-eater and the Puckle paragraph established a visual and textual alternative to the nearly naked "savior" hanging dead on the cross as the sacrificial lamb of God at the center of the sacred theater of the liturgy I'd grown up with as the child of practicing Catholics. The loaf and bowl consumed over a corpse, the sixpence paid by widow out of her want, the transfer of punishment from sinners to wandering sin-eater rather than a divine "savior," became the elements of a communion and tithe that fit nicely with my own insidious questioning of the church's principle faith claims. It fit nicely with my evolving sense that rather than a god in his heaven, it might well be another fellow human who, through offices performed over a corpse, eventually assisted the humans to whom the corpse had mattered. Furthermore, the enterprise of reconciliation and forgiveness was a business conducted among and between fellow humans, often out of their own self-interest, often out of nothing more complex than hunger and thirst.

Introibo ad altare Dei is what James Joyce had "stately, plump Buck Mulligan" intone on the opening page of his epic *Ulysses*, holding a bowl of lather aloft. And years later, reading that book for the first time, *Ad deum qui laetificat juventutem meam*, still formed in my memory as the cadenced response to the gods who'd given joy to my youth. Irreverence seemed a proper seasoning by then, the grain of salt added to articles of faith.

For all of my mother's and the priest's well-intentioned connivances, and though I kept my ears peeled for it, I never ever heard the voice of God. I remember seeing the dead priest's cassock hanging from a rafter in my grandparents' basement, a box with his biretta and other priestly things on a shelf beside it. I tried them on but nothing seemed to fit, and over time my life of faith came to include an ambivalence about the church that ranged from passion to indifference—a kind of swithering, brought on, no doubt, by mighty nature—the certain sense awakened in me when I was twelve or thereabouts that among the good lord's greatest gifts to humankind were the gifts he gave us of each other. Possibly it was meditating on the changes I could see in bodies all around me and sense in my own body, late in my grade-school years, that there were aspects of the priestly life that would be, thanks be to God, impossible for me.

I record these things because they seem somehow the ground and compost out of which Argyle rose, in that flash of recognition years ago, to become the mouthpiece for my mixed religious feelings. If I'd learned sin and guilt and shame and contrition from the nuns and priests, I was likewise schooled in approval and tolerance and inextinguishable love by my parents, earthen vessels though they were. Grace—the unmerited favor of Whoever Is in Charge Here—was the gift outright of my upbringing. It made me, like the apostle the priest I'd been named for was named for, a doubter and contrarian—grateful for religious sensibilities but wary of all magisteriums.

By the end of winter that first year I'd written three or four Argyle poems. I field-tested them at Joe's Star Lounge on North Main Street in Ann Arbor where boozers and poets would gather on Sunday afternoons to read their latest to one another. It was a kind of communion, I suppose, or potluck anyway: everyone bringing a "dish" to pass, their best home recipes of words. I liked the sound of them in my mouth, the cadence of Argyle's odd adventures and little blasphemies.

His name came easy, after the socks, of course, the only thing I knew that was reliably Scots, apart from whiskey, and the acoustic resemblance to "our guile," which sounded a note not far from "guilt," both notions that attached themselves to his invention.

These were the days long before one could Google up facts on demand, when writers were expected to just make things up out of the whole cloth of imagination: his loneliness, the contempt of locals, the contretemps of clergy—I intuited these, along with the sense of his rootlessness, his orphanage and pilgrimage. I'd spent, by then, enough time in the rural western parishes of Ireland and Scotland to have a sense of the landscapes and people he would find himself among—their "ground sense" and land passions, their religious sensibilities. And the two dozen lines of the first of these poems, each of the lines ranging between nine and a dozen syllables and thus conforming to an imprecise pentameter, seemed perfectly suited to the brief meditations and reliance on numbers and counts that were part of the churchy rubrics: stations of the cross, deadly sins, glorious and sorrowful mysteries, corporal and spiritual works of mercy, the book of hours. Hence this breviary: a couple dozen poems, a couple dozen lines each, a couple dozen photos, about which more anon.

By turns, of course, I began to identify with Argyle. As the only funeral director in a small town in Michigan, I was aware of the ambivalence of human sorts toward anyone who takes on undertakings involving money and corpses, religious practice and residual guilt. Both undertaker and sin-eater know that people in need are glad to see you coming and gladder still to see you gone. Argyle fit my purposes and circumstances. The work to which he had, by force of hunger, been called seemed in concert with my own summons and stumblings both religiously and occupationally. He is trying to keep body and soul together. And these poems articulate the mixed blessing and contrariety of my own life of faith—pre–Vatican II to the Current Disaster. I have been variously devout and devoutly lapsed.

The church of my childhood—the "holy mother" it called itself—has left no few of its children more damaged than doted over, more ignored than nurtured, orphaned and hungry, fed a thin gruel of religiosity rather than the loaves and fishes of spiritual sustenance. The ongoing failure of its management class, its up-line politics and old-boy malfeasances have done remarkable damage to generations of faithful servant priests and faithful people.

Of course, the life of faith is never settled, driven as it must be by doubts and wonder, by those experiences, losses and griefs that cast us adrift, set us to wander the deserts, wrestle with angels. And for Argyle, as for all fellow pilgrims, the tensions between community and marginalization, orthodoxy and apostasy, authority and autonomy, belonging and disbelief, keep him forever second-guessing where he stands with God. In this state of flux we are not alone.

The sin-eater is both appalled by his culture's religiosity and beholding to it. The accountancy of sin and punishment at once offends him and feeds him. He is caught in the struggle between views of damnation and salvation and the God he imagines as the loving parents he never knew—pure forgiveness, constant understanding, permanent love. He lives in constant hope and fear, despair and faith, gratitude and God hunger. In the end he isn't certain but believes that everything is forgiven, whomever God is or isn't, everything is reconciled.

If the English master, W. H. Auden, was correct, and "art is what we do to break bread with the dead," then the Irish master, Seamus Heaney, was likewise correct when he suggests that "rhyme and meter are the table manners." Prayer and poetry are both forms of "raised speech" by which we attempt to commune with our makers and creation, with the gone but not forgotten. Argyle's hunger, his breaking bread upon the dead, is a metaphor for all those rituals and rubrics by which our kind seek to commune with those by whom we are haunted—the ghosts of those gone before us, parents and lovers, mentors and heroes, friends and fellow outcasts, who share with us this sweet humanity, our little moments, the sense we are always trying to make of it in words. His is a sacrament of renewal and restoration. It is in such communion that our hope is nourished—the hope that is signature to our species—that there may be something in nature's harmonium and hush discernable as the voice of God.

Much the same with icon and image—the things we see in which we might see other things, the hand of God or the hand of man partaking in the same creation. Thus these photographs, taken by my son, Michael, in his many visits to our home in Ireland—the house his great-great-grandfather came out of, the house to which I was the first of our family to return, now more than forty years ago, the house my great-great-grandfather was given as a wedding gift in the decade after the worst of the famines in the middle of the nineteenth century.

When I first went to Ireland—a young man with a high number in the Nixon draft lottery and, therefore, a future stretched out before me—I thought I'd see the forty shades of green. And though

I arrived in the off-season, with a one-way ticket, no money or prospects, in a poor county of a poor country, as disappointing a Yank as ever there was, I was welcomed by cousins who could connect me to the photo that hung on their wall of their cousin, a priest, who had died years before. They took me in, put me by the fire, fed me and gave me to believe that I belonged there, I was home. If there is a heaven it might feel like that. In the fullness of time, they left the house to me: a gift, a grace. Everything in those times seemed so black and white—the cattle, the clergy, the stars and dark, right and wrong, love and hate, the edges and borders all well-defined. But now it all seems like shades of gray, shadow and apparition, glimpses only, through the half-light of daybreak and gloaming, mirage and apocalypse, a kind of swithering. And so these photos of home fires and icons, landscapes and interiors, graveyards and coast roads, asses and cattle, statues and stone haunts—all in black and white and shades of gray: like doubt and faith, what may or mayn't be, what is or isn't, happenstance or the hand of God.

IN THE END, Argyle is just trying to find his way home, burdened by mighty nature, life's work and tuitions; he's looking for a place at a table where he is always welcome and never alone. In the end he is possessed of few certainties or absolutes, his faith always seasoned by wonder and doubt. He knows if there's a god, it is not him. If there is one, then surely we are all God's children or none of us are. Either way, the greatest gifts are one another, the greatest sins against each other. To be forgiven, he must forgive everything, because God loves all children or none of them, forgives everything or forgives nothing at all, hears all our prayers or none of them.

At the end, all of his prayers have been reduced to *thanks.* All of the answers have become *you're welcome.*

MIRACLES

Our tribe did not read the Bible. We got it in doses, daily or weekly, from a priest bound by the lectionary to give us bits and pieces in Collects, Epistles, Gospels and Graduals, which, along with Confiteor and Kyrie, formed the front-loaded, word-rich portion of the Tridentine Mass. These were followed by sacred table work and common feed, to wit laving and consecration, communion, thanksgiving and benediction. On Sundays, it'd all be seasoned with some lackluster homiletics—linked haphazardly to the scriptures on the day. These liturgies were labor-intensive, heavy on metaphor and stagecraft, holy theater. Possibly this is why few priests put much time into preaching, preferring, as the writing workshops say, "to show rather than to tell."

Still, we knew the stories: Eden and the apple, the murderous brother, the prodigal son, floods and leviathans, mangers and magi, scribes and Pharisees and repentant thieves. I remember my excitement, the first time I heard about the woman washing the savior's feet with her tears and wiping them with her long hair and anointing them with perfume. My father, a local undertaker, was especially fond of Joseph of Arimathea and his sidekick, Nicodemus, who'd bargained with Pilate for the corpse of Christ and tended to the burial of same, in Joseph's own tomb, newly hewn from rock, "in keeping with the customs of the Jews." My father claimed this "a corporal work of mercy." This he'd been told by the parish priest, who furthermore gave him what my father called "a standing dispensation," from attendance at Mass whenever he was called, as he fairly often was, to tend to the dead and the bereaved on Sundays and Holy Days of Obligation.

The biblical narratives were told and retold through our formative years at school, by nuns who had done their little bit of editing and elaboration, the better to fit the predicaments of our station. And though we had a Bible at home—an old counter-Reformation, Douay-Rheims translation from the Latin Vulgate of St. Jerome's fourth-century text—we never read the thing. It was a holy knick-knack, like the statue of the Blessed Mother, the picture of the Sacred Heart, the tabletop manger scene that came out for Christmas, the crucifixes over each of our bedroom doors, the holy water font at the front door—all designed to suit our daily devotional lives. We prayed the family rosary in May and October, kept the fasts and abstinences of Lent and Advent along with whatever novena was in fashion and most likely to inure to our spiritual betterments. We abstained from meat on Friday, confessed our sins on Saturdays, kept holy the Sabbath, such as we knew it, and basked in the assurance that ours was the one true faith. Ours was a Holy, Roman, Irish-American, postwar-baby-booming, suburban family—sacramental, liturgical, replete with none-too-subtle guilt and shaming, the big magic of transubstantiation, binding and loosing, the true presence, cardinal sins, contrary virtues, states of grace and the hope for salvation. Litanies and chaplets stood in for scriptures and hermeneutics. That was a thing the "other crowd" did, God-help-them, bound to their idolatries about the Good Book, lost, we reckoned, in the error of their ways.

I memorized, through the weekly instructions of Fr. Thomas

Kenny, the responses to the priests' incantations at Mass, attracted as I was to the stately cadences of Latin and the mystery of a secret language. I took up my service as an altar boy at age seven, sharing duties for the 6:20 a.m. Mass with my brothers, Dan and Pat, a year older and younger, respectively, three weeks out of every four, at our parish church, St. Columban's. Then we'd hustle off to Holy Name School across town where the day's tutelage began with a students' Mass at 8:15 read by the saintly, white-maned Monsignor Paddock, beneath a huge mosaic on the general theme, the good sisters told us, of the Eucharist.

Old Melchizedek was on one side and Abraham and Isaac on the other, prefiguring the Risen Christ on his cross occupying the mosaic space between them—each a different version of priesthood, sacrifice and Eucharist. This was the image I stared at all through the mornings of my boyhood, never knowing the chapters or verses I might have read for a more fulsome understanding of it all, how Abraham's willingness to sacrifice his son prefigured the death of Jesus on the cross; how the bloody business of worship and communion became the loaf and cup of the Last Supper and the priesthood of Melchizedek became the holy orders of churchmen down through the centuries. Priesthood is something I understood in the cassocked and collared, biretta-topped celibates, the parish priests and curates, Jesuits and Franciscans in their habits who'd heard the voice of God—their vocation—and answered the call.

By twenty I was happily apostate, having come into my disbelief some few years after puberty, when a fellow pilgrim showed me all that she could on the exquisite mysteries of life. If the nuns had been wrong about sex, and they surely had been, it followed, I reasoned, they were wrong on other things.

"Why do you reason about these things in your hearts?" Jesus asks the naysaying elders in Capernaum, in Mark's telling of the healing of a paralytic. They are trying to catch his blaspheming out, in the way we are always conniving against our spiritual betters.

I'd been named for a dead priest—my father's late Uncle Tom—and for the famously skeptical apostle, whose finger and dubiety still hover over the wounds of Christ, waiting, in the words of that great evangelist and voodoo economist, Ronald Reagan, to "trust but verify." True to which code, I questioned everything.

The deaths of innocents, the random little disasters that swept young mothers to their dooms in childbirth, their infants to their sudden crib deaths, young lovers to their demises in cars, perfect strangers to their hapless ends, seemed more evidence than anyone should need that whoever is in charge of these matters had a hit-and-miss record on humanity.

My work—I eventually got about my father's business—put me in earshot, albeit over corpses, of some of the best preaching on theodicy available. The Book of Job, however god-awful and comfortless it is, remained for me a testament of faith: "Blessed be the name of the Lord." Nonetheless, I remained devoutly lapsed in my confession and praxis.

So I was fairly shocked when, years later, having achieved the rank of former husband and custodial father, small-town undertaker and internationally ignored poet, I got a call from one of my fellow Rotarians to say they were looking for "a good Catholic to join their Bible study."

"Let me know if you find one," is what I answered and we both laughed a little, but he persisted. "No, really, you'll like it. We're going to meet at the Big Boy Diner on Tuesday mornings at half past six. We'll be done by eight so everyone can get to work." Before I had time to construct a proper excuse he said, "See you then!" and hung up the phone.

What harm, I thought, it'll never last. A god-awful hour and a crummy eatery, not a great book, if a "good" one—like cocker spaniels, serviceable but ineluctably dull.

That was going on thirty years ago. Our little study has outlived the restaurant, the Rotary, a few of our roughly dozen charter members, our denominations and divided politics, and still we meet—at my funeral home now—every early Tuesday morning, every season, every weather, to read and discuss various books of the Bible. We've done everything from Genesis to Revelation, all of the Gospels, some extra-canonical texts, the letters of Paul. Job we've done three times, James maybe twice. We'll likely never do the Apocalypse again.

I only go to church now for baptisms, funerals or weddings. The mysteries of birth and death and sex are regular enough that I count as friends the neighborhood's clergy, whose personal charities and heroics I've been eyewitness to for many years. But dogma and dicta defy sound reason, and the management class of the Church, all churches, seems uniquely wrongheaded and feckless. What's more, my own views on same-sex marriage, the ordination of women, priestly celibacy and redemptive suffering would put me so sufficiently at odds with them as to render me, no doubt, an ex-communicant.

Oddly enough, the less observant I became, in belief or devotion, the better the "good" book seemed to me. I didn't need the religious epic so much as a good story, something to share, a party piece.

I can't remember not knowing about the healing of the paralytic, whether I heard it at Mass or from one of the nuns or Christian Brothers who were in charge of my education or read it as part of our Bible study. There it is, in three Gospels out of four, the details more or less the same. It is one of the three dozen or so miracle stories that punctuate the New Testament, from changing water into wine at Cana, calming the storm and filling the fishnets, to healing of lepers and the blind and lame and raising the dead, himself included. There are endless demons and devils cast out, sins forgiven, apparitions after his death. It was a poem in a book published a few years back that brought it newly to life for me.

The last time I heard Seamus Heaney read was in the Glenn Memorial Chapel at Emory University. It was and remains a Methodist church, which doubles as an auditorium for gatherings of a certain size. It was the 2nd of March of 2013 and I was occupying the

McDonald Family Chair, a cushy sinecure with the Candler School of Theology at Emory, teaching a course with the great preacher and theologian Thomas Long on "The Poetics of the Sermon." Dr. Long and I were just putting the final touches on a book we'd coauthored called *The Good Funeral*, due out later that year and written for clergy, mere mortals and mortuary sorts. And I was learning words like *exegesis* and *hermeneutics* and studying the dynamics of fiction, which Dr. Long regarded as a workable template for homiletics. We examined narrative arc and point of view, plot and character and setting. We read poems and short fictions and published sermons.

I was delighted that Heaney would be coming to town. His had been the most amplified and ever-present voice of my generation of poets. His work, since I first encountered it forty-five years ago, reading by the fire in the ancestral home in County Clare I would later inherit, had never failed to return a rich trove of the word horde and metaphoric treasures. Because so much of his poetry came out of a Catholic upbringing in rural Ireland, he became for me a useful guide for the parish of language and imagination.

Possibly because I first encountered prayer as poetry, or at least as language cast in rhyme and meter, addressed to the heavens as a sort of raised speech, poetry had always seemed sacerdotal, proper for addressing the mysteries of happenstance and creation. That Heaney held the natural world and human work—the chore and toil of the mundane, earthbound and near-to-hand—in awe and reverence, seemed more attuned to the holy than the politicized religiosity of the culture. Still, the Latin I'd learned as an altar boy in the 1950s, the sacraments, devotions and sensibilities I'd been raised with found many echoes in the early poems of the Irish master, even if my own life's experience and further examinations of scripture and secular texts had left me apostate. Though freighted with doubts and wonders and religiously adrift, I treasured the language of faith as an outright gift—the hymns of Charles Wesley, the angel-wrestling contemplations of John Calvin, the exile and anchoritic adventures of Columcille, and the rubrics of holy women and men—I retained some level of religious literacy given me by nuns and Christian Brothers, but I rejected the magisterium of the church. By the time I'd arrived at Emory in the late winter of 2013, I was deeply devoted to a church of latter-day poets, skeptics and noncompliant but kindly sorts. The irony of such a backslidden fellow as myself teaching at a school of theology named for the Methodist bishop and first chancellor of Emory, whose brother was the owner of our national sugar water, Coca-Cola, was not lost on me. Though I had been schooled in my apostasy by H. L. Mencken, Robert Ingersoll, Christopher Hitchens and Richard Dawkins, and by the feckless malfeasance of bishops and abusive priests, I had also witnessed, over four decades in funeral service, the everyday heroics of the reverend clergy and their co-religionists. These were men and women of faith who showed up whenever there was trouble. Their best preaching was done when the chips were down, in extremis, at death beds, in the hospitals and nursing homes and family homes and funeral homes. They pitch in and do their part even though they cannot fix the terrible things that happen. They are present, they pray, they keep open the possibility of hope. And I'd been schooled by my semester among the Methodists and seminarians at Emory, and by my friendship with The Reverend Thomas Long, whose scholarship and work in words has re-formed me in a way I thought impossible.

Thus Heaney's reading from the raised sanctuary of Glenn Memorial Chapel seemed a "keeping holy" of a Sabbath, and his poems, portions of a sacred text. And when he said, deep into what would be one of his last public readings, that he'd like to read some poems from his "last book," and then corrected himself to say, "my most recent collection . . ." I thought the insertion of the shadow of death was a deft touch by a seasoned performer of his work. It is also true that his "most recent collection," *Human Chain*, seemed so haunted a book, dogged by death and impendency and the urgency of last things.

On that day he read one of my favorites of his poems. "Miracle" proposes a shift of focus in the scriptural story of Jesus healing the paralytic, my favorite rendition of which occurs in Mark 2:1–12. Jesus is preaching in Capernaum and the crowd is so great, filling the room and spilling out the door into the street, that four men bringing the paralytic to be healed have to hoist him up to the roof, remove the roof tiles, or dig through the sod and lower him down on his bed by ropes, whereupon Jesus, impressed by their faith, tells the poor cripple his sins are forgiven. Of course, the begrudgers among them—and there are always begrudgers—begin to mumble among themselves about blasphemy, because "Who can forgive sins but God, alone?" Jesus questions them, saying which is easier, by which he means the lesser miracle—"to say, 'your sins are forgiven' or to say, 'Arise, take up your bed and walk'?" It is, of course, a trick question.

Because forgiveness seems impossible, whether to give it or to receive it, and impossible to see. It would always take a miracle. Nor is God the only one capable of forgiving. Do we not pray to be forgiven our trespasses "as we forgive those who trespass against us"? Who among us is not withered and weighed down by the accrual of actual or imagined slights, betrayals, resentments, estrangements and wrongdoings done unto us most often by someone we've loved. And in ways I needn't number, we're all paralyzed, hobbled by our grievances and heartbreaks, by the press of sin, the failure of vision, by fear, by worry, by anxieties about the end.

Whereas the scripture directs our attention to the paralytic, and to the quibbles between Jesus and the scribes, Heaney's poem bids us be mindful of the less-learned toil and utterly miraculous decency of "the ones who have known [us] all along," who lift us up, bear us in our brokenness, and get us where we need to go. On any given day it seems miracle enough.

The everyday and deeply human miracle, void of heavenly hosts or interventions, has special meaning for Heaney who, in August of 2006, woke up in a guest house in Donegal paralyzed by a stroke. He had attended the birthday party for Anne Friel, wife of the playwright and Heaney's schoolmate and lifelong friend, Brian Friel. After the night's festivities the Heaneys were spending the night with other friends and fellow poets in the local B&B. He awakened to paralysis on the left side of his body. So it was his wife, Marie, and Des and Mary Kavanagh, Peter and Jean Fallon and Tom Kilroy—ones who had known him all along—who helped strap him onto the gurney and get him down the steep stairs, out of the building and into the waiting ambulance to ride with his wife to Letterkenny Hospital. In the poem, which took shape in the weeks of what he called "rest cure" in the Royal Hospital, Donnybrook, in Dublin, the narrative power proceeds not to "the one who takes up his bed and walks," rather to "the ones who have known him all along and carry him in—" who do the heavy lifting of his care and transport. They are the agents of rescue and restoration, their faithful friendship miraculous and salvific. Their hefting and lifting and large muscle work is the stuff and substance of salvation. Here is the short poem.

MIRACLE

Not the one who takes up his bed and walks
But the ones who have known him all along
And carry him in—

Their shoulders numb, the ache and stoop deeplocked
In their backs, the stretcher handles
Slippery with sweat. And no let-up

Until he's strapped on tight, made tiltable
and raised to the tiled roof, then lowered for healing.
Be mindful of them as they stand and wait

For the burn of the paid-out ropes to cool,
Their slight lightheadedness and incredulity
To pass, those ones who had known him all along.

This language of shoulders, aching backs and waiting *for the burn of the paid-out ropes to cool* honors the hands-on, whole-body habits of human labor that the poet learned as a farm boy in Derry. From comparing his father's spade work in the turf bog to his own excavations in meaning and language in his poem "Digging," to the town and country indentures of blacksmithing, well-gazing and kite-flying at the end of *Human Chain*, Heaney's work upholds the holiness of human labor and the sacred nature of the near-to-hand.

Hearing its maker read "Miracle" from the pulpit at Emory put me in mind of my conversation with him at the funeral of our friend Dennis O'Driscoll, who had died less than three months before, on Christmas Eve, 2012, and was buried near his home in Naas, County Kildare.

Seamus had been Dennis's principal eulogist on the day, just as Dennis had been Heaney's most insightful interlocutor. His book of interviews with Heaney, *Stepping Stones*, is the nearest thing to an autobiography we will ever have of the Nobel Laureate and more thoroughly than ever examines the life of the man in relation to the work.

Following O'Driscoll's funeral liturgy, I walked with Heaney and his wife in the sad cortege from the church to the cemetery, half a mile or so, following the coffin and the other mourners. We chatted about our dead friend and the sadness we all shared. Maybe his stroke six years before and my open-heart surgery the year before eventuated in our bringing up the rear of the entourage. We were taking our time, huffing and puffing some at the steeper bits, as we made our slow but steady way up the town, out the road, to the grave behind the hearse. In Ireland the dead are shouldered to the opened ground and lowered in with ropes by the pallbearers. After the priest has had his say, the grave is filled in by family and friends. The miracle of life and the mystery of death are unambiguously tethered by a funiculus of grave ropes and public grieving, religiously bound by the exercise of large muscle duties—shoulder and shovel work and the heart's indentures, each a linkage in the ongoing, unbroken human chain. And the strain of pallbearers at O'Driscoll's open grave, as they lowered his coffined body into the opened ground with slowly paying out the ropes, seemed like the faithful and existential labor of the paralytic's friends, lowering his bed through the opened roof in Capernaum to the foot of his healer for a cure.

The witness of these things drew a catch in my breath, that New Year's Eve morning when we buried Dennis O'Driscoll, in the new row of St. Corban's Cemetery. Watching his pallbearers lower him into the vacancy of the grave, these mundane mortuary chores replicating the miraculous narrative of the Gospels where the paralytic's pals lower him into the place of his healing, the "slight lightheadedness and incredulity" perfectly articulated in Heaney's poem, remains caught in my chest, not yet exhaled, and like the scribes in Capernaum, that day in Naas, though I'd seen such things all my workaday life, I'd "never seen anything like this before."

And yet I saw it all again, months later in the late summer when Heaney's death stunned us all on Friday morning, the 30th of August, 2013. I woke to texts and emails from Dublin. "Seamus is dead," is what they read. "Ah, hell . . ." I wrote back. Ah, hell, indeed.

I called David Fanagan, the Dublin undertaker, and asked if I might ride in the hearse. Someone who knew the poems and the poet should ride along.

I flew to Shannon and stayed at my digs in Clare that night and drove up to Dublin on Sunday morning, stopping in Naas to visit Dennis's grave. At Fanagan's in Aungier Street, Heaney was laid out in Chapel 3, the corpse, horizontal and still, "silent beyond silence listened for." Marie greeted me and thanked me for making the long journey and was a little shocked to hear that I'd had my ticket in hand for more than a month, long before Seamus had any notion of dying. She told me she thought he must have had a heart attack on Wednesday, complaining of a pain in his jaw, then tripped leaving a restaurant on Thursday which got him to the hospital where they discovered a tear in his aorta. The only thing riskier than operating, she was told, was doing nothing.

He was in extremis. A team was assembled to do the procedure at half past seven on Friday morning, just minutes before which he texted her, calm and grateful for the long years of love, and told her not to be afraid. "Noli timere," he wrote at the end, the ancient language Englished: *be not afraid.* He was dead before the operation began.

All the way up there people lined the way, on the overpasses, and in the halted cars at intersections where they got out of their cars to applaud the cortege of the great poet. Women were weeping or wiping tears from their faces. Men held the palms of their hands to their hearts, caps doffed, thumbs up, everyone at their best attention.

"How did you get to be the one?" I asked the man at the wheel of the new Mercedes Benz hearse, no doubt hustled into service for the television cameras. "I drew the short straw," he told me. "We used to get extra to drive in the North, what with the Troubles and fanatics. Now it's just a long haul and a long day."

We picked up forty or fifty cars as we made our way, the roughly three-hour drive north from Dublin, then west around Belfast making for Derry, crossing the river that connects Lough Beg to Lough Neagh at Toomebridge, the crowds getting bigger the nearer we got. Police on motorcycles picked us up at the border, just outside of Newry, and escorted our makeshift motorcade all the way to the cemetery as we went down the boreen off the main road and drove by the family farm and onwards to Bellaghy, where a piper met us at the entrance to town and piped us through the village where the crowd spilled out of shops and pubs and houses and into the road, every man woman and child out applauding, crossing themselves, giving out with bits of "Danny Boy" and holding their hearts in signals of respect. The sadness on their faces and the tribute to the level man behind me in the box was like nothing I'd ever seen, and when we got to the grave, led there by a cadre of churchmen in white albs and copes and cowls, I took the family spray up to the grave through the cordons of paparazzi clicking photos of everything. I walked with Marie and her family behind the coffin as we went to the grave, where against my hopes that Seamus would pop out and proclaim it all a big mistake, his sons and his brothers and her brothers bent to the black ropes and lowered him into the ground, the paid-out ropes and the burn in their arms and hands and the hush of the gathered multitude notwithstanding. Leaves rustled in the overarching sycamores. The clergy struck up a verse of "Salve Regina" to re-insinuate their imprimatur on it all. We hung around in that sad and self-congratulatory way mourners do, after the heavy lifting is done. The limo had a slow leak in the right front tire that had to be tended to. Des Kavanaugh and his wife, Mary, came and spoke to me wondering if I'd be in Galway anytime soon. Brian Friel's car pulled away; he nodded. Michael, Seamus's son, came over to thank me for going in the hearse with his dad and I was glad of that. And grateful. I stayed until the sod was back on him, and the flowers sorted on top of that and then we drove back the road, arriving in Dublin right around dark. Anthony MacDonald, his short-straw, long day nearing its end, dropped me at the corner of Georges Street and Stephen Street Lower. I gave him fifty euros and told him to get something at the off license with my thanks for taking me up and back on the day, for getting Seamus where he needed to go, and for getting me where I needed to be. "No bother," he said. "Not a bit." Nothing out of the utterly ordinary, utterly pedestrian, a miracle.

Possibly these are the miracles we fail to see, on the lookout as we are for signs and wonders: for seas that part for us to pass through, skies that open to a glimpse of heaven, the paralytic who stands and walks, the blind who begin to see, the shortfall that becomes a sudden abundance. Maybe what we miss are the ordinary miracles, the ones who have known us all along—the family and friends, the fellow pilgrims who show up, pitch in and do their parts to get us where we need to go, within earshot and arms' reach of our healing, the earthbound, everyday miracle of forbearance and forgiveness, the help in dark times to light the way, the ones who turn up when there is trouble to save us from our hobbled, heart-wrecked selves.

MOVEABLE AND STEADFAST FEASTS

My old dog Bill will be dead by Easter. God knows, he should have been dead before now. The now of which I write—the moment to hand—is that no-man's-land of days between Christmas, New Year's and the Epiphany. I've gone beyond fashionably late with this essay, which I promised for the twelfth day of the twelfth month of the last year—an essay on Easter with an Advent delivery. I've promised it now for Little Christmas, hoping that like the magi of old, I'll come to see things as they are.

A member of the reverend clergy told me that the formula old preachers used to prepare their homiletics included three points and a poem. Montaigne would string his essays on a filigree of Latin poets. He worked in his library and when stuck for some leap into a fresh paragraph, he'd often quote Virgil or Catullus or Lucan and carry on as if the poem were an aperitif readying the reader for another course.

Which puts me in mind of the twelve days of Christmas I spent downstate being paterfamilias for our yuletide observations. This poem came into being in contemplation of a carol we always sing this time of year.

TWELVE DAYS OF CHRISTMAS

Some pilgrims claim the carol is a code
for true believers and their catechists,
to wit: four colly birds, four gospel texts,
eight maids a milking, the beatitudes,
and pipers piping, the eleven left
once Judas had betrayed the lamb of God—
that partridge in a pear tree, the holy one
and only whose nativity becomes
in just a dozen days the starlit eve
of three French hens with their epiphanies
huddled round the family in the manger,
tendering their gold and frankincense and myrrh.
The whole tune seems to turn on "five gold rings"—
the Pentateuch, those first books of the Torah
in which ten lords a leaping stand in for
the ten commandments cut in loaves of stone
which Moses broke over his wayward tribesmen.
Two turtle doves, two testaments, old and new.
Six geese a laying, creation's shortened week,
the swimming swans, gifts of the Holy Ghost
whose fruits become withal nine ladies dancing.
Twelve drummers drumming, the Apostle's Creed:
a dozen doctrines to profess belief in.
Still, others say it's only meant to praise
fine feathered birds and characters and rings,
our singing nothing more than thanksgiving
for litanies of underserved grace,
unnumbered blessings, the light's increasing,
our brightly festooned trees bedazzling.

Montaigne, the father of all essayists, himself a sort of preacher, to four centuries of readers and counting, was anxious to understand the human being and condition. It was, thanks be, his lifelong study. In his marvelous essay, "Of Repentance," a Lenten read and Easter anthem, he wrote in French a point that Englishes as *In every man is the whole of man's estate*, by which he meant we are all at once the same but different; to know the species, know a specimen. To understand the Risen Christ we'd better reckon with the wounds and miracles, betrayals and agonies. Study the scriptures and the poems.

The men in my Bible study took the day after Christmas off last week, but we met for the day after New Year's today, in the early morning dark at the funeral home, as we have been doing now for years. The price is right, the coffee's free, it's quiet in the early o'clock. Except for the ones gone to their time-shares in Florida, or the ones homebound with the seasonable woo, the turnout is a good one and we're glad to have survived into another year. We're reading from the 24th Chapter of Matthew when Jesus is giving the disciples a list of the signs that the end times are nearing. Wars and rumors of wars, false prophets, nation rising up against nation, earthquakes and famines in various places.

The sky has been falling throughout most of history. And for everyone predicting doom, the doom is certain. Whether we die en masse, in cataclysms of natural or supernatural origin, we die in fact, one hundred percent.

Possibly this is why one of us eases the talk around to declaring a win in the War on Christmas, reporting that people are saying "Merry Christmas" again in a way that political correctness prevented up until now. Another fellow heartily agrees. I mention that the War on Christmas was invented by a cable-news host to divert attention from the wars in Afghanistan and Iraq which were coming, alas too late, under scrutiny in the middle naughts. I suggest they go home and Google Barack Obama and Merry Christmas. And I wonder aloud, it being the feast of the Octave of Christmas which used to be observed in the Christian calendar, the Circumcision of Jesus, why these old white male and much-aggrieved Christians weren't willing to serve in the War on Circumcision. Why should we wish each other Happy New Year when Happy Circumcision is the more Christian, more religious greeting? They tilt their heads at what I am saying the way that Bill does when he hears an oddly pitched noise. But I digress. I was trying to relate Easter to Bill's slow demise. This is not about birth and circumcision and magi, rather betrayal, passion, death and burial, and then the Easter we claim to believe in.

HE'S LIVED WELL past the expectations—Bill, the dog—half again beyond his "use by" date. These latter days have all been bonus time and have taught me gratitude in the stead of the "poor me's" and the "why me's" and the "give me's," which have always seemed my usual nature. I'm easily beset by resentments and begrudgeries—a character flaw from which I've achieved irregular remissions over the years, occasional dispensations. I'm living through one such dispensation now, watching old Bill in his withering and bewilderments as the mightiness of his shoulders and hindquarters, the deep menace of his guardian bark, and the fathomless pools of his big brown eyes have given way to lame waltzing on his "last legs," a kind of castrato's cough at threats he senses but cannot see through a cloud of cataracts, nor hear in the dull chambers of lost itching ears. His nose still works its cold damp magic. He finds his food and good places to squat to the duties of his toilet. His soft black curls of fur are full of dander and dry skin beneath despite the designer mash of essential oils and my wife's tender correctives. So long as he eats and craps and can be medicated against the pain, I won't exercise the lethal dominion over him I wish I did not have. Yes, dead by Easter I'd wager, or sooner, much sooner, as the gyre of demise works its tightening, ineluctable damage.

Back when I was researching his breed, the Bernese mountain dog, or as I joked when he was a puppy, "an AKC Registered Pain in the Ass," the Wikipedia on my old laptop promised six to eight years of life expectancy for dogs of his prodigious size. All to the good, I remember thinking, at least I'll outlive him. I was fifty-seven years old that late winter I got him, now twelve years ago. I was well into my last trimester of being. My father, my grandfathers, the men in my line had all died in their sixties, of broken hearts: a bad valve, clogged arteries, congestive heart failure, some embolism—quick, convincing "failures," or "attacks," or "infarctions."

Bill's gone half again older than we expected. And even that might have been a miscalculation. My wife never really wanted a dog. After the kids were grown and gone and out on their own on automatic pilot, throwing in with partners of the same species, taking mortgages, signing leases, making plans and car payments, after we breathed the sigh of relief that they all seemed poised and provisioned to outlive us, Mary settled in with *Law and Order* reruns and I kept to my old customs of splitting my time between the day job undertaking and the preoccupation with language, writing and words.

I remember sitting with her one Sunday afternoon, watching the episode where Lennie and his estranged daughter, Kathy, meet up for lunch—she keeps her distance because of his drinking and the two failed marriages, one to her mother. The episode, "Aftershock," involves Lennie and Ray Curtis, his young partner, along with Jack McCoy and Claire Kinkaid, the legal team, witnessing an execution of someone they put away. Lennie's life was always complex. And I was thinking what a good thing a dog would be to get me out of the house and walking on a regular basis and I said, on one of the commercial breaks, "What would you think about my getting a dog?"

"Are you out of your (expletive deleted) mind?" she responded. "Finally we have the place to ourselves, we come and go as we please, we've got some peace and quiet and you want a dog!" I took this to mean she didn't want one.

IN THOSE DAYS I would occasionally write a poem that borrowed from a famous poem for the kernel of creation that brought it into being. This is how I'd come to write a poem called "Corpses Do Not Fret Their Coffin Boards," which borrowed unabashedly from William Wordsworth's sonnet "Nuns Fret Not at Their Convent's Narrow Room," which I'd encountered that morning, possibly on the radio, listening to the voice of Garrison Keillor, who used to do "The Writers' Almanac," a five-minute diamond of daily bits and pieces that ended with the reading of a poem. Wordsworth's sonnet is in praise of sonnets, in observation of the truth revealed to him, some centuries back, that formal constraints—"the narrow room"—often produce an unpredictable freedom. The sonneteer knows all too well that the work in words to make a sonnet is but fourteen lines of ten or so syllables, organized to rhyme in some predetermined way—a code that poets map out as AABB or ABAB or maybe, as Wordsworth did for his wee sonnet, ABBA, with the twist that the sound of A in lines one and four repeats itself in lines five and eight. There are other embellishments of sound and sense to bring it to an end in line fourteen, but what I can say is that one comes to the close of a sonnet with a sense that it must have been a loving God that brought old Wordsworth into being to speak to me years after his demise in a different century, millennium and nation.

WORDSWORTH AFFIRMS THE snug hugging and liberation of the sonnet's terms in the last half of his, to wit:

> In truth the prison, into which we doom
> Ourselves, no prison is: and hence for me,
> In sundry moods, 'twas pastime to be bound

Within the Sonnet's scanty plot of ground;
Pleased if some Souls (for such there needs must be)
Who have felt the weight of too much liberty,
Should find brief solace there, as I have found.

My own sonnet, while crediting Wordsworth, albeit sub-titularly, has less to do with space and nature than with time and money, preoccupations of my advancing years.

CORPSES DO NOT FRET THEIR COFFIN BOARDS

after Wordsworth

Corpses do not fret their coffin boards,
nor bodies wound in love their narrow beds:
size matters less to lovers and the dead
than to the lonely and the self-absorbed
for whom each passing moment is a chore
and space but vacancy: unholy dread
of what might happen or not happen next;
this dull predicament of less or more's
a never balanced book, whereas for me,
the worth of words is something I can count
out easily, on fingertips—the sounds
they make, the sense, their coins and currencies—
these denouements doled out in tens, fourteens:
last reckonings tapped out on all accounts.

Fresh from its typing, this is the page I posted to the fridge with a kitchen magnet back in the day before stainless-steel appliances made magnets redundant, the better for my missus to see it in her own good time and possibly ink some edits in as marginalia. I loved it when she read my poems and commented for better or worse because it sang to me a song of hope beyond the everyday desolation of long consortium, often marked by romantic indifference and connubial blahs in the stead of bliss.

But days after I'd posted the draft, alas, no corrections or comments had appeared. No cross-outs or smiley faces, no affirmations scribbled in passing, no nothing.

It was another Sunday afternoon when, being as I am a man of habits, I said into the general silence of the day that was in it, "What would you think about my getting a dog?" To which she replied without enthusiasm, "Maybe you could name it Wordsworth."

My heart leaped inside my bosom. I couldn't believe my ears. What meaning ought I to take from this expletive-free and contingent utterance? Surely, it seemed, she had read my poem, or at least the title and citation line. Was this some signal of approval, some sign that my efforts had not been for naught? At the very least it was not disapproval, no rhetorical about the state of my (formerly expletive-ridden) mind. No, this was, if not full-throated approval, a willingness to consider the prospect, a nod toward tolerance if not the full embrace of the notion. I moved immediately into my office, where my computer, ever at the ready, soon had me Googling for "Bernese Mountain Dogs, Michigan." Two days later I was driving up the highway with my middle son to mid-Michigan where a man claimed to be weaning a recent litter.

"What about 'No!' didn't you understand?" she said, when I brought the puppy in the door. "But honey," I coaxed her, "we can call him Wordsworth! Just like you said. William Wordsworth."

"Let's just make it 'Bill W.,' " she said, insinuating the name of the founder of the fellowship of Alcoholics Anonymous, a fellowship to which we both belonged. Was she insinuating that the puppy might shake the serenity that our long sobriety had produced?

It is hard to know, but "Bill" it has been ever since—from the eleven-pound puppy he was that Ash Wednesday of 2006, that first of

March I brought him through the door on the day of my only daughter's birthday, to the hundred-and-ten-pound giant of kindliness he in time became, to the withering, arthritic, ninety-some-pound geriatric pooch snoring on the floor next to my shoes as I type these truths into the computer.

In the twelve years since, so much has happened. If I take stock, it is an inventory of losses. My daughter, now in her middle years, has disconnected from her family. She is estranged from her mother, my first wife, and from me, her stepmother, her brothers and her brothers' families, her aunts and uncles and cousins, everyone from her family of origin. In the email asking us to keep our distance and not to initiate any contact with her, she said she was going out west for therapy to treat what she called her codependence. She said that she felt that she never got enough time as a child, that she had to grow up too soon, what with the divorce between her mother and me when she was nine and ten years old. I wrote back saying that such insights were hard got and that I supported her eagerness to get right with herself and would follow her directives and stood ready to assist in any way I might do her some good in her efforts. Except for the occasional text message to wish happy birthdays or best for holidays, we've had no substantial communication since. Her family of choice, near as I can figure, includes her husband, her horse, her dog, some friends? Before this happened, I spent two years in weekly therapy with her in an effort to discern what might be done to let this cup pass. The shrink thought we'd arrived at a plan for what to do to keep us in each other's futures. But soon after that, my daughter wrote to say her well-being required that she keep her distance from us all. I said I wanted her to be well. It feels like a death without any of the comforting, buffering infrastructure of mortality—a known cause and certification, a ceremony, a grave, a place I can go and weep. There's none of that. Her absence, her choice of absence, her riddance of us all is everywhere. On holidays and birthdays there's a text that comes more or less as a proof of life. For years it seemed I was left with a choice between assigning this sadness to evil or mental illness. I chose the latter. There is no succor in it.

Whether this grief is coincident with, correlated to, or the cause of our lackluster marriage—the second one, or maybe the first—I do not know. But what I do know is we've lost our way. We live, for the most part, separate lives and have slowly ceased to share our lives, our dreams, our meals, our bed, our whereabouts, our hopes and fears, our plans for the future. The desolation is as palpable as our bliss once seemed. All of this after many years of joyous intimacy, shared purpose, real partnership makes it more the pity that we both live now like widowed people, bereft of a spouse that, though still alive, is gone from us in measurable ways. We share bank accounts and an estate plan and rise to the occasion for holidays, but otherwise are in every meaningful way alone, and what has grown between us is what Heaney called a "silence beyond silence listened for." It seems I've ended up like Lennie Briscoe—a two-time loser at marriage, estranged from a daughter who chooses to remain out of contact with or from her family of origin. We text our affections or proclaim them to anyone within earshot, but it makes no difference. When I compare my lot to men I've buried, whose flaws and imperfections seemed amplified compared to mine, and yet whose wives still went along for the ride, whose daughters doted on them till the end, like a hurt dog howling at the emptiness, I shake a fist in the face of the God I don't quite believe in anymore.

The poor-me and why-me lamentations, variations on the Book of Job, leave me with a choice between hurt and anger. I tend toward the latter and fear the worst. I keep working the program, the fellowship and twelve steps of AA, because it keeps me from adding a class-A depressant to the gathering sadness, the tears of things. I do not want to live in fear.

MY PAL GEORGE is what we call a "sponsor"—someone in the fellowship to reach out to when the ways of things threaten to overwhelm. He's been sober longer than anyone I know. And he's bookish and very well educated: he's a JD and a CPA, and for a good few of my books, he was the proofreader I sent the roughest of drafts to. He'd fix the spelling and punctuation and errors of thought and construction. We've been friends and neighbors for decades now. For years he's been losing his short-term memory. The arc of his infirmity has been slow but steady. Dithering gave way to a sort of discombobulation, which in time gave way to chronic disorientation, which became what seems now a cruel advancing dementia. Beyond the indignities of age, his condition rightly frightened his family. They got him into assisted living. Attendant nurses see to his meds and meals. There are bingo nights and socials. I call and visit when I can. I live upstate now three weeks out of four, at a lake house with Bill for whom the remove and the quiet are like balms. He doesn't have young suburbanites to bark at out the windows as they stroll by with their toddlers, infants and designer dogs. Downstate, my wife occupies the house next to the funeral home where I lived for forty-five years and into which she moved, when my sons and daughters were school children or teenagers and I was the family court's designee as the "more fit" custodial parent—all of us hobbled some by the end of the marriage that brought them into being.

I CALL GEORGE a couple times a week to see how he's doing. When I asked him how he was adjusting to living there, he told me what I guess I needed to hear.

"I'm doing fine," he said. "You can't be angry all the time." It makes me believe in a loving God when deep in my resentments about living alone, I hear my sponsor, though addled and beset, bewildered really and yet making perfect sense to me. Good to have just such a sponsor. You can tell him anything and he'll likely forget. Sometimes I think it might be a gift except when I see the thousand-yard stare he sometimes gets, like combat soldiers who have seen too much, or keep getting a glimpse of what they can't remember anymore. I took him to the movies a couple months ago. We saw *Dunkirk*, ate popcorn and Milk Duds. It was fun. On the way out of the theater he quoted some lines from Churchill's speech to Parliament regarding Dunkirk: "*We shall defend our island, whatever the cost may be, we shall fight on the beaches, we shall fight on the landing grounds, we shall fight in the fields and in the streets, we shall fight in the hills; we shall never surrender*"—something he'd remembered from his lifelong studies and erudition. By the time I dropped him back at his quarters in the care facility, he could not remember what movie we'd seen.

Surrender's a big part of staying sober. "Let go," we alkies often say, "let God." LG, LG! Or "not our day to watch it," meaning we are not in charge. It's why I address my supplications to Whomever's In Charge Here, because the article of faith I hold to is provisional, to wit, if there's a God, it isn't me. The fellowship has ruined my religious certainty—that One True Faith-ism we all are raised with. But the fellowship of wounded, variously damaged goods who've shared their experience, strength and hopes with me have illumined for me, however dimly, a life of faith. It's made me wary of certainty and open to hopes and loves I never before imagined. It's made me grateful and rheumy eyed so that I find myself weeping at the ways of things. *De Rerum Natura*, Lucretius called it—the glimpses of godliness we sometimes get in the otherwise quotidian, dull happenstance of life. Lucretius was a disbeliever, whereas I'm a happy ignoramus—in either case, we do not know.

The things George still remembers best are often things that happened years ago, like the woman who told him at his mother's funeral how his mother "understood life's higher callings." He remembers that as the high praise it was of a woman who took to heart the hardships of others and did what she could to make their situations better. I tell him I think he has that too, an understanding of life's higher callings, how he's been a source for me of good orderly direction, if not the voice of God, at least a goodness in him that is undeniable. He looks out the window at the birds in the snow—chickadees and nuthatches, titmice and a cardinal—and asks if I believe it means an angel is near, to see a bright red cardinal in the chill of winter. Perhaps, I tell him, it's his mother, or mine. He looks away; I'm getting rheumy eyed.

I had Bill's grave dug two years ago, fearful as I was of getting caught by frost deep in the ground, with a dead dog on my hands in Michigan's winter. And I started collecting the soup bones, littered everywhere over the yard, which he had worked the marrow out of over the years. It got to where I'd have them custom cut at the butchers, a few dozen at a time. I found a couple hundred of them and strung them on a line of rope and wound some solar-powered lights around the rope and hung the whole assemblage from the fulcrum that overhangs the water's edge and by which the former tenants' dock was swung out into place each spring. The bone rosary is what I call it, this blinking string of bones and lights that's meant to mark the spot where Bill will be interred sometime in the coming spring, I reckon, when his age and infirmity come to the certain end all living things come to. I've even written a brief lament and asked my son to have it cast in bronze so I can bolt it to a stone over his grave.

LITTLE ELEGY

for a dog who skipped out, and after XJ Kennedy

Here lies loyal, trusted, true
friend for life, Bill W.,
named for Wordsworth and the guy
by whose twelve steps I've stayed dry,

sober even, these long years,
like the good dog buried here
who could bark but never bit;
never strayed too far or shit

indoors; never fell from grace.
God, grant him this ground, this grave,
out of harm's way, ceaseless rest.
Of all good dogs old Bill was best.

They laugh at me, of course, my sons, for all the planning for Bill's demise—the hole at the corner of the lot, the rosary of bones blinking in the dark over the water's edge, the stone, the little poem. Preparing for Bill's death they figure is a way of preparing for my own or diverting my attention from fears about what lies ahead, in the way that Easter has, for true believers, been a blessed assurance of eternal life, a contingent balm, in its alternate narrative, in the gaping maw of mortality.

I've a friend who says we've lost our "eschatological nerve," the certainty that heaven awaits the good and perdition the evil doers. With the loss of a sense of eternal reward or damnation producing justice in a world so often unfair, we've begun to uphold the so-called prosperity gospel, to wit, success is a sign of God's favor, as if grace was deserved or earned like the poverty the poor are said to have coming to them. The good news formerly proclaimed by the evangels has been replaced by their enthusiasm for Donald Trump and his zero-sum, winners and losers agenda.

This year Easter falls on April Fools'. Some feasts are moveable, some steadfast. It'll also be, if my friend George remains, as he has since April 1st, 1974, quit of the booze that made him crazy, his forty-fourth AA birthday, proving, as he often says, that any fool can get sober if he or she works the program. Whether March Madness or April Fools', Easter is for those who believe in second acts and second chances, another go, mulligans and do-overs. Easter is for repentance and forgiveness, amends and abundant life. Easter is when the lost are found and the dead arise, transfigured, glorified by what is possible. The Easter I believed in as a boy was a sort of zombie apocalypse. It never mattered much to me whether Jesus was really raised from the dead. Like Lennie Briscoe I was damaged at the specter of the capital punishment. The broken, bloody body of the Christ that hung center stage in Catholic churches was more a spectacle to me than narrative. Perhaps that's sacrilege. Perhaps not. Nor have I much interest in whether the Moral Influence or Substitutionary Atonement models of redemption most apply. My faith in a loving God, keeping a count of the hairs on my head, comes and goes with changing realities. It is as if I blame every outrage, every evil not averted, every sadness that might have been undone, on the God I hardly believe in anymore. Some days I see the hand or hear the voice of God implicated in the things that happen; others not so much. Begrudgery and resentment are the crosses I bear, and I find them much heavier than just giving thanks. This Easter I'm not looking for an empty tomb, triumphant savior or life eternal. Rather, some spiritual progress, instead of perfection; a little repair if not redemption, some salvage south of full salvation. "No appointments," an old-timer used to tell me, "no disappointments." No expectations, no vexations.

Truth told I see sufficient triumph in the way that Bill still makes the climb upstairs at night, despite his sore hips, cloudy eyes, and the withered muscle mass in his shoulders and hindquarters. It comes with age. Is he driven by loyalty or an old fear of sleeping alone? Is it love or fear of loss? Impossible to know. He carries on but does not speak.

I see an Easter in George's getting through another day of his assisted but nonetheless bewildered living, in good humor though utterly out of sorts. I sense it in the texts I get from my long-estranged daughter, those proofs of life; the flickering of tenderness I still feel toward my distant wife, our genial courtesies.

The meeting I go to on Sunday nights up at the lake is in the basement of Transfiguration Church. And that's what I'm after this Easter, I think. That's what I'm after most of the time, the momentary radiance of the divine beaming out of God's creation. Old dogs can do it, old friends, old wives; old sorrows borne patiently, old grievances forgiven, old connections restored.

New ones too, like the other night at the meeting when Lilah was talking. She's the youngest pilgrim at the table. She's paid her dues and is working on sobriety. She's talking about how she came to know that she was beloved, when her girlfriend, noticing how badly sunburned Lilah got when they were gardening one August afternoon last summer, did not scold. Rather, she carefully peeled the dry shreds of skin off Lilah's reddened shoulder, bent and tenderly kissed the spot, and held the desiccated remnants of her darling's flesh in the palm of her hand, like viaticum, a sort of holy grail that she brought to her mouth, ate and swallowed.

Her sharing this intimacy and its intelligence quickened my breath and then caught it up. Gobsmacked is what I was, my mouth agape as if trying to hold my breath and let it go. My eyes were getting red and rheumy yet again, welling with a glimpse of the divine, the beautiful, the redeemed and atoned for, manifestly forgiven beings, all of us assembled around the table, we had shown up broken and bewildered and disconnected and were suddenly beatified, illumined and made new, transfigured in the shimmering moment; my catching breaths were shortening and I was fearless suddenly, cavalier about the scene I was on the brink of making.

It was then I was remembering that Jesus wept.

WHENCE & WHITHER

Some Thoughts on Uteri, on Wombs

The contemplation of the womb, like staring into the starlit heavens, fills me with imaginings of Somethingness or Nothingness. It was ever thus. If space is the final frontier, the womb is the first one—that place where, to borrow Wallace Stevens's phrase, the idea of the thing becomes the thing itself. It is the tabernacle of our expectations. The seedbed and safe harbor whence we launch, first home and habitat, the garden of delight's denouement. A place where the temps are set, the rent is easy, the food is good and we aren't bothered by telephone or tax man. That space we are born out of, into the world, where the soft iambics of our mother's heart become the first sure verses of our being, the first poetry of our life, Cavafy said. "Sometimes they speak to us in our dreams; sometimes in thought the mind hears them . . . like distant music that dies off in the night."

When I first beheld, as a student in mortuary school, Plates 60 and 61 in Book Five of *De humani corporis fabrica libri septum* (The Fabric of the Human Body) by the great sixteenth-century physician and anatomist, Andreas Vesalius, I was smitten with ontological and existential awe. A disciple of the first-century Greek philosopher and medico, Galen of Pergamon, one sees in the Belgian's handiwork the male gaze on female parts he examines at autopsy and vivisection. There is such tenderness in the splayed cavity and skinned breast of the headless woman of his scrutiny, such precision to his illustrations of her innards.

By then I'd had a rudimentary acquaintance with the bodies of women. I knew what to touch and rub, fondle and savor, hug and hold, loosen and let go, lave and graze. But the frank exposure of the human fabric that Vesalius's images detailed were wondrous to me, unveiling as they do, apocalyptically, the beauty of both form and function. Had I not found his drawings so sumptuously instructive—corresponding as they did to the focus of my own gobsmacked gaze—I might have considered then what I consider now, here in my age and anecdotage, to wit, the notion that, though each gender has its own specific parts to play in our species' drama of "reproduction," such issues are neither male nor female solely. Rather, they are human in scope and nature, requiring, in both meaning and performance, the two it always takes to tango. We are, it turns out, in this together.

Still, it is impossible to behold a woman's parts without gratitude and awe. Likewise I am often chuffed—a word that means both one thing and its opposite—by the sense such encounters invariably include that we are all, in fact, the same but different; the anatomists' renderings of our private parts show the male member is nothing so much as a vagina turned inside out, so that the adventitia, smooth muscle and mucosa of the latter reflect, actually, the phallic urgency of the former, almost as if they were made for each other, bespoke, custom fit—like sword to scabbard, hand to glove, preacher to pulpit or corpse to opened ground.

And, lest any man assume the sword more salient than the scabbard, consider science, that great leveler:

In utero, we all start as female and only the random happenstance of the Y chromosome and its attendant hormones makes some of us male. Still, testes are unambiguously fallen ovaries and the scrotal raphe a labial scar from the fusion of one's formerly female lips. The penis is a clitoris writ large, the nipples sans lactating, ornaments for men to remind them of the truth they are mostly boobs that do not work. So, whether penetration, ejaculation, ovulation, uterine contraction, fertilization or gestation seals the reproductive deal, each is essential to this essential mystery, we are brought into being by the fervent collaboration of both male and female. Science provides stand-ins for the stallion and sire. "They bring the bull in a suitcase, now," my cousin Nora in West Clare informed me years ago, speaking of her small troupe of milking Friesians, which had a withering effect on my rampant mannishness. Men are easily made redundant, but female mammals still do the heavy bearing. Far from the second, weaker sex, the female seems the first and fiercest, like poetry to language, the one without which nothing happens.

I WENT FOR stillborn babies, as a boy. Well not a boy, exactly, but not yet a man. My apprenticeship to my father's business meant I'd go to hospitals to get the tiny lifeless bodies, transported in a small black box, such as one might take fishing or to keep one's tools. I'd return them to the funeral home: wee incubates in various stages of incompleteness and becoming. Sometimes they were so perfectly formed in miniature that they seemed like tiny icons of humanity, their toes and fingers, noses and eyes, their little selves too small, too still, but otherwise perfectly shaped and made. As with Galen and Vesalius, as with Wallace Stevens, the thing itself outweighs the idea of the thing. Thus these little fetal things, stillborn or born but not quite viable, were freighted with a gravitas, fraught with sadness, laden with a desolation born of dashed hopes and grave-bound humanity. The body, the incarnate thing, is critical to our understanding. The uterus is wellspring, headwater, home ground of our being.

In time I'd learn to sit with the families of dead fetuses, dead toddlers, dead teenagers—the parents who'd outlived the ones they'd made, the fathers who remembered the night of bliss they'd had, the kissing and embraces, the mothers who recalled their first intuitions of gravity, their gravidness, its gravitas, the grave consequences of impregnation—an ill-at-easeness in their lower core, tenderness in the breast, the momentary hot flash of a future changed or changing utterly.

"It's only been maybe a hundred years," says my young assistant, halfway through her childbearing years, "that women have actually owned their uteri." And even now, she adds, the agency of men—of husbands and fathers, bishops and politicos, no less moguls and marketers—have too much a say in what goes on in the hidden places of a woman's body, the womb and its attendant, adjacent parts: cervix, ovaries, fallopian tubes, adventitia, clitoris, labia major and minor, mons pubis, all of which conspire, as it were, to raise a chorus of praise to the mighty nature whereby we renew, repeat, reproduce and replicate ourselves.

In the panel *Eve Tempted by the Serpent* by Defendente Ferrari, who was painting in Turin while Vesalius was dissecting in Padua, the pale-skinned, naked teenager's mons veneris is obscured by the filigree leaf frond of the sapling she is plucking an apple from—the tree of knowledge of good and evil. The leering, bearded, lecherous, old-mannish-faced snake, slithering up the adjacent tree, is hissing his temptation in her ear. It is the last moment of Paradise, the girl is her girlish innocence, oblivious to the ramifications, her genitalia, her tiny breasts, her consort's parts are not yet shameful. Time will eventually blame everything on her: the Fall of Man, the pain of childbirth, the provocations of her irrepressible beauty, death itself. But for now, God is still happy with Creation. He has looked about and seen that it was good. It's all written down in Genesis 3. The diptych panel with Adam, perhaps erect and prelapsarian, has been lost to the centuries, so we do not see how happy he is, how willing and ready and grateful he is for her succor and company, her constancy.

IT WAS A drizzling morning in the winter of 1882, in Washington, D.C.; a retinue of black-clad pilgrims gathered around a small grave in the Congressional Cemetery to bury little Harry Miller, a toddling boy who had succumbed to that season's contagion of diphtheria. The small coffin rested on the ropes and boards over the open ground while the mother's sobs worked their way into a rising crescendo. The undertaker nodded to the man at the head of the grave to begin. He shook his head. The mother's animal sobs continued. She was bent over, like someone stabbed, wrapping her small arms round her uncorseted middle, holding herself together by dint of will at the point in her body where she felt the blade of her bereavement most keenly.

"Does Mrs. Miller desire it?" the speaker asked. The dead boy's father nodded his assent.

The officiant on the day was Robert Green Ingersoll, the most notorious disbeliever of his time, his age's Christopher Hitchens, Richard Dawkins or Bill Maher. Though stridently unchurched, Ingersoll was the son of the manse, the youngest son of a Congregationalist minister who preached his abolitionist views and had, as a consequence, been given his walking papers by congregants around the East and Midwest. Robert spent most of his youth shifting from church to church because of his father's politics. Because of his father's mistreatment at the hands of Congregationalists, Robert turned first on Calvinism and then on Christianity and, by the time he stepped to the head of the grave that rainy morning in Washington, D.C., he was the best known infidel in America—an orator and lecturer who had traveled the country upholding humanism, "free thinking and honest talk" and making goats of religionists and their ecclesiastical up-lines.

"Preaching to bishops," a priest of my acquaintance once told me, "is like farting at skunks." And I wonder now if he wasn't quoting Robert Ingersoll. As he stepped to the head of the Miller boy's burial site, Ingersoll began his oration.

I know how vain it is to gild a grief with words, and yet I wish to take from every grave its fear. From the wondrous tree of life the buds and blossoms fall with ripened fruit, and in the common bed of earth, patriarchs and babes sleep side by side.

Every cradle asks us "Whence?" and every coffin "Whither?"

They who stand with breaking hearts around this little grave, need have no fear.

We have no fear. We are all children of the same mother, and the same fate awaits us all.

We, too, have our religion, and it is this: Help for the living, hope for the dead.

Help for the living. Hope for the dead.

EVERY CRADLE ASKS us whence indeed, and every coffin whither. The abyss we consign our dead to—opened ground or fire, pond or sea or air—is incubation of a sort our sacred texts make faith claims for, hoping they are like the space, pear-shaped sometimes, no more than centimeters, hormonally engaged, impregnated by mighty nature—a primal station in the journey of our being.

WHAT BENT THE dead boy's mother over was the grief, felt most keenly in her most hidden places, the good earthen, opened seedbed of her uterus, vacated with pushing and with pain, and vanquished utterly by her child's death. It is the desolation Eve must have felt when one of her sons killed the other. And the wonder Andreas Vesalius beheld when looking into the bloody entrails of the Paduan girl who first unveiled for him the mystery of our coming into being, and by the sound and sense we humans get, examining our lexicon, that "grave" and "gravid" share their page and etymology, no less gravitas and gravity, "grace" and "gratitude." And that the surest human rhymes of all are "womb" and "tomb."

THE DONE THING

By getting the dead where they need to go, the living get where they need to be. This seems, after half a century of undertaking, the essential brief, the task most manifest, the raison d'être for a funeral. If these outcomes are not accomplished, whatever else takes place, however pleasant or wretched, meager or sumptuous, is of no real consequence. The accessories amount to nothing—the requiems and mum plants, the shaky brace of pallbearers, coffin plates and monuments, five stages of grief, seven deadly sins, ten commandments, umpteen eschatologies and apostasies—if the essential job's not done, the rest is senseless. To deal with death we must deal with our dead, to get our riddance of the corpse, beloved though it might be, and get ourselves to the edge of the life we will be living without them. And this is coded in our humanity: when one of our kind dies, something has to be done about it, and what that something becomes, with practice and repetition, with modifications and revisions, is the *done thing* by which we make our stand against this stubborn fact of life—we die.

By bearing the dead to their abyss, by going that distance, the living hope to bear the loss of them. By processing the mortal remains, we endeavor to process mortality's burdens and heartbreaks. This amalgam of corporal and spiritual works, an effort to deal with the manifest and mysterious life, has been the work that separates humanity from the other animals.

And here some sort of motion, some movement and tasking, some shifting of conditions and circumstance are implicated. Where, the discerning reader will likely wonder, do the dead need to go? Where indeed! Let me say that what the dead most need, in the moment of their death, is to be gotten, coincident perhaps with hurried and heartfelt farewells, en route to their riddance, their oblivion and abyss, whatever form it takes—the ground, the fire, the sea or air—that elemental disposition that ensures they will not embarrass themselves further by putrefaction or decomposition or any of the postmortem indignities that creatures of bone and blood and meat are prone to. Whereas the mother of Jesus was assumed into heaven, a feast in mid-August in the Western church, most of us will find the opened ground or the chambered fire or tomb sufficient to the task of final disposition, a word the etymologist will inform proceeds from *dispose*, which itself proceeds from the Latin *disponer*e meaning "arrange," influenced by *dispositus* "arranged" and Old French *poser* "to place." Which is to say, we must arrange to place them elsewhere, thus the shoulder and shovel work, the pecking birds that pick the dead thing clean of its rot, the fire, the depths, the tree's high branches: each an end of the done thing somewhere. There are others, we know, but in their final dispositions they are all the same.

I FIRST LANDED in Clare on February 3, 1970. The inky, oval welcome in my first passport has long since dried; still, I get a glimpse of it again every time I pass through Shannon or Dublin now, as I've done many dozens of times in the intervening years, going on half a century now, though we don't feel the time going.

The man in the customs hall in Shannon chalked an X on my bag and waved me on saying, "The name's good." I was twenty-one and possessed of a high number in the Nixon draft lottery—a surreal exercise in the existential that had been drawn a couple months before, giving me a pass on becoming fodder for the American misadventure in Vietnam. A lackluster student without goals or direction, I thought I'd better make a move, a gesture to put some distance between my effortless mediocrity at school and my parents' scrutiny. I'd read Yeats and Joyce and reckoned to reconnect with what remained of our family, "on the banks of the River Shannon," as my grandfather had always prayed over Sunday dinners throughout my youth. His widow, my grandmother, a Dutch Methodist who converted to "the one true faith," as she called the idolatrous superstitions of the crowd she'd married into, still sent Christmas greetings to "Tommy and Nora Lynch, Moveen West Kilkee Co Clare," which is what I told the taximan in the big Ford idling outside the arrivals hall.

"Can you take me here?" I asked him, proffering the places and names scribbled in my grandmother's sturdy cursive.

I REMEMBER NORA LYNCH, nearly seventy then, in the doorway of her home, shoulder leaning into the jamb, arms crossed, a study in contemplation, figuring to what use she might put this young Yank on his holidays. Her brother, Tommy, was holding back the snarling dog. I was dressed like a banker's apprentice in my one black suit, polished wing tips and my dead grandfather's watch fob, trying to make a good first impression, a little hung over from the drinks on the plane and the compression of a night crossing. And, despite my efforts, I was as disappointing a Yank as ever showed up in Clare, without property or prospects, cash or complete education. I had Yeats's *Collected Poems* and Joyce's *The Dubliners.* They had a newly wallpapered room with a narrow bed and a straight-back chair.

I was their first American cousin to return; they were my Irish connections, twice removed.

"Come in," she said, "you're perished with the journey. Sit in by the fire. We'll make the tea."

Nora and her brother were living on the edge—of Ireland and County Clare to be sure; the north Atlantic just over the road, the Shannon estuary below. Likewise they were, late in their sixties, at the narrowing edge of the lives they'd been given in the opening decade of the twentieth century. First cousins of my late grandfather, to my twenty-one-year-old self they seemed relics of another time entirely, Bruegel-esque, premodern, ever, as Yeats claimed, "the indomitable Irishry."

Nora could not have seen her brother's death, of pneumonia, coming around the corner of another year, nor her own long and lonesome vigil by the fire that would come to a close twenty-two years hence. She could not see the trips she would make to Michigan or my many returns to Moveen, nor the family, immediate and extended, who would, in the fullness of time, make the trip "home" with me. All of it was the mystery the future always is, rhyming as it does with the history of the past. The moment we're in is a gift, the bromide holds, that's why we call it the "present."

And in that moment, that gray, midwinter Tuesday morning in the yard in Moveen, gift that the present tense of it was, I could not see how it would change my life, to have followed the frayed thread of family connection back to its source and headwaters to this distant townland of Moveen West, a thousand acres divided by families and hedgerows and ditches, the open palm of treeless green pastureland, dotted with shelters and stone sheds, hay barns and outbuildings, stretching from the high cliffs edging the Atlantic down-land to the gray, shingly banks of the Shannon estuary.

IN TIME I would learn all the place names, find the wells and scenic routes, flora and fauna, the mythic and epic accounts of things—

how Loop Head was named for the mighty leap the Hound of Ulster, Cuchulain, made with Mal the Hag in hot and lecherous pursuit of him; how the Montbretia that blooms up the boreens and ditch banks, coast roads and villagescapes, through July and August leaped over the stone walls of the Vandeleur land lords' walled estate in Kilrush like liberty itself, like water, escaping every effort to keep it in, propagating by mighty nature, a new reality.

THE LEAPS AND tributaries of reconnections that I pursued all those years ago were bound to place and people and the ties that bind. In Tommy and Nora I found the last and steadfast remnant of a family sept that had remained while others sailed out of Kappa Pier in Kilrush and Cobh in Cork, a century before when a nineteenth-century Thomas Lynch crossed the Atlantic on a steerage fare and found his way from Clare to Quebec and Montreal, thence to Michigan where he'd heard of a place called Jackson where the largest walled prison in the country was being built and maintained by the unskilled, gainful labor of poor immigrants. "Tom Lynch—Wanted" it read on the tin case he brought his worldly possessions in. He gave that case to his son, who gave it to his son, who gave it years later, now empty, to me.

"Tom that went," said Nora Lynch, speaking about the uncle she never knew and handing me a glass of whiskey, "and Tom that would come back. So, now for you." She admired the circularity of time and happenstance. The way what goes around, etcetera.

AND NODDING BY the fire after the welcome and the whiskey and the talk, so brogue-twisted and idiomatically rich, I began to feel the press of hitherto unknown forces—cultural, religious, familial and new—like Dorothy in Oz, I was a long way from Michigan and suddenly and certainly home.

It changed my life, those next three months hunkered over the sods, observing lives lived nearer the essential edge of things, keeping body and soul together, making sense of the elementals, the social and seasonal nuances, the register of imaginative and emotional dynamics, the stories and poems and songs and performances that everyone brought to the evenings' "cuirt"—that gathering of neighbors around hearth and table, each with a party piece, a pound cake, tobacco or drink to add to the evenings' effort to give thanks for another day that was in it. I belonged to a culture of isolates who gathered around our individual, glowing screens to connect with virtual realities. Tommy and Nora lived actual lives on life's terms, which included both the gossip and the goodwill of neighbors, come what may. This was a time before country people could escape the contingencies of their geography, before the Fords and Vauxhalls lengthened their range of travel. In 1970 the ties that bind could only be slipped so far as "shanks' mare" or the Raleigh bike, the pony trap or ass and cart could take them. They married over the ditch, caroused within the townland or village, got their sacraments within the parish bounds and got their income from their hard labor in their land and the local creamery. That I had come from across an ocean many of their people had crossed and never returned, that I spoke with a Midwest American brogue, that I'd experienced things that were different from them made me momentarily a minor celebrity. But only momentarily. After a while I was just Tommy and Nora's "Yank."

So when Tommy died the following year, in early March of pneumonia, Nora rode her bike into Kilkee to make the call to let me know. When I showed up the following morning to join the wake in progress in Moveen, it upped the ante of our connection.

"Most Yanks," a local bromide holds, "wouldn't give ye the steam off their water."

So a Yank who comes running at the news of "trouble," that deftly understated Irishism for a death in the family, seemed to them another thing entirely. But Ireland had taught me things about the ties that bind—the press of family history and place, all the rooted behaviors conditioned over generations.

And when Nora Lynch, in those first months that I spent in West Clare, took me to the graveyard at Moyarta, near the banks of the River Shannon in Carrigaholt, it was to the vaulted grave of our common man and the flagstone cut by Mick Troy with the particulars of a sadness eighty years before I ever landed.

> Erected by Pat Lynch *[it reads]* in memory of his beloved wife, Honor alias Curry who died October 3rd 1889 Aged 62 years may she R.I.P. Amen.

The erector named in the stonecutter's work was Nora Lynch's grandfather, my grandfather's grandfather, thus, my great-great-grandfather, thus, our common man. His wife, Honor, for whom the tomb was built, was a grandniece of the Irish philologist and antiquary, Eugene O'Curry, whence, according to Nora, any later genius in our gene pool. And it was Pat's wife's slow dying of a stomach cancer that gave him the time, in cahoots with his brother, Tom, to fashion this stone vault at the western side of the burial ground, with the great graven flagstone to cover it giving the details of his wife's demise and his grievous love for her. He would follow in the fullness of time, as would his son and heir, Sinon, Nora's father, as would Nora's twin brother who died in infancy, and finally Nora, her long lonesome vigil quit in March of 1992, her tiny corpse in its wooden coffin lowered into the stone-lined, opened ground to be comingled with the bones and boxes of her ancestors.

THEY ARE ALL dead now, of course, the bed of heaven to them. And I am long since into that age when the wakes begin to outnumber the weddings and we think of ourselves as maybe mortal too. I mostly go for funerals now. Word comes by Facebook or furtive text or a call from the neighbors who look after my interests there—the house, the donkeys, the ones who come and go.

When I got word in June that the poet Macdara Woods had died, I knew I'd have to make another trip. He was, along with Leland Bardwell, Pearce Hutchinson and Eilean Ni Chuilleanain, a founding editor of the Dublin literary journal *Cyphers.* Whereas my poetry had been pretty much ignored in my own country, publication in a Dublin literary journal made me suddenly, internationally unknown. The tiny society of poets who write in the English language would not overfill a minor-league sports stadium. More people get chemotherapy every day than read or write poetry. So, with some few exceptions, we matter almost entirely to ourselves.

Some years ago, on New Year's Eve, I walked with Seamus Heaney behind the hearse and cortege that took the body of Ireland's most bookish man, the poet, critic and biographer Dennis O'Driscoll, from the church in Naas to St. Corban Cemetery where he was buried. Nine months later it was Heaney in the hearse and me riding shotgun from Donnybrook in Dublin to Bellaghy in Derry, three hours journey into the north to bring the body of the dead poet home, helpless as the few hundred who gathered around the grave, having gone that distance with the great voice of our time because it was all we could do, to be with him who could no longer be among us.

Last October it was a neighbor woman's death by cancer, in June my friend Macdara Woods by Parkinson's, then early in August I boarded the plane again in Detroit, making my way to JFK to connect to the late flight to Shannon and thence to Cork City because the poet Matthew Sweeney died of motor neuron disease. This year the catalog of losses seems inexhaustible and I'm thinking it must be the advancing years that put me in the red zone of mortality. In February it was the poet Philip Casey, who died in Dublin of a cruel cancer; in April my dog, Bill W., long past the eight-year life expectancy of his furry mammoth breed; he was the only mammal over 100 pounds who could bide with me. He was going on thirteen when his hips and shoulders all gave out. I'd had his grave open for two years plus, fearful of getting caught with a dead dog in the deepening frost of a Michigan winter.

And there's truth in the bromide that by going the distance with our dead, the principal labor of grief gets done, in the deeply human labor of laving the body and laying it out, lifting and lowering, watching and witnessing, having our says and silences. Which is why I'm flying tonight a day late, alas, but nonetheless, to get my friend's body where it needs to go, from Cork City in Munster to Ballyliffin in Ulster, six hours north, where I once caddied for him. I have a hat I bought in the pro shop on the day. I keep it in the clothes press in Moveen and I'll wear it to his obsequies on Wednesday. I've read with Matthew in England and Scotland, Dublin, Galway, Cork and Clare, Adelaide, and Melbourne and Wellington, Australia, New Zealand; we tutored together several Arvon Courses, at Lumb Bank and elsewhere and in Michigan. He's been on trains and boats and planes with me and to each of my principal residences in southeast and northern Michigan and my ancestral stones in County Clare. My heart is fairly desolate these days, with a long-estranged daughter, a long-distant marriage, the low-grade ever-present sense of what Michael Hartnett called the great subtraction. I've been badly subtracted from these last few years. Only for the fact that I banked such friendships against the howling winter of age, that I did not miss the best years of their being and their beloveds' beings and the times of our lives that we caused on purpose to frequently intersect. Two Octobers ago, he made me lamb chops in my own kitchen on the south shore of Mullett Lake where he sat up nights making poems that became the last ones in the last books he published this year. He called it "The Bone Rosary," which was the name I gave to the rope of old soup bones I'd had the butcher cut from the femurs of cows and given to my dog, Bill W., to chew the marrow out of. I thought they would make a suitable memorial. The poem ties the dead dog and the dead poet together in my imagination.

THE BONE ROSARY

The big dog's grave is already dug, a few
yards from the lake, and all the bones he's
sucked the marrow from are strung on a rope
draped over the porch railing, a bone rosary,
waiting to be hooked to a rusty chain hung
from a metal post stuck in the ground, poking
out over the water. I can already imagine
the reactions of people in boats who'll pass,
what they'll think of the resident of the house.
there might be more to tickle their fancy—
I have a BB gun and ball bearings in a cupboard
that would kill as many black squirrels as I
wanted. And I might just commission a black
totem pole. And although there are no records
of anyone walking on the waters of Mullett Lake
I think I may visit a hypnotist in Harbor Springs
to see if she can facilitate this. I'd love to run out
into the middle of the lake, carrying the Stars
and Stripes and make all the folk in boats
I meet faint and fall into the water, maybe to
drown there, and befriend the big dog's ghost.

After his burial I came to West Clare where the summer is winding to a close for another year, the last of the holiday makers are walking the strand line in Kilkee, whale watchers peer through their telescopes at Loop Head, the dolphin boat and charter fishing boat take the last of their passengers out the estuary in Carrigaholt, the pubs are frantic with late-season revelries. The pope is coming to a nation that has changed religiously in forty years since the last papal visit. There are worries, after the hot, dry June and July, that there won't be enough fodder for the coming winter. Round bales of hay and black-wrapped silage and heaps of fodder are filling the barnyards, hopes for another cutting abound. Limerick wins the All Ireland Hurling Match, a man in the townland succumbs to his cancer; we're passing through life is what is said. We're passing through.

In many places they've lost the knowledge of the done thing and try to reinvent the ritual wheel every time a death occurs. Dead bodies are dispatched by hired hands, gotten to their oblivions without witness or rubric while the living gather at their convenience for bodiless obsequies where they "celebrate the life," as if the good cry and the good laugh, so common at funerals, had gone out of fashion or lost its meaning. But the formula for dealing with death hasn't changed. It is still essential to deal with our dead, to reconfigure but reaffirm the ties that bind us—the living and dead. It was the Irish connection that convinced me of that.

The reading of poems and sharing remembrances over Matthew's dead body in its box in Cork were good to be a part of, likewise to beckon the mourners to their last look at him, close the coffin lid at the wake the following morning in Ballyliffen at the other end of the island nation, which was his home place of the many places he'd called home. He was shouldered from the house and up into the town by family and friends taking their turns at sharing the burden of his remains. Large muscle work prepares the ground of precious memories. It is not the other way around.

I rode in the hearse with Matthew Sweeney's corpse out of town to the grave in Clonmany New Cemetery between showers and the tributes of the couple hundred fellow humans who stood out in the rain to see the poet's body lowered into the ground. It is the done thing here, the only thing that we can do in the maw of rude mortality, the shoulder and shovel work, the words work, waling, waking, walking and witnessing, the vigil and chitchat, the hold and beholding these sad duties occasion, the stories we remember before we forget. These ties that truly bind, these sad done things uphold by focusing our diverted intentions on the job at hand, to wit, to get the dead where they need to go and the living where they need to be.

Acknowledgments

The author is grateful to Jill Bialosky and the team at W. W. Norton for bringing three collections of essays, two collections of poetry, and a book of short fictions into being, and to Richard McDonough, agent extraordinaire, who found good digs for these projects. Robin Robertson, likewise, through his offices at Jonathan Cape in London, has been essential to these efforts. David Dobson at Westminster John Knox Press brought *The Good Funeral*, coauthored with Thomas G. Long, and, most recently, *Whence & Whither* into being. Gordon Lish published my first poems at Alfred A. Knopf, Inc., and commissioned my first essay for *The Quarterly* more than thirty years ago. For their scrutiny and attention to this work in words, the author is permanently grateful.

Thanks too to the editors of journals and periodicals, radio producers, academics, journalists, seminary presidents, and conference programmers for their interest in my reviews, commentaries, and opinions, where some of these essays first appeared, in broadcast or print or spoken word venues, in various incarnations of the texts found in this volume, among them:

The Candler School of Theology at Emory University

The Austin Presbyterian Theological Seminary

Notre Dame University

The Wellcome Collection, London, UK

Commonweal magazine

The Journal for Preachers

BBC Radio 4 and Cast Iron Radio and Kate Bland

RTE Radio Ireland

NPR USA

PBS Frontline

Southword Journal (Munster Literary Center) Cork, Ireland

For many years my work has been enriched by friends and close readers, sons and daughter, colleagues and artists, the reverend clergy and family members, without whose ongoing conversations these essays would not have taken shape, among them Michael Heffernan, Keith Taylor, Richard Tillinghast, George Martin, Julie Young, Mary Tata, Colonel Dan Lynch, Patrick Lynch, Corrine D'Agostino, Emily Meier, Carolyn Belknap, Thomas Long, Doug McMunn, Eric Lorentzen and anonymous others—all fellow pilgrims in love's bewilderments and life's sustaining grace and mercies. No amount of thanks is sufficient to their generosities, nor catalog of gratitude complete without their names.

Permissions Credits

"How We Come to Be the Ones We Are" and "The Theory and Practice of Cremation": Excerpted from *The Good Funeral: Death, Grief, and the Community of Care*. © 2013 Thomas G. Long and Thomas Lynch. Used by permission of Westminster John Knox Press. All rights reserved.

"Bone Rosary" by Matthew Sweeney. From *My Life as a Painter* (Bloodaxe Books, 2018). Reproduced with permission of Bloodaxe Books. www.bloodaxebooks.com.

"Miracle" from *Human Chain* by Seamus Heaney. Copyright © 2010 by Seamus Heaney. Reprinted by permission of Farrar, Straus and Giroux.

Excerpt from "Voices" from *The Complete Poems of Cavafy*, translated by Rae Dalven. English translation copyright © 1961, and renewed 1989 by Rae Dalven. Reproduced by permission of Houghton Mifflin Harcourt Publishing Company. All rights reserved.

Excerpt from "Under Ben Bulben" from *The Collected Works of W. B. Yeats, Volume I: The Poems*, Revised by W. B. Yeats, edited by Richard J. Finneran. Copyright © 1940 by Georgie Yeats, renewed 1968 by Bertha Georgie Yeats, Michael Butler Yeats, and Anne Yeats. Reprinted with the permission of Scribner, a division of Simon & Schuster, Inc. All rights reserved.

"In Memory of W. B. Yeats," copyright 1940 and © renewed 1968 by W. H. Auden; from *Collected Poems* by W. H. Auden. Used by permission of Random House, an imprint and division of Penguin Random House LLC. All rights reserved. Reprinted by permission of Curtis Brown, Ltd.

"Audenesque" from *Electric Light* by Seamus Heaney. Copyright © 2001 by Seamus Heaney. Reprinted by permission of Farrar, Straus and Giroux.

Excerpt from "Tract" by William Carlos Williams, from *The Collected Poems: Volume I, 1909–1939*, copyright © 1938 by New Directions Publishing Corp. Reprinted by permission of New Directions.